Autism – An Inside–Out Approach
An innovative look at the mechanics
of 'autism' and its developmental 'cousins'

Donna Williams

Jessica Kingsley Publishers
London and Bristol, Pennsylvania

First published in the United Kingdom in 1996 by
Jessica Kingsley Publishers Ltd
116 Pentonville Road
London N1 9JB, England
and
1900 Frost Road, Suite 101
Bristol, PA 19007, U S A

Second impression 1997

Library of Congress Cataloging in Publication Data
A CIP catalogue record for this book is available from the Library of Congress

British Library Cataloguing in Publication Data
Williams, Donna, 1963-
Autism : an inside-out approach
1. Autism 2. Autism - Patients - Biography
I. Title
616.8'982'0092

ISBN 1–85302–387–6

Printed and Bound in Great Britain by
Biddles Ltd, Guildford and King's Lynn

Contents

Acknowledgements

I would like to thank my husband Paul for staying up whilst I was deep in sculpting this book and for coming to my assistance whenever I needed to borrow his mental structures to make sense of and hold together something that I couldn't. I would also like to thank him for the herbal tea and snacks he brought me whilst I was mentally chained to this book and for making sure I stopped to eat and brush my teeth and put my slippers on. I would like to thank him too, for letting me grill him about his own condition, which helped me to put my condition, 'autism' into perspective and draw first hand contrasts and comparisons where they came up between 'autism' and its cousins such as 'Asperger Syndrome'.

Foreword

Some people who have read my books, *Nobody Nowhere*, *Somebody Somewhere* and, most recently, *Like Color to the Blind* just read them as stories and have no particular interest in disabilities, psychology, neurology, language or development. Other people pick up those books to see if the pages hold answers for them about their own 'differentness'. For some, they do, for others, they don't.

Some people have picked up those books to try to understand the experiences of people they live with or work with. It is some of those people who have written, asking where this book is; a book which will outline what worked for me and what didn't and what I think of the techniques, therapies and treatments that are out there now.

I am diagnosed as having 'autism'. If you ask me what that word means, I would tell you that, for me, it is about having trouble with connections. I would tell you that having trouble with CONNECTIONS also causes me to have trouble with TOLERANCE and trouble with CONTROL. The word 'autism' doesn't tell anyone this, any more so than the labels of some of its 'cousins'.

People with difficulties like mine are not meant to be capable of being so intentionally self-expressive, so insightful, so aware and certainly, throughout large chunks of my life, I too appeared to be none of these things. Yet, when I write I am all of these things. This is because my writing, unlike speaking, is (both fortunately and unfortunately) a largely automatic skill so I don't have to be aware of what I am unknowingly aware of. If it is in there, it just comes out. The same thing happens for me with music and art and it has been through these things that I have discovered who I am inside and all the knowing and awareness I didn't know I had. Some people call these automatic, almost unconscious, skills, 'savant skills'. I call them useful.

Having spent the last four years corresponding with and meeting people diagnosed with 'autism' (whatever that means) who work in professional fields, have written published articles or their own autobiographies (as I did), drive vehicles or are even married with children, I know that the stereotypes about what people can and can't do may be more about where you look for your stereotypes and how you look at them. Having sat around with 'autistic' people who have more empathy, curiosity, imagination or ingenuity than most so called 'normal' people, I think it is time the myths that hover over these people were not just uncovered but unravelled.

Not all of these people started out as 'high functioning' as they ended up being. That raises the question of why others with the same label don't also grow up to be so 'high functioning'. The answer to that question, for some people, is in waving an equally questionable label of 'mental retardation'. Yet, it may just be that when people see people with 'autism' fitting 'autistic' (and generally 'low functioning') stereotypes, they just might be getting shown exactly what they are expecting to see and little more. The battle against 'autism' is a big one and if no-one expects you to be capable of climbing a mountain, then maybe you wouldn't even consider doing so, nor look for the tools with which to do so. My philosophy is that it is not everyone who is a good mountain climber but that with the right coaching, everyone is capable of taking a few steps more than they might if not challenged nor expected to do so.

Ultimately I cannot speak on behalf of anyone but myself. Yet having discovered the awareness and insight I have into my own condition is, ironically, a kind of advantage in recognising when I see the same compensations and adaptations at work in other people. I have lived these things from the inside in a non-autistic world which can only view and describe them from the outside.

Perhaps it is not that I dare to speak about other people who share conditions like mine but how I dare to that is important. Parents and professionals may describe with great empathy what someone with 'autism' does but can they then assume that the perceptions, sensations, logic, or wants of the person are comparable to their own or even work by a similar system? I have never found morally digestible the arrogance of those who do not admit to being ignorant. I hope to be neither of these things, but inevitably, because I am human, will probably at some point be both. For this, I apologise in advance.

I speak as a person who has had to learn many things in different ways from most people and who, therefore, may not only dare, but be able sometimes to view things in a way others are sometimes blinkered from daring to imagine or admit. .

In the writing of this book, I speak as a Nobody, as a Somebody, as an Anybody, not at, nor in front of, nor even to, but among you all.

Donna Williams

CHAPTER 1

A Bucket Full of Jigsaws
How I learned what made up my 'autism'

An interesting tumble
of boggle-dee jumble,
this weed full of gardens,
this door to the key,
this dish-load of sinks,
this pea full of pods,
this backward gone forwards,
this me.

'Autism' is spoken of by some people as a jigsaw with a missing piece. I experienced my own 'autism' as one bucket with several different jigsaws in it, all jumbled together and all missing a few pieces each but with a few extra pieces that didn't belong to any of these jigsaws. The first dilemma for me was sorting out which pieces belonged to which jigsaws. From there, I had to work out which pieces were missing and which ones weren't supposed to be in my bucket at all.

When I was an infant, my senses didn't work right and my response to light and sound and touch were not just meaningless but too acute. I could not only not understand the world, but I also could not stand it.

Up until I was about three years old, I don't think I knew I had problems. I had no consistent processing for meaning through any of my senses and no consistent meaning for anything that happened to me within the immediate context in which it happened. I made no consistent meaning out of touch that happened to me and made no consistent meaning out of what I touched beyond a texture. I made no consistent meaning out of what I saw or of other people's responses to seeing me or of what I heard, including what I said, or of other's responses to hearing me. I made no consistent meaning of my body in space or what I looked like or of my body messages or emotions or the behaviour they sometimes drove me to. I couldn't understand the meaning or significance of what was expected of me because other people's words, intonation, facial expression, body language and touch had no consistent meaning and, therefore, little or no significance. I couldn't understand much about consequences or effect. The inability to get consistent meaning through any of my senses in an environment that demanded that I did, meant I developed an acute ability to respond, not to meaning, but to patterns. I don't remember thinking of these things as problems.

In fact, as far as I can remember, my first idea that there was any problem was that the problem wasn't with me, it was with the thing that was stuck on me that I came to know as my body. It was with the intangible, uncontrollable and overwhelming assaults I came to know as emotions and it was with the unpredictable, incomprehensible, illogical actions of what I came to know as people and their expectations. But me...I probably figured that I wouldn't have had any problems if I could have got rid of all of those things.

The expectation to respond when I didn't understand or want or feel safe with the emotions that are meant to drive the interest, need or want to communicate, was a problem. The expectation to use a body and face and voice I was perceptually disconnected from, was a problem. The expectation to respond immediately with understanding when my ability to process anything for meaning was slow, out of context and incomplete, was a problem. My initial answers to these problems was to fight them off, ignore them and run away from them.

Within a few years I found that no amount of rejection on my part, no amount of tuning people out, no amount of retaliation was going to make these stubborn and persistent expectations go away. My answers now to the problem of expectations were to learn to feign the emotions I was expected to have but didn't feel safe with, to feign the interest I didn't have, to communicate with a copied voice and to move with mirrored movements in the absence of personal connection to my own and to learn to look as if I understood even if I didn't.

Around the age of ten when consistent (though generally delayed) meaning started coming more consistently through my senses, the problem was that my mind was bombarded with placeless fragments of literal meaning that I hadn't had the interest or want or need to find and didn't know what to do with. My answers to this were to find structures with which to use these things. I expanded the only things I had in place of interest and want: obsession and compulsion.

Because my processing for meaning had been happening but was very delayed and out of the context in which meaningful events happened, most of my processing for meaning was subconscious and not even I knew it was there. Mid childhood was a time of having all of this processed but subconscious; knowing and awareness were triggered and what came out surprised me as much as other people. Mid childhood was also a time when the old reliance upon patterns and the newly developing reliance upon meaning became a psychological, emotional and social battle most children never have to face. This was a time of realising the irony of a sanctuary that is also a prison. It was a time of experimenting with the boundaries of meaning and the boundaries of pattern.

That reliance upon and triggering by patterns, combined with sensory fascinations in the absence of efficient processing for meaning or personal significance, fed into the hands of compulsion and obsession, the control over which had already been pushed to the limit because of the degree of chronic stress I was under. 'Compulsion' and 'obsession' can be your friend or your foe and at different times they were both. On the one hand, I was being swept along with the tide of my own sensory pleasures and cognitive hiccups. On the other, I got glimpses of the hidden constraint of these addictive and out-of-control drives and tried sometimes to stop myself, just to prove who was in control and whose life it was.

Without an awareness of my own self, the intense sensitivity that had compelled me to reject closeness and personal and intentional self-expression came to have a name. That name was fear of emotions. It was named among so many other fears, such as fear of losing control and fear of others seeing the me in me (fear of self-exposure).

By my teenage years, I began to be too aware of the feeling of being alien. Unable to have even consistently shared true self-expression or real felt emotions with anyone, I grasped the absolutely emptiness of what the world held for me. My answer to this was to follow and mimic anybody who would take me along for the ride and to move through life as fast as possible so I didn't have to stop to feel how bad and out of control it all felt.

After several years I began to find out just how much passing for 'normal' doesn't stand up to the measure of consistency and having tried my best and still found failure, I had to look elsewhere for hope. I looked for answers and after many years of finding bits of them, found some.

By the age of thirty, I knew what jigsaws were in my bucket; problems of connection, problems of tolerance and problems of control. I know which of my jigsaws have a lot of pieces and which ones have a few. I know how these jigsaws have worked together to help or hinder me in functioning and in knowing and being close to myself and the world around me. I know how these jigsaws collectively form some of my identity and expression and some of what is not my identity or self-expression but comes from my connections nevertheless; intentional or not.

From knowing all these things, I have been able to weed my own garden; to sort through the difference between what is useful, feels good or feels like 'me' and what is counter-productive, doesn't feel right and doesn't feel like 'me'. Where I could get the weeds out, I did. Where I couldn't, I looked for what might have caused the weeds in the hope of undoing their cause.

At the age of twenty-five, a name was put to my bucket of jigsaws and that name was 'autism'. I then spent time with others who had this label (and some who had other, related labels or no labels at all) and I saw my own systems at work; sometimes more, sometimes less, in most of these people, but not all.

I saw people wading through their own collection of mixed up jigsaws. I saw some people trying to sort through them or put them together or pretend they didn't exist.

I saw some carers and professionals helping some people to sort through their jigsaws when they were still only wading. I saw others helping people to ignore their jigsaws when they'd been doing such a good job at sorting through them. I saw carers and professionals helping people to work with a type of jigsaw they didn't have when they actually had every other jigsaw but the one the carers and professionals were helping them to work on. The most surprising thing of all that I saw was that most of the carers and professionals couldn't tell one jigsaw from the next most of the time.

So many people live in a world where reading 'appearances' is their focus. I move in a world where the necessity for me to do so many so called 'normal' things happens 'unaturally' and mechanically and this means that I have come to rely on seeing 'systems' rather than 'appearances'.

That is what this book is about. It is about helping carers and professionals to recognise all the different jigsaws that can be in a bucket and to take them on the sort of journey that my own life took me. It just may be that in being able to tell one jigsaw piece from the next, they might be able to put one or two of them together and have a little more consistent success than they might presently be having.

My 'autism'-related difficulties took me on a journey where perceptual problems and systems integration problems made the world seem empty, meaningless, insignificant and without interest or reward and made my own body, voice, movements and emotions estranged from me, overwhelming and alien.

These problems took me on a journey where I learned to act as though I had a sense of 'us' and 'we' even if my systems integration problems made it very difficult to consistently process internal 'self' and external 'other' at the same time; an experience that is essential to grasping what 'social' is, how to be it and why you might want to be.

My 'autism'-related difficulties took me on a journey where sensory hypersensitivities made certain sounds, textures, patterns and colours my personal and private heaven. In the hands of other people who would indiscriminately inflict upon me the sounds, textures, patterns and colours I found overwhelming and intolerable, my sensory hypersensitivities became my social hell.

It was a journey where emotional hypersensitivity made having a self difficult and showing it to be almost impossible and like being choked or suffocated from the inside. Emotional hypersensitivity made contact with gentle affectionate people give me the effect of being force fed with a box of lemons. It made being social a sick joke where the only life possible was a non-experienceable one on a stage where one cannot be oneself except at the cost of losing thought or connection to intentional expression.

It was also a journey where attention problems made life seem like a whirlpool, where an idea couldn't be held and connection couldn't be held and I got pulled and tugged in an oblivion of activity.

It was a journey where a sleep disorder put me to 'sleep' with my eyes open and either froze my connection to my body or put my body and voice on automatic pilot after any attempt of sustained attention. These things often put me into the compromising position of being a suggestible, mirroring puppet or a zombie.

It was a journey where the addiction of compulsions, and the adrenalin 'highs' they caused, drowned out any remaining residue of REAL interests or wants, thoughts or emotions and made me an accomplice to the actions and expressions of a body, face and voice I didn't even feel was mine.

Obsession and ritual demanded that the world worked within my boundaries or was discarded, as was interference of anything so redundant as REAL emotions or closeness.

On the journey, fear dominated choice and practicality and each fear conquered merely replaced itself in a new form.

My 'autism'-related difficulties took me on a journey where my physical health fell apart from a combination of inherited faults, bad management and the chronic stress of dealing with an incomprehending world which taught this camel to walk straight instead of taking the lorry-load of straws off its back for the thirty years before it realised there was a choice.

These are the reasons why, to me, there is no single thing called 'autism'. Some camels have a lot of one type of straw on their backs. Some camels have a whole collection of different types of straws on their backs.

CHAPTER 2

What is This Thing Called Autism?

Nobody has the copyright on 'autism'. 'Autism' existed long before it got its label, long before there were charities and organisations for it and long before there were books or films about it. Its remnants can be found in fairytales and folklore about fairies and fairy possession and magic spells. They can be found in old stories of 'feral children' and famous 'fools' and, more recently, in works of science fiction.

'Autism' was around long before the American, Leo Kanner, 'discovered' it or the German, Hans Asperger, 'discovered' its more 'high functioning' cousin, 'Asperger Syndrome', back in the 1940s. 'Autism' was around long before all manner of professionals cropped up to study it, work with it or claim to be able to treat or cure it.

Over the years 'autism' has been considered a form of spiritual possession, a mental illness, an emotional disturbance, a personality disorder, a communication disorder, a mental handicap, a social communication disorder, a developmental disability and, more recently, an information processing problem, a movement disorder, or a sensory or perceptual condition and professionals of different sorts evolved within each of these camps.

Professionals from each of these different camps didn't become extinct as new camps arose. They are still out there beating their drums and beating down each other's doors. Like dinosaurs some professionals have believed their ideas are the only ones which are right. Others have been a bit more open minded, wholistic, imaginative and less resistant to change. Some professionals are the dinosaurs of today and some are the dinosaurs of tomorrow and some try hard not to become dinosaurs at all.

The professionals in different camps each focused on a written or unwritten collection of symptoms by which they could diagnose or treat the condition of 'autism' and even though they couldn't agree on what sort of condition they were looking at, many of them relied on roughly the same handful of identifiable symptoms.

Looking at 'autism' as a collection of symptoms, at a very basic level, people with 'autism' could apparently be distinguished from people with other types of problems on the basis of sharing a handful of basic features:

(a) an impairment in the ability to interact socially

(b) a 'communication disorder'

(c) certain 'bizarre behaviours'

(d) 'bizarre' responses to sensory stimuli

(e) impairment in the use of imaginary play.

Some professionals also looked at types of responses. Three basic types of responses were found; 'aloof', 'avoidant' and 'odd'. Now, 'autism' probably began to not look so similar after all. Some people seemed to fit one category in some aspects or at one time and fit another category in some other aspects or at another time. Still, looking with the intention of categorising, enough people probably seemed to fit one category more than another.

Different places have developed different public, or 'media' representations, of 'autism' and these public representations of out-of-date stereotypes continue today in articles, radio and television documentaries and film.

'Autistic' People as 'Odd'

In some places, the media representation of 'autism' has singled out those who had 'odd' responses rather than those who had mostly 'aloof' or 'avoidant' responses – the American film 'Family Pictures', for example, focused on the 'odd'. Because of their 'incomprehensible' and 'odd' or 'bizarre' behaviour, 'autistic' people were sometimes portrayed as 'alien' and 'uncomprehending', and this portrayal sometimes leaned on elements of shock and alienation rather than of mystery. This may have been a tidied up, well presented, rehash of the 'circus freak' concept and its popularity may be based upon the attraction of 'freaks', who challenge the fiercely guarded and generally accepted myth that there is such a thing as 'normality' and that 'most people' have it.

One of the results of focusing on how 'odd' or 'bizarre' or 'incomprehensible' or 'incomprehending' people with 'autism' were, may have been that it has left people with little ability to see how these people, who were so obviously 'abnormal', could be fitted into mainstream society and no reason why 'normal' people might want them to. Perhaps there is an assumption that these people either wouldn't care about their non-inclusion or wouldn't have the intelligence to think much about it.

The 'bizarre', 'odd' image may have created the same impression as any media 'monster'; that these 'creatures' needed to be controlled and pitied but also politely shovelled out of the way where people didn't have to look at them. Rather than 'angelic', the 'odd' impression seemed to portray people with 'autism' as wild or animalistic. The public impression this created may have been that parents who had such children and didn't put them in institutions had to be pitied or commended for their commitment.

'Autistic' People as 'Aloof'

In other places, the 'aloof' impression was more widely exploited and 'autistic' people were portrayed as being unreachable, fairy-like and off in their own worlds. This was portrayed in the recent film 'House Of Cards', in which the 'autistic' child is miraculously 'rescued' from the allure of 'her own world'.

The 'aloof' image had an air of mystery that possibly provoked ideas that perhaps these 'autistic' people had discovered depths of the universe that the rest of the world hadn't. The general portrayal may have been that these 'fairy-like' people were somehow 'beyond' 'normal' society and so had no interest in it. This was an attractive image that seemed to play on the lure of 'other worlds' and also on the mentality that 'if it is that good, I'd like to get a taste of it too'.

Aloof 'autistic' people were sometimes portrayed as being fallen angels or somehow closer to God. Rather than finding them repulsive, some people were attracted to them, perhaps as though this might be a way to get an express ticket to some sort of spiritual realisation.

This may have led people to feel spited or 'snubbed' in being 'left behind' and somehow 'unworthy' of these 'autistic' people who showed no interest in them. Perhaps this was why some people treated recognition by an unrelated 'aloof' 'autistic' person as a kind of advertiseable status or honour and 'yearned' to be acknowledged.

Where some have imagined or sensed a yogi, others have imagined or sensed hidden genius, a sociopath or even a psychopath. These ideas may have brought out a kind of awe and expectancy in people as well as a combination of attraction and caution or even fear.

'Autistic' People as 'Avoidant'

Where the 'avoidant' image was exploited, there was the impression of 'autistic' people as frightened and somehow victim-like. This impression may have brought out people's protective feelings but also social judgement of those who were seen as either causing these 'victims' or appearing not to have 'helped' them.

Generally, it left spoken or unspoken blame resting on the parents, with the assumption that 'obviously', if the parents were kind enough and gentle enough and caring enough (as other people sometimes figured they themselves might have been), their 'autistic' child mightn't be so avoidant. This impression puts people with 'autism' into a category similar to abused children. It fostered ideas that such parents needed to be reprimanded or scorned, have their children removed, or go into counselling to learn how to relate to them. The effect of this on parental self-esteem and mental and emotional state must be devastating, particularly when, despite years of trying to 'improve' themselves, there was no apparent effect on their child's autism. Some have even been encouraged to look back to what they did to cause it. Some, not finding anything substantial, have gone back to trivial events such as having shouted once at their infant for making noise or having had a stressful month during their pregnancy, as though these things had somehow had a shattering impact upon their child, enough to cause 'autism'.

Some of the 'avoidant' (and many 'aloof') children seen in this way were put through hours, months or years of psychotherapy or hug therapy to try to get them to release the frustration and pain that therapists assumed they harboured. When any of these 'autistic' people did begin to express themselves, it may have been presumed to be evidence that the original assumptions had been correct and the therapy appropriate. It was probably never questioned whether access to art materials in the therapist's office may have been the real key to their expression; whether it was just quieter in the therapist's office without a TV blaring or any distracting social blah-blah in the background; whether progress may have come down to something as simple as the therapist's office not having fluorescent lights in it like home did; or even whether the 'autistic' person (as some do) had spontaneously outgrown their developmental difficulties.

One film which seems to reinforce this unfortunate impression of 'autism' is a fairly recent American film called 'Back Street Dreams'.

From Stereotypes To 'Facts'

In the hands of the media, impressions became stereotypes and those stereotypes started to be treated as though they were 'facts'.

One impression was that people with 'autism' generally appeared to lack empathy towards others in any expected non-autistic way. It was generally not questioned that to the person with 'autism', the ignorance demonstrated by many non-autistic people sometimes made them appear far from having empathy themselves. Articles appeared and were quoted far and wide, not saying that many 'autistic' people appeared to lack empathy towards others in any expected non-autistic way (or deserved way), but, instead, less carefully, stating things like 'autistic people lack empathy'.

Another impression was that people with 'autism' appeared rarely to express emotion or pain in any expected non-autistic way. This became 'autistic people lack emotions' or 'autistic people lack a sense of pain'.

Also, people with 'autism' appeared rarely to understand non-autistic jokes and joking in any expected way. But the humour they were expected to share in was often directed at themselves. The general observation became 'autistic people lack a sense of humour'.

It was noticed that people with 'autism' appeared rarely to display interest and curiosity in their surroundings in any expected non-autistic way. This impression became the statement, 'autistic people lack imagination'.

People with 'autism' appeared to move and behave differently in response to their surroundings, quite differently from any expected non-autistic way of moving and behaving. Rather than acknowledging that these might simply be *different* ways of moving and behaving, people generally assumed them to be incomprehensible and, therefore, unquestionably 'bizarre', and this became, 'autistic people engage in bizarre movements and behaviours'.

It was noticed that people with 'autism' appeared to not understand many things in any expected non-autistic way. It was generally not understood that some 'autistic' people might have a form of information processing strikingly different from that of non-autistic people and that this different form of processing might make it difficult to understand information presented in a conventional non-autistic way. Unquestioned, the observation turned to 'fact' and became, 'autistic people have some degree of mental retardation'.

Now, the observation of these 'symptoms' might have been fairly harmless except that people stopped looking at them as observations of symptoms and started taking them to be 'facts'. Instead of noticing all the people who *did* seem to get jokes or show curiosity or be emotionally expressive or express 'normal' intelligence, these people were considered 'exceptions' to the 'rule' and only those who fitted the outlined symptoms were considered the 'true' 'autistics'. However, this may not have singled out one subgroup among the 'autistic' population, it may have created one.

These attitudes did injustice not only to those people who did not fit these stereotypes, but also to those people who *did* appear to display these things. Though unexpressed, some of these people *did* have empathy, emotions, a sense of pain, a sense of humour, imagination (and interest and curiosity). Their otherwise 'bizarre' behaviours not only made sense to them but, in some cases, were actually adaptations they'd discovered to HELP them to make connections, calm themselves down and remain in control better than they may otherwise have been able to.

These stereotypes had a number of repercussions. One was that many people who did not fit the media representations or the stereotypes were turned away when approaching GPs, social workers, teachers and therapists for referrals for a diagnosis on the grounds that they 'couldn't possibly be autistic'.

I have heard from many people who deal with their own serious difficulties with social interaction and communication and have sensory, perceptual, attention, obsessive, compulsive or phobic 'difficulties' that cause them to display 'autistic' behaviours, who are denied a referral on the grounds that they 'couldn't be autistic' because they didn't fit these stereotypes. One such woman who has an 'autistic' son and whose mother also appears to have had Asperger Syndrome (a high functioning relative to 'autism'), approached a professional with a view to getting a diagnosis for herself for problems she shared in common with her son and mother. She was turned away because she cried during the consultation and was, therefore, considered to have expressed too much emotion to have been autistic. Other people have been turned away because they have a wider range of interests or more acquaintances than the stereotypes portray or because, like many people diagnosed with Asperger Syndrome, they complain of having an overactive imagination that distracts them all the time. It is worth questioning whether it is here, where these people are turned away, that the stereotypes become self-fulfilling prophecies.

One of the other repercussions of the stereotypes is that more often it is those who fit the stereotypes who are given ongoing support, keeping them in the client/patient role. There are others people with 'autism' who are too accepting, too gregarious, too acceptance-seeking and compliant who are equally at risk and need support just as much.

People who are considered to lack empathy, a sense of humour, emotions or imagination are not likely to be invited to speak at international autism conferences or to be interviewed on TV. The result of this is that professionals and parents remain the spokespeople for people with autism, that the world doesn't hear about the exceptions except as 'exceptions' and that the stereotypes (and the jobs and organisations that rest upon them) remain neither shaken nor stirred.

Another repercussion of the pervasiveness of stereotypes is that people do not expect people with 'autism' to be anything contrary to the stereotypes. For people who DO feel and have empathy, humour, emotions, understanding and imagination but are seriously inhibited, blocked or disconnected from expressing or displaying these things, this might mean several things. Some get away with not trying as they otherwise might to battle with or find strategies around what is blocking or inhibiting them in the expression of their empathy, humour, emotions, understanding and imagination.

Another repercussion is that some people with 'autism' might listen more to what you do than what you say and might think they are actually meeting your expectations by adhering to what they perceive as your assumed limitations to their capabilities. I heard from one man with 'autism' who wrote about not being able to show his understanding or to speak because he didn't want to 'shock' his parents! (who had been told he was severely intellectually retarded and often referred to his 'inability to speak').

These stereotypes may also have particular repercussions for so called 'high functioning' people with 'autism' who are afraid to admit to not fitting the stereotypes. Some 'autistic' people I have corresponded with over time were reluctant to admit to having 'imagination', either assuming they might be considered not 'truly' 'autistic' on the grounds of having it or assuming that having creative or fantastic thoughts or mental images (imagination) is 'odd' and that 'nobody else has anything like this'.

There is a view that such people are merely demonstrating a lack of knowledge of the existence of other minds. This may be true, and may even be a reason why people who have even an excess of imagination do not find any reason to express it (because 'nobody else has anything like this'). It may, however, also be true that some people with 'autism' have imagination but don't know how the word 'imagination' applies to what they have.

The word 'autism' can broken into two parts. The first part, 'aut' comes from the Greek prefix, 'autos', and means 'self'. The second part, the Latin suffix, 'ism', means 'a state or quality'. This means that the literal translation of 'aut-ism' is 'self-state' or 'self-ness'.

Perhaps this word came about to describe the apparent rejection or aversion to other people which was at the heart of the original stereotypes of 'autism'.

The assumption that those who seemed to be self-focused were actually in a 'self-state' seems to be a sweeping one. People can be intensely focused on their body parts or sensations or workings, specifically *because* they perceive them as foreign, incomprehensible, ever new and 'other' and generally not aware that these things are part of themselves. As a teenager, I spent many of my lunch breaks at my first secondary school trying to shake a hand off an arm without the perception that both were part of my body. I had spent a childhood trying to get away from my own body, finally accepting that the damned thing wasn't going to stop making me aware of its clinging attachment to me.

I spent most of my life with a jumble of sounds going through my mind that were the regurgitation of sounds of the world around me and devoid of much that was generated by me.

I spent the largest percentage of my life trying to cope with what the world around me had bombarded me with, with little or no extra processing time for the luxury of having any conscious thoughts about that world. If anything, my 'autism', like that of so many others like me, was often an example not of a kind of 'self-ism' but of a kind of 'other-ism' where any conscious and conjoined or consistent sense of selfhood doesn't come easily at all.

Whilst this little play on words might seem like an irrelevant load of hoo-ha, it has a point to it. That point is that right from the start, from the time someone came up with the word 'autism', the condition has been judged from the outside, by its appearances, and not from the inside according to how it is experienced. As we have seen, that has big implications for how people try to deal with the condition and big implications for 'success' or a lack of it.

People have imagined all sort of things about how the body got ill. At one time, it was imagined that washing made people ill. Instead of washing themselves, people powdered themselves up and sprayed themselves with fruits and other nicer smelling things that kept the stink-level down (or disguised it).

At another time, it was thought that the physical problems of women were due to their pursuit of intellectual knowledge. The solution was that women shouldn't pursue a formal education. Mental problems in women (including the 'mental problem' of pursuing intellectual knowledge) were once perceived as being due to trouble stemming from the womb. In many cases, the 'cure' involved setting leeches upon the body (they thought this cleaned out the 'bad blood'). Strangely enough, it sometimes worked (if it didn't kill you). I think that if someone tried to set leeches upon me, I'd pretty soon learn to stop displaying whatever it was I was being 'treated' for.

The point is, that once people better understand how things actually work, progress is usually made. For some people a label has the power of unquestionability. For others, it is only as good as its usefulness. Labels are basically answers to the question 'WHAT?'.

If you look at a reddish, rectangular, solid, mass that is embedded among other reddish, rectangular, solid, masses that collectively form a big flat surface, it doesn't help much to know that that thing you are looking at is a brick. The word 'brick' tells you 'what' it is but 'what' doesn't tell you much at all.

When people ask, 'what does this label mean then?', they are generally directed to look at its description (its symptoms). They look at its 'appearances' rather than considering it by its 'experience'. The description of something tells you a whole load of more 'what', and all that 'what' doesn't mean a lot. Some people get a diagnosis and they are handed a label. They might look for more and they get descriptions of the symptoms that go with the label. For many, that doesn't get them anywhere.

'What' puts a name to something that you maybe didn't have a name to but it doesn't tell you anything you aren't already experiencing. It doesn't tell you what the 'what' is made up of. It doesn't tell you what caused the things that the 'what' is made up of. It doesn't tell you what to do about the 'what'. It doesn't even really give you any idea of where to go or who to ask about the 'what'. Having a word for 'what' might inform you a bit but it doesn't empower you much at all.

I think this is why some people aren't content with just a label; sooner or later they feel like they got nothing at all. They might know what they are looking for, or they might not. If they do know what they are looking for, it is probably answers about 'why'.

Causes are answers to 'why'. 'Why' can feel mind-boggling if you find the causes but don't know what to do about them. That 'what to do about them' is the 'how'.

The 'what' and the 'why' and the 'how' are all part of the mathematics of life and from there you can find out 'where' to go and 'who' to look to without chasing your tail as much as you might have. There's no point trying to start at the middle or the end of the equation; life is full of sidetracks but you can get to your destination quicker and easier with a map. Right tracks are about being in the right place, with the right person (or thing) at the right time. The problem is, how to tell the right ones from the wrong ones and that is all about avoiding the advertisements and the flag wavers and the ego trippers and just reading the signposts along the way.

'WHAT?', 'HOW?', 'WHY?', ('WHO?' or 'WHICH?' and 'WHEN?' or 'WHERE?') can be not just different types of questions but different levels of questioning. Here's an example that might help to explain this.

The condition of: 'the dog which wouldn't move'

The WHAT (the condition):
Canine inability to move.

(the symptoms):
Dog appears unable to move from one place to another.

The WHY (the cause):
  ◦ dog is glued to the floor
    ◦ dog is dead
  ◦ dog is made of wood
    ◦ dog is asleep

(The HOW / WHEN / WHERE / WHO or solutions):
    ◦ Unglue the dog
  ◦ Bury dead dog and get one which does move
    ◦ Stick wheels on the feet of wooden dog
      ◦ Wait till dog wakes up.

Looking at this example, you can see that if you just focused on the condition, it wouldn't help at all in changing the condition. If you focused only on the symptoms, that wouldn't give you any solutions either. If you stopped at the causes, that also wouldn't tell you how to deal with the condition. Dealing with a condition involves looking beyond labels and symptoms and beyond causes yet any journey to find which solutions will work has to go through all of these things.

CHAPTER 3

Tackling the Bogie-Man of 'Autism'

Professionals get paid to tackle 'autism' and one thing that most of them *have* shared is viewing 'autism' as the enemy.

Although many parents share this view, there are also those who don't. Among people with 'autism', too, there are those who identify with their condition and do not seek to change it. There are also those who don't have the motivation to change their condition and those who either see no hope or ability to cope with trying to change or work with it. On the other hand, there are also those who feel constrained, distorted or imprisoned by their condition who fight or need help to fight the constraints or discomforts of their 'autism' and to push out its constricting boundaries.

Those who do see 'autism' as the 'enemy' do so for all sorts of different reasons:

- because it is not what they see as 'normal'
- because they feel that a disability is unquestionably a burden that they should assist in the unburdening of
- because they just don't have the energy, personal resources or social support to cope with someone's 'autism' as it is
- because they imagine that, like peeling a banana, beyond the 'autism' there is some sort of 'normal' child
- because they think they have seen a trappedness in the eyes of someone with 'autism' that tells them that, whoever the person with 'autism' is, that person is more than just a bag of 'autism' with no personality independent of the effects of their condition.

There are people with 'autism' who look into the mirror and see, or imagine they see, all these things too. There are also people with 'autism' who look into the mirror and see no-one beyond their autism.

For whatever reasons someone is motivated to do battle with the bogie-man of 'autism', they might fight it on one or more of several levels; as a label, as a collection of symptoms, as an experience and/or as a cause or causes needing to be dealt with.

Symptom and Stereotype Approaches

Approaches to 'treatment' based on symptoms and stereotypes are usually aimed at taking away the offending or disturbing symptoms/stereotypes to leave a semblance of something that more closely resembles 'normality'. These approaches forget that symptoms are not causes.

When people attempt to 'treat' people by getting rid of the appearance of symptoms it is not so much that people are expected to *become* 'normal' as that they are expected to learn to *act* 'normal'. Within this approach there is generally no suggestion that so called 'normal' people should become more tolerant and accommodating or even work *with* the condition rather than *against* it. Ironically, such people generally find this idea to be 'unnatural'. In my view, teaching an amputee to walk without artificial limbs, a frame, or a wheelchair is also pretty unnatural even if it amounts to the same sort of treatment some people with 'autism' find themselves getting.

Some people with 'autism', like anybody else, identify with their behaviour and consider it a part of themselves and their personality. To people like this, attempts to make them behave in a way that is unnatural to them may be a demonstration of a non-comprehending world that is lacking in tolerance and empathy.

The eradication of symptoms may often be a relief to parents, professionals and carers, and even to some people with 'autism' themselves, those who welcome the achievement of self-control and functional ability and some of the (albeit conditional) acceptance, acknowledgement, dignity and inclusion this entails. At the same time, this approach is like seeking to 'cure' epilepsy by teaching people how to 'act normal' during an attack.

'Cure' Approaches

Some people seek 'cures' as though there is a 'normal' person within an 'autistic' shell just waiting, like sleeping beauty, for the spell to be broken.

Some look only for causes, forgetting the 'now' that people with 'autism' and those who support them, have to tackle today and again tomorrow.

Some 'treatments' based on a 'cure' approach include kinds of 'hug therapy' or 'holding therapy' where 'love' is somehow meant to 'get through to' the 'autistic' person. These treatments assume that all sensory and perceptual systems are intact and integrated and that information processing for the person with 'autism' is basically 'normal', except that issues like 'love' and who is in control have not yet reached that person.

Experiences-Based Approaches

Experiences-based approaches acknowledge that viewing a condition from its outside appearances is not enough. These approaches acknowledge that if you're having trouble leading the horse to water, you have to understand how it feels about the water and whether it understands its body messages to do with thirst and what the significance of those body messages is for action.

Experiences-based approaches try to understand not so much the 'appear' of a condition (what it looks like) but the 'be' of the condition (what it feels like).

Cause-Based Approaches

Cause-based approaches attempt to look at various possible underlying causes of various symptoms of 'autism' and other related developmental conditions. Usually, this is with a view to avoiding or lessening the plod-plod of working with the condition of 'autism'. Cause-based approaches look at identifying the straws on the camel's back and finding out how to remove them rather than teaching the camel to act as though it doesn't have those straws on its back or teaching it to walk 'normally' in spite of its heavy load. One of the problems of some cause-based approaches is that they assume a single type of 'autism' with a variety of underlying causes when, in my experience, there are several different types of 'autism' and sometimes more than one type of 'autism' present.

My view is that all of these approaches have their time and place, and *person* but none of them is useful all the time, in all the places, with all the people. The question is, how to know when and where that time and place is and who these approaches will work with to gain the most 'success' and cause the least damage or fewest set-backs. By lifting the covers on the symptoms of 'autism' and having a look at what is underneath, this question might have some answers.

Looking at 'autism' from the point of view of a collection of symptoms generally makes the mistake of assuming there is one only type of underlying problem.

I don't see 'autism'. I see compounding collections of 'autism'-related problems. I see different adaptations to different types of 'autism'-related problems. I see different personalities dealing with different types of 'autism'-related problems. And, I see different compensatory flow-on effects in people where a problem that affects one system of functioning will cause a weakening in another system as it tries to compensate.

I see people identifying personally with their type of 'autism'-related problems and I see people rejecting their type or types of 'autism'-related problems. I see people encouraged to pretend that their type of 'autism'-related problems doesn't exist and others encouraged to flag-wave or hide behind or use their type of 'autism'-related problems as their excuse for giving up. I see these things in the 'autistic' people I have met and read of these things in the letters of many 'autistic' people who have corresponded with me over the past four years, and I have seen these things in myself.

There are mild forms and more severe forms of the different types of 'autism'-related problems but severity does not make one person have a 'purer' form of 'autism' than another, even though I have heard of and from parents who have advertised their children in this way.

Some people appear to be only mildly affected by their problems because they have become masters at adaptation and managing compensations but, in fact, actually have a greater degree of impairment. They function at a higher level than their actual abilities to monitor, process or comprehend this functioning.

Some people, on the other hand, appear severely affected by their 'autism' but, in fact, have very low motivation to develop functional adaptations which would help them manage what is actually only a mild degree of impairment. They function at a lower level than they are capable of monitoring, processing, comprehending or coping with.

Some people ARE exactly as they appear and some people are not.

There are people who identify with 'autism' but have only one or two of its impairments and people who fall on the 'autistic' side of 'normal' who have a range of 'autism'-related impairments but have these in such a mild degree as to pass for 'normal' under most circumstances.

There are also some who have other problems who wish they had 'autism' instead and probably just as many people with 'autism' who wish they had something else, perhaps more manageable or curable than autism.

There are those who have 'autism'-related problems but have been passed off as having a condition other than 'autism' – even encouraged to believe they are insane or mentally retarded, for example.

The most important reason for distinguishing between types of 'autism'-related problems is not in order to exclude anybody but in order better to understand how to help people in a way that will waste fewer resources (including mental energy and emotion) and have a greater and more consistent degree of 'success'.

Just as there is no point treating broken, or clotted or severely bruised or burned legs by merely sticking them all in a plaster cast, the cause of 'autism'-related problems and the successful treatment of those problems will not be found until people understand more specifically what it is they are looking at and whether, in spite of a shared label, they are all looking at the same thing.

Misplacement

A misdiagnosis doesn't help anybody, nor does a misplacement. Too many people with 'autism' have been testimony to ignorance and arrogance or lack of services or funding. Too often these things have resulted in hammering square pegs into round holes. The dumping of people with 'autism' into other categories such as 'emotionally disturbed', 'mentally ill' or 'intellectually retarded' doesn't help the people with 'autism'.

On the other hand, there have been those in whom conditions like Tourette's syndrome or aphasia or dyspraxia have been diagnosed in people displaying 'autistic' symptoms. Where these diagnoses were correct, they may have been more helpful in getting appropriate services than sending these people along to 'autism' services where the particular underlying cause of their 'autistic' symptoms is generally not addressed.

Understanding things like pervasive 'anxiety states' or where 'obsession' or 'compulsion' exist as two separate or possibly compounding conditions without psychological cause or association, is a direction for the future rather than a thing of the present. Whilst certain branches of psychiatry or psychology or neurology have some idea about these things in communicatively able adults, there is a general lack of understanding of them in children and functionally non-verbal adults, in whom these conditions may be seriously compromising their ability to communicate and the formation of identity and the ability to interact socially.

Similarly, although there is some understanding of attention problems in children, particularly related to diet, nutrition and biochemical or hormonal problems, there are few adequate educational or family support services specific to dealing with this condition. Some of these children, too, are to be found in 'autism' services. Unfortunately, those staffing these services are generally not trained to handle problems particular to this condition or to manage their special diets adequately (so many of these children get 'high' on sweets and cordial full of additives and sugar given to them by professionals to 'reward' them, only to find they are then punished for the resulting behaviour or attention problems).

There are a handful of 'autistic' children in some deaf–blind schools who have *no* sight or hearing impairment. Some of these children have perceptual problems, or systems-integration problems in processing what they see and/or hear.

The recognition of perceptual problems and systems-integration problems is a new field and many teachers and other professionals are unaware or unknowledgeable about the problems, how to recognise them or what to do about them. Some of the same types of children who are doing well enough in deaf–blind schools have counterparts in 'autistic' schools who the staff find generally harder to 'get through to' than some of their other 'autistic' children. 'Autistic' children with recognised perceptual problems or systems-integration problems in deaf–blind schools seem less likely to be considered intellectually retarded than when the same types of children are in 'autistic' schools. Many children with perceptual problems, therefore, are found not just in deaf–blind schools and 'autistic' schools but in special schools for people with marked intellectual disabilities when, in fact, a large number of them may have 'normal' intelligence.

Children with sensory hypersensitivities or emotional hypersensitivities may appear to have difficulty being able to stand what they see or hear or in sharing or expressing awareness or understanding of what they see and hear. Sometimes, these problems are mistaken for emotional damage, or these children's seemingly incomprehensible and apparently unjustified responses are mistakenly taken as indications of emotional disturbance. Because of this children with severe sensory or emotional hypersensitivities are as likely to end up in schools for emotionally disturbed or damaged children or for children with challenging behaviour as anywhere else. In my view, this is like putting pigeons in with cats. Emotionally hypersensitive children, limited in their ability to express themselves or demonstrate need or felt emotion, are at an even greater risk of being bullied at these schools than in mainstream schools. Sensorily hypersensitive children, likely to run from noise or touch, become easy scapegoats. What is more, among such a disruptive, disturbing or out of control population, the less confrontational behaviour of children with sensory or emotional hypersensitivities may mean that they may be more likely to get overlooked because they don't seem to be causing problems to the staff.

'Autistic' schools, too, are generally limited in helping these children. The staff at 'autistic' schools are generally not informed about the nature of sensory or emotional hypersensitivity, nor about how to identify it or what to do about it.

In order to provide better services for people with 'autism', people need to be better trained and educated so they can deal with more than just symptoms. Attacking symptoms does not get rid of the causes and for many people with 'autism' if symptoms are suppressed, the causes just create new symptoms to replace the old. That frustrates everybody. It frustrates parents who put their faith in those working with their children. It frustrates the teachers and professionals who put effort into helping people with 'autism' only to see the same or similar problems recurring. Most of all, it frustrates those adults and children with 'autism' who want REAL help.

The training and education needed is already happening among people with 'autism' who are able to communicate verbally or through writing. Around the world, people with 'autism' are sharing their experiences with each other and sometimes with the professionals, with parents or with the general public. People with 'autism' are trying to tell people what is going on, rather than telling them what they expect or want to hear. These people are sharing tips and training and educating each other.

What parents and professionals need, more than fluffy 'success' stories of 'autistic' people who have learned to 'act normal', is information about the experiences people have of their particular 'type of 'autism'-related problems. What parents and professionals need is an understanding of how they might be able to identify different types of underlying problems so that they can work with the causes and not just the symptoms.

Taking three of the recognised features of 'autism':

- 'impairment in social interaction'
- 'communication disorder'
- 'bizarre behaviours'

I would like to focus on a handful of specific problems that can result in all three of these features. These can roughly be grouped together into three basic types of problems:

Problems of Control
- ○ 'compulsion'
- ○ 'obsession'
- ○ 'acute anxiety'

Problems of Tolerance
- ○ 'sensory hypersensitivity'
- ○ 'emotional hypersensitivity'

Problems of Connection
- ○ 'attention problems'
- ○ 'perceptual problems'
- ○ 'systems integration problems'
- ○ 'left-right hemisphere-integration problems'.

Problems of control are about being able to respond with intention to the world and/or oneself. Problems of tolerance are about being able to stand the world and/or oneself. Problems of connection are about being able to make sense of the world and/or oneself.

CHAPTER 4

The Mixed Bag Found in a Hypothetical Classroom

In the case of two people showing all three symptoms associated with 'autism', one person may have one underlying problem but the other may have a different underlying problem resulting in the same three symptoms. To understand this a bit better, I have sneaked into the fictional office of a fictional school for children with 'autism' to look at some fictional files on some fictional children (who are all diagnosed as having 'autism') who are all in the same fictional class.

Joanne: A Case of 'Compulsion'

Joanne sits in a seat up in the front area of the classroom in this school for children with 'autism'. Joanne, like all the other children in this classroom appears to have the three features of 'impairment in social interaction', 'communication disorder' and 'bizarre behaviours'. In Joanne's case, these symptoms are the result of compulsion.

Joanne does not have just a handful of compulsions. Her compulsions are pervasive and intense and dominate every aspect of her thinking and emotional responses. Because of this, Joanne is generally unable to control her behaviour.

Because she can't control her behaviour, she feels helpless and alienated from her own body. She also feels without hope because nobody seems to realise that she doesn't mean to do the things she does but she always seems to be blamed for them and other people act as though the things she does are *intentional*.

Being judged by her unintentional expression and behaviour, Joanne has generally become fed up with people who don't seem to be able to see 'the real her' and she perceives them as treating her unjustly as they seem not to help her.

Another reason why Joanne doesn't like being around people is because she has learned that every time she is compelled to do things she doesn't mean to, she feels guilty and full of self-hatred because she was unable to control herself and stop herself inflicting these things on others, especially those she likes.

There also doesn't seem much point in trying to engage other people in interaction because their words and actions just trigger more unintentional compulsive behaviours and responses in her. She has learned that people seem to 'cause' her to be out of control and so she learned that interaction is not comfortable or enjoyable. She has also learned that there is no point trying to share her thoughts or feelings with other people or trying to do things with them because, inevitably, if she tries to express things with intention, things come out messed up.

When Joanne is on her own she puts a lot of energy into trying to stop her compulsions taking over so sometimes she tries to 'freeze' her mind and her body and when she does this she looks like a statue. She tries to stop her body from destroying things, striking out at her or giving out unintended impressions to other people. She tries to stop her mind from unintentionally repeating sound patterns and jingles and making it hard for her to concentrate when she wants to. She tries to listen to people but she can't fight the compulsion to click the muscles in her ears non-stop so she can't concentrate or understand what people are saying. Joanne tries to speak but her compulsive thoughts push their way in front of her intentional ones and she says things that make her look silly or as if she doesn't make sense.

Joanne knows other people think she is probably mad or stupid and annoying and even though her true self-expression is limited, there is a depth and sadness in her eyes because she feels like a tortured prisoner.

Joanne is so caught up in compulsion that she has had little time to understand her own thoughts and feelings. Whenever she tries to reflect on something, she finds herself compulsively playing with the patterns in things. Without reflection, she has not yet had much chance to explore or understand how she, nor other people might think or feel so she appears to have no real awareness of how other people think, or that they think at all.

Joanne's frustration results in her hitting herself because she is sick of the lack of control she feels (and sometimes she is just compelled to hit herself and she then feels abused by her own body). Joanne also rocks a lot and jumps a lot and taps herself a lot to try to give herself a rhythm to calm herself down and try to get some order to her thinking and some control over it. She has also been compelled to lash out, tear her clothing and tear paper and smash things. She has been compelled to spin things (by definition 'spinable' objects themselves seem to be irresistibly commanding her to spin them). Other objects seem to demand physical recognition of their presence and not to be 'left out' which drives her to tap things compulsively to acknowledge them. Joanne's mischannelled emotions compel her to throw her body about and put it into a variety of poses and make a variety of unintentional noises and sound patterns.

Joanne has developed rituals about everything, which is her way of trying to gain control over her life. Once established, she has an aversion to the threat of chaos that breaking rituals seems to entail.

Joanne has a ritual to do with food and eating in order to get herself through a meal. If anything interferes with these rituals she finds herself so compelled by the lack of symmetry of what is on the table and her plate that she cannot properly attend to eating until she 'takes care of it'.

Joanne has sleep rituals that involve checking the entire room and this helps her to fight off the compulsion to check intermittently through the night. Her feelings of being out of control also drive her to make sure the covers of the bed are all entirely without creases (this used to make it impossible for her to stand sleeping in the bed as she caused it to be messed up). She has the same compulsion to do with her sleeping clothes which make it very hard for her to stand wearing any as they never stay perfectly uncreased. Even once under the covers, Joanne is compelled to place herself symmetrically in the bed and if she doesn't she feels gripped with anxiety for not having order and control. She has attempted to fight this compulsion but found herself then compelled at different times to place herself exactly diagonally across the bed, lie along the side of the bed where she was neatly and conservatively preserved in the hanging pouch where the blankets were tucked in, or packaged as tightly as possible in a tidy bundle at the foot of the bed where she took up the minimum space possible. All of these compulsions made it very difficult to be free to go to bed and sleep as she might 'naturally' and by contrast she can see her life is clearly not as easy as it is for other children, though she doesn't know why.

(Joanne has another classmate called Janine who has the same three features of 'autism' which are the result of the same 'compulsion' problems. Janine, though, is not as self-aware as Joanne, so Janine actually feels that her compulsions are part of herself and her self-expression.

Instead of feeling out of control, Janine thinks that her compulsions are 'wants' and 'needs'. This means that Janine doesn't feel as trapped and helpless and without hope as Joanne does. Also, Janine feels upset when people try to stop her from being compulsive because instead of knowing people are trying to help her, Janine feels they don't care about what she 'wants' or 'needs' or 'enjoys' to do.

Janine assumes she 'likes' saying word patterns and lines from jingles. She assumes she 'wants' to avoid listening to people and indulge, instead, in the hypnotic rhythm of her own repetitive thinking.

Because she feels 'stopped' by other people this makes Janine feel other people are unreasonable and unfair so she has learned to avoid them because she knows they will try to stop her doing things.)

Jed: A Case of 'Obsession'

Jed sits across the room from Joanne and also has the same three features of 'autism'; social interaction problems, communication problems and 'bizarre' behaviours. The problems underlying these things for Jed is related, but different, to the problems for Joanne and Janine. Jed has an 'obsession' problem.

Jed's obsession makes him intensely interested in a very limited number of things to the exclusion of all else. In Jed's case, it is bath plugs and plumbing.

Jed cannot think about anything but bath plugs and plumbing fixtures because bath plugs and plumbing fixtures make personal sense and feel personally significant. For Jed, bath plugs are like floodgates that he has control over in sending water away in such a consistent, predictable and clearly purposeful and seemingly intentional direction. Because of this, Jed has no interest in anyone or anything else because they don't have the same clear meaning and significance and they can't compete with bath plugs and plumbing fixtures. He cannot control the direction of people and they never act in any clearly defined consistently predictable, intentional and purposeful direction.

Jed will only communicate with people as a means of getting near bath plugs and plumbing fixtures, to which he is attracted as though they were 'friends'. He will say 'go to the bathroom', 'the plug', 'turn on the tap' and 'where's it going' (talking to the water) which he says in response to questions, remarks or suggestions regardless of the topic.

Because of Jed's obsessions, his thinking is not free to make use of anything he hears *unless* it reinforces, challenges or adds to his obsession with bath plugs and plumbing fixtures. When forced to repeat a word or phrase that is unrelated to Jed's obsessions, his total lack of interest in what he is being made to say comes through in the way he says it which is generally in a bored or flippant, generally expressionless and mindlessly compliant tone.

The significance of Jed's obsessions gives them a dominance over his life that means Jed hasn't found an interest in knowing what other people think or feel or are interested in. Because of this, Jed is seen to have no awareness of other people as having minds.

Jed will also not sleep without his personal collection of bath plugs in bed with him because they make him feel secure and as though something in the world is comprehensible and feels 'real'. If he is denied the ability to sleep with his special things, he prefers to go and be where his 'special things' are than to sleep in bed, even if it is not as warm or comfortable and even if he is clearly tired. For Jed, security is the greater comfort.

It is difficult to lead Jed away from bathrooms and plumbing fixtures and he throws tremendous tantrums, throwing and tearing things and striking out (even at himself) and screaming, when forced to leave them, because he feels this forced separation personally.

Jed will sit and study his collection of bath plugs for hours. Jed has no interest in using the toilet and is so involved in his obsessions that he feels distracted by, and therefore annoyed, at any need to go to the toilet. Because of this, he generally holds on for ages.

Similarly, Jed has no interest in eating unless it is a means of getting back to his obsessions and will only come to the table to eat if he can bring some of his collection of things with him.

(Jed's cousin, Joe has the same three features of 'autism' which result from the same obsession 'problem'. Joe, however, is self-aware and tries to tear himself away from the domination of his obsession: locks. Locks make personally significant sense to Joe because they are used to keep things out and that gives him a feeling of control, even if it is just to carry them as symbols with him as their possessor.

Joe tries to be involved with other people but he has to force himself to do this without any interest in doing so. He also tries to force himself to say things that are not related to his obsessional topic of locks, so he tries to work out what people want to hear him say. However, because the DISPLAYED interest did not originate with him, he speaks without purpose and his obsession drags him repeatedly off track. Joe knows that intonation is meant to demonstrate interest and emotions about things and because he wants to be interested in other things but isn't, he sometimes forces himself to put some 'interest' into his voice, which, to the listener, sounds like an inappropriate use of intonation.

Joe also gets very disappointed in himself at not being able to force himself to be interested or expressive in 'appropriate' ways. He sometimes gets so fed up at himself that he is self-abusive. At other times he gets apathetic and stares into space, refusing to indulge in his obsessions, but otherwise interested in nothing and motivated to do nothing. Sometimes, Joe thinks he has found another interest, but it turns out to be just another obsession. When he recognises this, he generally drops it but finds himself reverting back to his original one.)

Jasmine: A Case of 'Acute Anxiety'

Jasmine sits across the room from Joanne and Jed. Jasmine also has the three features of 'autism'. In her case, these things are not the result of one or two sources of anxiety but of an intense and pervasive anxiety state. Jasmine has never been abused nor neglected, publicly or privately.

Jasmine is afraid of hands (even her own) which seem to jut out of sleeves as though they are not connected to the people who have them. She runs away when anyone tries to reach for her or touch her and also refuses to use her hands except to instinctively push away.

Jasmine is also afraid of eyes which seem to be saying or expecting things or looking for things and she doesn't know what. So she can't stand to look at them. Jasmine is afraid of people and has trouble eating around them so she sometimes appears to be refusing to eat. Then people try to hold her to force feed her and then her terror of hands makes her panic.

Jasmine is also afraid of animals which seem unpredictable and demanding of her. She has a fear of stairs which seem to disappear off into nothing and a fear of the dark. She has a fear of sleep and of toilets which all feel as if they rob her of control. Jasmine's family's house has all of these things in it and in the garden and at school Jasmine is confronted by other things that cause her acute anxiety. She is so constantly gripped by anxiety that she cannot consistently concentrate, pay attention or find her thoughts. She is so constantly gripped by fear that she cannot consistently connect properly with her body and understand her body messages or emotions. Because of these things, she cannot communicate efficiently most of the time. She can, however, be made to repeat words that are said to her but is usually in too great a state of anxiety to attend to the meaning of what she is being taught to repeat.

Jasmine's constantly dominating anxiety means that she has little time for reflection or curiosity about what other people think or feel and so she appears to have no awareness of other people's thoughts or feelings or that they have minds at all.

Jasmine does a lot of things to try to calm herself down. She rocks and tries to hypnotise herself in various ways to get away from her anxiety (and the compulsive attraction she has in attending unintentionally to what makes her anxious).

When she is anxious, Jasmine sometimes strikes out suddenly or bites her finger or flaps one of her hands. Jasmine generally refuses to go anywhere near the toilet because it causes her acute anxiety. Jasmine's anxiety means that she will not sleep unless there is a light on and she will not stay in bed if she can't watch the doorway. Even after all of this, she is usually too gripped by anxiety to sleep and appears to have no awareness of the need to sleep.

(Jaqueline has the same three symptoms resulting from the same problem as Jasmine. Jaqueline, however, has more self-awareness, which leads her constantly to challenge her anxiety, knowing that the anxiety has no real basis in spite of the feelings. In spite of this, Jaqueline can't seem to get ahead because every time she conquers one source of anxiety, it merely gets replaced by a newly acquired one.)

Jake: A Case of Sensory Hypersensitivities

Jake is seated at a table towards the front of the classroom even though he would prefer to be off in the corner or not in the classroom at all. Jake is a person with all three features of 'impairment in social interaction', 'communication disorders' and 'bizarre behaviours' who has severe and pervasive sensory hypersensitivities.

Jake sometimes appears withdrawn because he can't stand the sound of people's voices and the sounds of their movements and even the sound of their breathing makes them sound invasively closer than they actually are. He also can't stand the texture of their skin and clothing and the smell of their perfume and this makes him avoid people. He also refuses to eat with the family as he can't stand the smells of sitting next to them or the smells of the food they have. He also can't stand the textures of many of the foods they eat so, instead, he helps himself to things in the cupboard which he can stand.

Jake also generally finds it difficult to stand listening to people because of their pitch or volume and is generally non-communicative because he cannot sensorily bear the sound of his own voice.

In order to avoid being engaged in conversation, Jake generally only makes an attempt to communicate verbally when he is forced to do so or when doing so will make people leave him alone. Here, he often uses only the minimum words necessary and speaks in a whisper which is sometimes so inaudible that he appears almost only to mouth the words.

Because Jake has such a sensory aversion to involvement with others he has never found the desire to understand them or have much empathy for them and because of this, he has never thought much at all about how they might think or feel about anything. So, basically, he appears to have little awareness of minds other than his own.

Jake rocks a lot to calm himself down from the stress of his painful sensory hypersensitivities. He also covers his ears and shields his eyes a lot to keep out light and sound (but people taught him not to do this which confused him even more about them and made them appear to not understand or care). Jake also sometimes makes noises to try to drown out other sounds that are even less tolerable than his voice (and, surprisingly, people let him do this because they think he is experimenting with communication).

Jake refuses to take off his coat most of the time because he feels protected from the touch of other people this way. On the other hand, some types of fabrics irritate him so much that he will not keep them on and has torn some of them up in an effort to avoid being made to wear these uncomfortable things. He also has trouble pulling woollen jumpers over his head because the fabric touching his hair affects him like fingernails scraped on a blackboard disturb some people (Jake has this response too to the sound of anything chalky used on an abrasive surface and this makes regular classrooms difficult to handle).

Jake also holds his breath much of the time because he can't stand the smells around him and the taste of these smells gets into his mouth and makes him feel yukky.

Jake has an aversion to textured food so he will only eat a very limited number of things like soft plain bread, custard and bananas. When he will eat a full meal, he is particularly fussy about its texture, insisting on mashing it until it is mushy with no lumps. When people try to stop him 'protecting' himself from his sensory hypersensitivities (as the ways he attempts to do so are often seen as 'bizarre' behaviours to those who don't comprehend them) he appears to throw tantrums because, to him, this feels as though these people are intending to inflict upon him the discomfort of his otherwise controllable sensory hypersensitivities.

Jake has an aversion to using the toilet because of the irritating sound of flushing. He doesn't like the imposition of many of the sensations that are inflicted upon him by the world around him including the texture of toilet paper and the temperature and texture of the toilet seat itself.

Jake has difficulty sleeping sometimes because the noise of things like the fridge and the airconditioning, the passing traffic and even the sound of his own blood rushing in his ears can make it hard for him to relax. Also, he can't stand the texture of anything near his face, like the tufty blankets, and spends much of the night keeping uncomfortable textures away from himself (he also had this trouble with his pyjamas but he solved the expectation to wear them by tearing them to pieces). The abrasive rubbing together of fabrics, such as cotton and wool, also grates badly on his nerves (although he copes fine with satin). The only way Jake can find to relax enough to sleep is by touching his body parts, which other people actively discourage him from doing.

Jasper: A Case of 'Emotional Hypersensitivity' (and/or Exposure Anxiety

Jasper often sits as close to the corner as he can get. Jasper also has the three features of 'impairment in social interaction', 'communication disorder' and 'bizarre behaviours'. In Jasper's case, all of these problems are the result of intense and pervasive emotional hypersensitivity and/or exposure anxiety. Jasper's environment didn't cause these things and he has had these difficulties for as long as he can remember.

Jasper appears generally withdrawn because he found that feelings overwhelmed him and were more than he could stand. The unexpectedness of them felt like unpredictable, unintentional onslaughts and so he gradually learned to avoid any ongoing contact which would provoke these sensations.

At this stage, Jasper didn't have names for these feelings and didn't know what they were for or why they were there. Those connections didn't happen. All he knew was that they made him feel intensely out of control – like a butterfly in a hurricane. If he'd been able to name the feelings, he'd have recognised that even happiness and excitement were too much for him to bear but he couldn't distinguish between them; they were all just sensations.

Feelings made Jasper feel so out of control that this made him fearful of other people's involvement (because involvement made him feel and also made his face respond unintentionally and unpredictably with expressions he didn't understand or intend and made his body respond the same way).

Even the provocation of happiness or excitement felt like an invasion. To be caused to laugh at something made him feel angry that people were making him lose control. Being told he was 'loved' made him feel people were trying to inflict emotions on him, which he associated with being overwhelmed or even drowned; they couldn't seem to understand this and the more he pushed them away, the more they kept trying. It is not that Jasper is fragile, it is that his brain can't process or disperse his emotions efficiently, so they feel too big for him to handle, even though they might feel 'normal' and meaningful and personally significant for anyone else.

Jasper developed not only an aversion to being affected but also a fear of emotions themselves similar to a fear of flying or falling or letting go. He felt suffocated by the limitations this put upon him and sometimes experimented privately with the boundaries of these fears by letting himself fall through space and by jumping from heights and deliberately soiling himself, just to privately (and within control) experience letting go and being free.

Jasper also couldn't handle being shown how to do things because this made him feel watched. This made him feel too exposed. It felt as if people could see the 'him' in him and could somehow 'touch' this 'him' through sharing things with him. People also seemed to always be looking for what he felt and that made him feel trapped like a caged animal. He couldn't understand why they continued to do this when they could see it caused him difficulty and this made them appear insensitive and uncaring and made their declarations of caring seem all the more hypo-critical and unable to be trusted.

Jasper's emotional hypersensitivity makes it hard for him to look at people or sustain the effect of directly paying attention to them or listening to them so he walks away from them when they speak to him, or looks about the room when he starts to feel too much. This has meant that he hasn't learned good communication skills, not because he lacks intelligence, but because he can't stand the impact of the interaction.

Jasper couldn't stand to be touched, either, because it resulted in him having feelings and he didn't like having feelings because they over-whelmed him and scared him (because he didn't know what they were, why they were there or who had made these unintentional things happen or what their motivations were in doing so) and they made him feel out of control.

Jasper couldn't fix his dilemma because he didn't know what to do about his emotions, how to resolve them or how to share them or even what they were or that other people had them (because they didn't seem to have these problems). He couldn't ask for help in learning these things because asking for help would result in him having feelings of exposure and invasion too, and he hadn't learned to trust the seemingly alien and hypocritical people around him. This meant that Jasper didn't speak unless he had to, or unless it would make people go away or stop affecting him. On the one hand, he wished that interaction didn't feel so bad, on the other hand he avoided it and tried to manage it in a way that wouldn't make him feel anything.

Jasper was afraid to show his own voice because the self-exposure of hearing it in his own ears resulted in him having feelings. Even daring to think about saying or doing something with intention from his own interest or want would result in such an intense feeling of exposure and vulnerability that he often could not even dare think about expressing himself.

If made to answer, Jasper would often answer as the other person or in a voice that wasn't his own or using formal language that gave him a sense of personal distance or in a flat and expressionless detached and impersonal way.

Because Jasper has such an emotional aversion to being involved with others, he has never been motivated to understand the thoughts and feelings of other people. Because of this, he appears to be unaware that he might be confusing other people or hurting their feelings.

He rocks a lot to soothe himself because he feels trapped and isolated and bored and helpless and without hope because he can't cope with interaction or dare expression, nor even explain himself to others who might be able to work out how to make it easier for him.

He stares into space a lot as his mind races with a variety of emotionally non-threatening ideas of factual things and machines and systems and inventions and cartoons, and these thoughts sometimes make him giggle to himself.

Jasper sometimes mentally repeats something over and over again, trying to lose awareness of the people around him, and he closes out what people say by humming in his head or out loud or by grinding his teeth. He also sometimes stares into space for hours in an effort to lose awareness of himself and any feelings of humanness, including awareness of his own body.

Jasper went through a stage of intentionally soiling himself and wilfully excreting in his room to experience freedom and test the boundaries of the constraint of his emotional hypersensitivity. At this time he thought no-one would trace these things directly to him (thinking that even if they blame him, they won't actually *know* he did these things).

Aside from this, his general aversion to losing control or expressing himself in any way in front of others means he feels vulnerable and exposed in demonstrating any need. This includes the need to go to the toilet and he is often too anxious to let go the control required to go at will and is annoyed at unintentional and unpredictable body messages that try to rob him of control and make him do things. Because of these things, Jasper often holds on for days at a time and this sometimes results in 'accidents' (which he dissociates from as though nothing has happened that came from him).

Jasper also often refuses to acknowledge his own hunger as an act of control and out of an aversion to acknowledging need or dependence upon others. Because of this, he often appears not to care if he starves to death although he will sometimes take things from the cupboard when he thinks no-one is aware. If people make a point about him liking something, he sometimes automatically and unconsciously stops eating that thing altogether as though the exposure of his liking something was some form of self-expression and a channel through which someone might try to connect with him and cause him feelings.

Jasper's fear of losing control also results in him having difficulty sleeping. He cannot bear being tucked in as he feels helpless and out of control (and can't cope with the involvement). Instead, he insists, where possible, in sitting up all night, dressed. When made to lay down, he often insists on lying on top of the bed, where he is not enclosed or controlled in any way. When made to sleep under the blankets, Jasper will not keep his arms under the blankets but, instead, will place his arms over the blankets, rigidly by his sides. He will not sleep on his side, except where it helps him to keep an eye on the room to be aware and in control of anyone entering it who might look at him. Because he so fears losing control, he also avoids losing control to sleep, which he perceives as a weakness. Instead, he stares into space for hours whilst fighting the urge to close his eyes, and, sometimes, he falls asleep this way with his eyes open. Both asleep and awake Jasper holds onto his thumbs or the cuffs of his sleeves or keeps the top of his trousers clenched in his grip which makes him feel 'sealed up' (as though there are no loose ends through which things can 'get in'), 'self contained' and 'in control'.

(John doesn't go to Jasper's school even though, on the surface, he sometimes behaves a bit like Jasper. John is not emotionally hypersensitive and he has no problem

*processing the meaning and personal significance of feelings or the motivations of
people in provoking these.*

    *John is emotionally and psychologically damaged. John did not always have these
problems. John's problems were acquired because John had been badly abused and
neglected for a long time since early infancy and too much had happened to him for
him to be able to make up for these things yet. These things had interfered with John's
emotional and psychological development and John lacks confidence and is immature
but he is not emotionally hypersensitive. In John's case, it has made him feel vulnerable
and without confidence and this makes him avoid people or respond defensively to
them if they insist on trying to engage him. This vulnerability, however, is not an
inherent thing for John, and he would not have been this way if he hadn't been through
what he has. After years of counselling and therapy John might be able to 'recover'
from his difficulties and have his self-esteem and his trust of others restored.)*

Josh: A Case of 'Attention Problems'

Josh doesn't sit much at all even though he is meant to sit in his seat near
Jed. Josh also has the same three features. His are the result of an 'attention
problem' which means that even if he tries to pay attention, he can't.

    Josh is very self-aware and knows that he doesn't want to be distracted
by things but he just can't seem to slow down and everything just seems
to *grab* his attention.

    Josh finds himself to be like a robot that is complying with the demands
of everything around him. He tries to think but then a thought jumps into
his head because of something he saw out of the corner of his eye. He
manages another thought and goes to act upon it but then his ears hear
a sound and his body heads off in the direction of the sound even though
he isn't interested in it.

    Josh tries to look into his mother's face but the pattern of short hairs
that make up her eyebrow distract him and he stops being able to think
about her as a person. His father tried to cuddle him but Josh appeared
uninterested because he got distracted by the feeling of his own shirt collar
against his neck and then by a piece of cotton dangling from the button
on his shirt cuff.

    Josh is often on the way to the bathroom or to get something to eat
but can't seem to get there because he sees, hears, feels or smells too many
things on the way and each one of those things leads to another that take
him into rooms and places he didn't mean to go.

    Josh tries to listen to his father's voice but the ticking of the clock
competes for his attention and he only hears a few words here and there

with meaning and the rest of what he heard was a series of clock ticks. Because of this, Josh has learned to use all forms of sound as though they are equally language and will sometimes answer people using the sounds of machines or animals without considering that others will not perceive these sounds as language, or how they might feel being responded to in this way.

Josh tries to ask for something or say something but he can often only stay undistracted long enough to get out the main word and even then he doesn't seem very interested in the response because he is too distracted by something else. Because of this, what he has to say sometimes comes out in a rushed jumble that is difficult to decipher for meaning.

Josh is so constantly distracted and unable to hold onto and follow through with a whole thought that he has not had much time to consistently understand his own thoughts or feelings yet. He has also not been able to hold onto any sustained well-formed interest or curiosity in how other people think or feel and this means he appears not to realise that other people even have minds.

Josh gets frustrated and upset with himself at not being able to pay attention. Sometimes this frustration makes Josh attack himself. Sometimes, he just tries to close out all the distractions by running repeatedly around in circles very very fast.

He also jumps on the beds a lot because this makes him feel as though things are not so chaotic and he can sometimes think a bit this way. These things make him feel in control and like he is not being pushed and pulled by all the sights, sounds, textures, smells and sensations around him.

Josh feels so dominated by his feelings of lacking control that he is overly sensitive to anybody else trying to control him as well, so he often throws tantrums when he feels other people are trying to control him.

Josh has difficulty following through with the actions motivated by a need to go to the toilet and his constant distraction means he often doesn't get where he needs to go. When Josh does try to follow through with the need to go to the toilet, he has established a ritual of pulling his trousers down on his way to the toilet as an indication and prompt of where he is going in order to ensure he is less distracted from his intended course. At the same time, he is so distracted that he often comes back out untucked and occasionally attached to the toilet paper.

Josh is so 'over-active' and easily distracted that it is very difficult for him to relax enough to sleep and, even when he does sleep, it is more as though he collapses from exhaustion (and anywhere is as likely as in bed for this to happen). He sleeps for only a short time and, even then, does not seem to sleep peacefully. One of the things that he does to try to relax is to shake one of his feet very very fast and this sometimes keeps him active enough not to be driven to get up constantly. He has, however, often been stopped from doing this by people who see this as 'rocking' and don't want him to look 'autistic'.

It is also very difficult for Josh to get through a whole meal and he often finds himself distracted by the plate or the wallpaper or the table more than he is attracted to the food. He is also distracted away from his meal so often that it takes him a long time to get through it so it is usually cold by the end and he has had little chance to focus on its taste and process whether he enjoys it or not or whether he is full or wants some more.

(Jerry is similar to Josh but much less self-aware. Jerry isn't so hard on himself or so frustrated. Jerry also doesn't try to fight the distractions of his attention problems and so he is even more active than Josh and seemingly more oblivious.)

Jenny: A Case of 'Perceptual Problems'

Jenny is in the same class as the other children with 'autism' and has all three same features. In Jenny's case, her apparent 'impairment in social interaction', 'communication disorder' and 'bizarre behaviours' are all due to perceptual problems.

Jenny refuses to look at people because although she can *see* an entire person, she can only visually *process* the meaning of one bit of them at a time and only forms a mental impression from the bits of what she has seen rather than forming coherent mental images. Seeing in bits also means that Jenny defines people and places and things by these bits and she can suddenly find once familiar things to be strikingly unfamiliar if slight components are changed, such as when someone moves the furniture or doesn't wear the same coat as usual.

These perceptual problems mean that Jenny finds facial expressions and body language meaningless or even scary so she generally doesn't trust people or show much interest in them *as people*. She doesn't find any meaningful experience in looking into their faces or eyes for sustained amounts of time.

Jenny also has perceptual problems with touch so she can't tell properly where she is being touched or what she feels about it or even who is doing the touching and her visual perceptual problems give her no help in even knowing why she is being touched so generally Jenny avoids the confusion of the *social* (as opposed to purely sensory) experience of touch.

Jenny also has difficulty consistently perceiving her own voice with meaning so she either doesn't use it at all or she just uses it to play about with sounds and patterns. Although she can hear sound just fine, she can't make consistent meaning out of words or intonation so she avoids listening to people talking unless the patterns are sensorily arousing.

Because she has not been able to process consistently the meaning of words as she hears them, she sometimes uses phrases she has heard in certain situations, thinking these phrases will always bring the same consequences, but often using the phrases incorrectly out of their original context. She has learned to use many phrases meaningfully this way but because she learned them embedded in the situation she first heard them in, rather than through processing the words for meaning, she speaks these sentences with the same intonation and emphasis in which she first heard them, regardless of any change in her own mood or any understanding of the meaning carried by things like pitch, volume or intonation.

Because Jenny can't consistently get full messages from what she sees or hears or feels, she has a fragmented perception of people as people (as opposed to people as a form of sensory objects) and this impairs her ability to imagine how they might think or feel or what motivates them to do the things they do. This means that Jenny appears to have no awareness of the minds of others.

Because what comes in through Jenny's eyes and ears and sense of touch doesn't make much consistent meaning, she plays around with her sensations a lot to occupy herself and experience something in her generally meaningless and personally insignificant world. Because of this she pushes her eyes in and flicks the light switches on and off, she plays with the volume control on the TV and plays about with her lack of depth perception by moving things near to and away from her face repetitively.

Because she can often make better meaning out of what she hears or sees by looking or listening peripherally (such as out of the corner of her eye or by looking at or listening to something else) she often appears not to be looking or listening at all (and sometimes people make her look or listen directly which makes all the meaning fall out for her and this makes these people appear not to care or understand).

Jenny also bites and slaps herself, pulls her hair and chokes herself to experiment with the sensations and try to work out where they are coming from, what they mean and what their boundaries are. She also taps herself and other things and sometimes, more intensely, slaps things or constantly runs her hands or cheek over surfaces or 'mouths' objects or her arms in an attempt to try to connect some meaning with these objects she is in contact with.

Because Jenny takes a great deal of time to process the meaning or significance of what she feels, she often doesn't interpret fullness as needing to go to the toilet, or hunger as needing to eat, or being cold as needing to get out of wet clothes or put on warm ones, or that discomfort can be taken away by moving away from its source. Because of this, she often goes without eating, going to the toilet, going to bed, getting changed, putting on warmer clothes or undressing unless prompted and sometimes fails to remove herself from the source of having burned herself or to remove herself from interpersonal situations that feel abusive (such as bullying).

When Jenny does go to use the bathroom, she is confronted with three white porcelain receptacles; the toilet, the bathtub and the hand basin, all within close proximity of each other, all with running water and somewhere for it to run to. Because Jenny often has difficulty quickly interpreting the meaning of what she perceives, she is sometimes as likely to go to the toilet in the bathtub as she is in the toilet, without realising until later (if at all) that she went in the 'wrong' place. When she manages to go in the toilet, rather than in the bathtub, there is a white hand towel on a ring next to a white toilet roll on a ring and this poses the same kind of problem for her.

Jenny also plays with and explores her food as it sometimes takes her time to make meaning out of its appearance or smell and translate this into the intention and action of eating. Even when she does realise what to do with it, if she gets distracted she is back to wondering what it is there for and what she is meant to do about it.

In a world that makes little consistent sense in context and holds little personal significance, it often feels to Jenny that people are relentless in expecting her to behave in ways that often feel perceptually unnatural and meaningless to her (so called 'normal' ways). Because of this, she generally experiences life as an endless expectation to comply where she is unreasonably denied the right to 'be herself'.

Jessica: A Case of 'Systems Integration Problems'

Jessica is meant to sit in her seat (she has a seat across the room from Josh) but she either sits there without trouble or is found everywhere except her seat. Jessica also has all of the three features of 'autism' and for her, these are due to systems integration problems.

Jessica's brain works like a whole load of separate departments where the managers of each department do not co-operate well with each other, and they take days off here and there when enough of the others come to work. Jessica's brain works in 'mono' (working on only one track at a time) where so called 'normal' brains work on 'multiple tracks' (working on several tracks at the same time).

Jessica's systems, her functions, don't stay integrated very well. This means that Jessica's brain sometimes registers the meaning of what she sees but only as long as it disregards (and fails to process) the meaning of what she hears. She sometimes understands the meaning of everything she hears as long as her brain doesn't process the meaning of what she sees (and she sometimes assists this switching by not looking directly at anything as she is listening).

Similarly, she sometimes understands the meaning and location of what her body feels as long as her brain is not processing the movements of any touching that she is doing at that time. She can also generally move across a room with awareness of her body but then can't monitor (keep track of) and process her thoughts at the same time so she often doesn't 'know' what she crossed the room for.

She can sometimes be aware of and experience her feelings but only so long as she isn't aware of nor processing her own thoughts. If she becomes aware of and comprehending of her own thinking, her emotions abandon her.

Jessica can generally perceive herself but only as long as she does not process the experience of other people in relation to herself. When she processes her perception of other people, she generally loses the ability to process any sense of herself within the context of their company so she often does things like walking away in the middle of a sentence or action. In this aspect, being 'mono' for Jessica means that she swings between having *either* a sense of 'self' *or* a sense of 'other' but, unlike most people, does not have a simultaneous sense of both.

Because of these things, Jessica can't really understand what being 'social' is meant to be all about because she has never cognitively been able to experience it consistently. She has been taught to emulate appearing 'social' but is generally unmotivated to be truly social from her own wishes or interest and doesn't understand why other people expect it of her.

Jessica finds people to be tiring, unreasonable, demanding and unrelenting and so, by choice, would generally rather have nothing to do with them. Even though she sometimes finds amusing the illogical and alien nature of their behaviour and responses (because they have 'multiple tracks'), she mostly finds this 'differentness' overwhelming, confusing, frightening and alienating at some level even if she often cannot properly fathom the significance of these feelings she is having in the context they were provoked in.

Jessica often can't think and speak at the same time so she sometimes speaks in thought in her head rather than out loud (and sometimes doesn't realise that other people can't 'hear' her this way or that she hasn't actually connected thought to physical expression – which requires two channels – and said her thoughts out loud). Then she sometimes puts her body into action to speak what she mentally heard herself say in her head and this sometimes brings consequences, but then she generally can't process those consequences properly (because her voice is still 'on line' but her hearing isn't).

Even when Jessica speaks, she often can't process what she is saying as she speaks because her brain can't process what her own ears are hearing at the same time as she is involved in the mechanics of speaking. This means that unless she says exactly and only what she thought about saying, she often goes way off track, says the same things again, or doesn't seem to have much purpose to what she is saying. Also, because she generally cannot consistently monitor how she sounds at the same time as she is putting all her energies into speaking, she often fluctuates between using 'inappropriate' volume, pitch or pace and speaking in a combination of monotone or 'odd' intonation (all of which can make her sound as if she is uninterested in what she is saying or as though she takes no account of her impression upon the listener).

Because Jessica can't consistently process her own feelings at the same time as she is processing what she is seeing or hearing, she doesn't have much of a sense of what she feels about anybody. Because of this, she generally has never been socially curious or motivated to understand other people or feel for them and so she appears to have no real awareness about how they think or feel, and nothing has ever driven her to have to find out as a matter of survival.

With her systems unable to operate consistently in an integrated way, Jessica has sometimes 'forgotten' that her hand belongs to her and has become very amused at its rediscovery and has explored it and tried to shake it off. She has also become amused at the sounds inside her body and has shaken her head violently for long periods of time to hear the internal sound (without realising the significance of the sound being connected to herself and that she might damage herself). She has also played a lot with body sensations by biting herself and holding her breath, because she doesn't understand she *is* her body and is experimenting with its relationship to her as though it were a separate thing.

She also constantly touches things and experiments with textures to try to test out the boundaries of her body and where her touch sensations are coming from. At the same time, if she is touched whilst her sense of touch is not 'on line', she either seems to 'ignore' or purely tolerate it, rejects it as a distracting and incomprehensible annoyance, or finds herself suddenly and shockingly tuned in to it with all the associated disorientation of this jolt and the loss of what else she had been previously processing.

Jessica's inability to use consistently several systems of functioning simultaneously with feedback makes it difficult for her to learn fully in the same learning environments as so-called 'normal' children and, knowing this, her learning is basically on a track of its own rather than on that of others who clearly do not use their senses and systems of functioning in a way that makes sense to her – one that is like her own. When people try to make her 'learn' in ways that restrict learning, she either fights them, or complies with them and learns far less that she otherwise might.

Jordon: A Case of 'Left–Right Hemisphere Integration Problems'

Jordon sits in his seat by the window. Jordon also has all three features of 'autism'. For Jordon, these are due to a left–right hemisphere integration problem. The left part of Jordan's brain doesn't consistently know what his right part is doing and vice-versa so he generally appears to be unaware of what he has heard or seen or done and this makes him look like an idiot.

Even though Jordon can learn, it is difficult for Jordon to have much conscious awareness of what he thinks or feels about anything he is learning, until his thoughts or feelings are triggered externally at some later point (15 minutes/ an hour/ a day/ a week/ a month later) when (at least preconsciously) his brain has had time to process them. Because of this, Jordon doesn't *appear* to learn well, even though he seems sometimes to 'surprise' people with what he has somehow 'picked up'.

Because of Jordon's left–right hemisphere integration problems, things generally take longer for him to process than other people so his brain accumulates a lot of things (quite indiscriminately at times) for later processing. Because Jordon is still busy taking in new information when some of this processing of old information is taking place, much of the processing is not on a conscious level and a lot of it happens whilst he sleeps (so he is generally unaware of what he knows unless it is triggered by something outside of him). Because Jordon's brain generally doesn't process information at the same time as it comes in, the effect of context on filtering this information for significance is mostly lost. He picks up a lot of peripheral information but, unlike other people, his brain actually processes this peripheral information along with everything else it has stored up. Because of this, even if Jordon is unaware of all the information that his brain has processed subconsciously, he actually carries about more knowledge and understanding than most so-called 'normal' people.

One of the disadvantages of this for Jordon is that, because he generally doesn't get to process information *in the immediate context in which it happens* he only accumulates understanding *about* things. This is like gathering a huge repertoire of facts but not using them to form 'common sense' (which is often related to learning in context). Because of this, his wealth of understanding (all his consciously unknown preconscious knowing) generally doesn't translate easily into practical situations (which has the disadvantage of people wrongly assuming he is intellectually retarded, lacks 'appropriate' affect and is generally uninterested in his environment).

Jordon's left–right integration problem makes it difficult for Jordon, himself, to access information about what he has learned or experienced. He often can't, for example, tell you what he thinks or feels about something, even though he can correct you if you say something that is incorrect or incomplete according to his information (this is a triggered response rather than conscious accessing).

Because he often can't access information voluntarily and consciously, Jordon relies very strongly upon the external triggering cues of others which trigger actions and expressions in him that he can't easily access on his own or at will. This way, Jordon can do a lot of things on 'autopilot' even though he has a lot of trouble putting a thought into action or expression. Without people to trigger him into action or expression, Jordon sometimes appears 'stupid'.

Jordon's left–right problems affect his ability to connect feelings and thoughts. This means that when his recall of experiences is triggered, this recall is generally without real felt affect (even though he can be taught to portray socially expected affect). This also means that he sometimes has great undispersed bursts of contextless emotion that accumulates and is discharged rather than stored in some connected way to his experiences.

Jordon's left–right problems also affect his ability to connect his thoughts to words or actions. This means he often has to rely on triggered stored language more than the true self-expression that comes from personal thought and he often gets a whole load of responses that he doesn't really want or even like. When he then doesn't seem to appreciate or even understand the responses he gets, he appears ungrateful, contrary and unthinking, so he has learned to act sometimes as if he likes and wants things even if he is unaware of whether he actually likes/wants them or not.

Jordon's left–right integration problems also mean that he can't easily get anything he wants or even use the toilet when he needs to unless he automatically mirrors someone else doing, or on their way to doing, these things. This means that even though Jordon may not be able to move or speak as himself, he can do these things as someone else (or a whole array of someone elses). He has, however, often been told off for copying and following people as well as being told off for not doing and getting for himself the things he needs or wants. This no win situation causes Jordon a lot of anxiety and makes people appear confusing, insensitive, torment-ing and unworthy of being deeply trusted or relied upon.

Some of these stored mental 'videos' and 'audios' have come from watching TV and this makes Jordon look and sound quite 'odd' sometimes. People try to correct him and make him look less 'odd'. Unless they actually overtly demonstrate at this time other 'less odd' ways to say or do things (without expecting him to extract this information within its 'natural' context), their 'helpful' corrections sometimes only make Jordon more helpless and less able to function.

Jordon's difficulty in accessing how to move or speak as himself also means that he is generally unable to form a mutually felt, close relationship with anybody (in spite of a learned ability to perform the semblance of one) and, has never experienced interaction consistently as himself, even with his parents. Because of these things, Jordon has developed a very different identity from most people. On the one hand, he lives inside his head as his 'true self' (where he is in the company of a whole repertoire of stored copies of the selves of other people) and, on the other hand, he lives in the world outside his head as people other than himself. This has resulted in Jordon feeling an intense sense of helplessness and aloneness for, no matter what he achieves as these stored copies of other people, he cannot feel belonging or pride among other people because he feels other people have not seen, or even cannot see, the 'real' him.

By contrast with how able he can sometimes appear when moving and speaking as others, Jordon's comparative problems, when trying to do things as himself, have sometimes made him appear to have a mental problem, to be acting or to be going backwards in his development. This sort of response from others, in turn, confirms for Jordon that nobody knows or cares about the real him and it stops him from trying to develop connections as his real self. He continues to put all his energies into disguising his problems (which results in severe chronic stress).

Unless Jordon can find a cue to follow to get something done that he wants or needs, he may use a stored repertoire or question to cue other people to respond, which in turn will cue him. Because of this he sometimes indulges in a whole range of behaviours that result in other people reacting to him (and result in 'him' reacting back). Jordon also often relies on real or living 'mirrors' to monitor or cue movement or expression. It is not that Jordon imitates people intentionally, so much as he allows himself to move and speak and even appear to think or feel *as* them by allowing an automatic tendency to copy to run its course.

(Jordon has a neighbour a few streets away, named Jamie, who also has a left–right hemisphere integration problem. Jamie is affected not just in his ability to move or communicate consciously and voluntarily, but is equally impaired in his ability to move or communicate subconsciously and automatically. This means that, unlike Jordon, Jamie is unable to follow through subconsciously and automatically in mirroring or copying other people (echopraxia: in movement; echolalia: in verbal expression), nor to store these actions or expressions and use them as his own maps to externally trigger action or communication. Because of this, although Jamie is not an idiot, he is seen to be intellectually (as opposed to functionally) retarded.

When, with help, Jamie does manage the connections to complete a simple action or utterance, the people who have helped him act as though his success was a display of the small amount of intelligence they suppose he possesses rather than a display of the huge determination, application and control he has put into making the connections to express even the tiny bit of the considerable intelligence he actually has.

Even though Jamie can't connect properly, he has still accumulated a lot of information about the world around him. Much of this he has absorbed peripherally and incidentally. Because of this, he not only has far more intelligence than is credited to him but he knows, too, when he is being treated as or spoken to as intellectually retarded. This makes him feel his isolation and entrapment even more strongly and makes him feel as though nobody knows him. It also robs him of what he already has so little of: dignity.)

CHAPTER 5

Approaches to 'Autism'

One way or another, people are going to try to tackle 'autism'. Some will do it through institutionalisation. Some will do it through drugs. Some will do it through behaviour modification or a whole range of other 'treatments', 'therapies' or 'techniques'. Ideally, whatever is used to tackle 'autism' should be appropriate to the particular problems of the person they are dealing with.

I have known of people without sensory hypersensitivity who have received 'therapy' meant to aid a condition they didn't suffer from (at great expense). I have known of people with no psychological or emotional disturbance or damage being 'treated' for having it (and convinced it is in their interests to believe they had it so they could 'get better').

I have known of sensorily and emotionally hypersensitive people who are already suffering from extreme information overload who have been put through the emotional and sensory bombardment of 'hug therapy'. I have known of sensorily hypersensitive and people with perceptual problems and problems of systems integration being put through behaviour modification programs to teach them to behave as though their problems do not exist or even punished for displaying any signs or compensatory adaptations to their problems.

What I think was missing in all of these cases was a proper understanding of what these 'autistic' people were dealing with and enough humility for carers and professionals to admit when they weren't sure or didn't know how to help a particular person.

What is needed generally are suggestions of how to deal specifically with each of these underlying conditions (types of 'autism'-related problems) so that people get services that don't waste their time, their money or cause further set-backs to a person who has enough to cope with already.

A Look at Some Modern Approaches

'Therapies', 'techniques' and 'treatments' used with people with 'autism' present themselves like shops along the High Street; they have little relationship to one another and each shop will encourage you to shop at their store and tell you why their product is THE product.

But each of these shops sells something quite different from the next. Some deal with behaviours, some deal with communication, some with perception, some with brain development, some with biochemistry, some with cognition or with the mind and some with the soul – and some don't deal with anything but make a good job of appearing to.

The problem with services behaving like High Street shops is that people with 'autism' don't just have problems with behaviour or communication or perception or their senses or with brain development or biochemistry, or with stress levels or with troubled souls. Because people with autism are whole beings, most of them have trouble with the whole lot, which all interconnect and feed into each other at some point.

To get any kind of all-round service, people with autism don't need a High Street full of competing shops, they need a department store where each department is aware of what the others offer and points people in the direction of other services which complement their own.

Perhaps, some time in the future, 'autism'-related therapies, techniques and treatments might work like a clinic full of specialists who can work at a great variety of levels with approaches to cater for the particular stage of development relating to each problem in a way that works best for a particular person at a particular time. In the absence of this I will now, for better or for worse, take a brief look at some of the High Street 'therapies', 'techniques' and 'treatments' currently being used with people who have 'autism'.

Behaviour Modification

This attempts to tackle two types of problems in people with 'autism'. One of these problems is about how people FUNCTION. The other type of problem is about how people APPEAR.

Behaviour modification in all of its forms is primarily aimed at behaviour rather than perceptions or experiences. People using behaviour modification can take a tough, firm, approach or a gentler approach. They can rely on a system of punishments (sometimes including the use of what are called 'aversives') or a system of rewards, or a combination of the two. Some of the problems with this approach start here as what is experienced or responded to as a reward or punishment depends on your own perceptions. As non-autistic people generally design the rewards or punishments based on their own experiences or perceptions, these don't necessarily fit with an 'autistic' perception.

I have seen people for whom touch is invasive and unwelcome being 'rewarded' with pats and strokes and hugs. The result is that, where they can, they will learn to avoid doing what will bring them these 'rewards'.

I have seen people with receptive language problems or trouble with pitch and volume, being 'rewarded' with fast, animated outpourings of verbal praise that clearly either make no sense at the time or are sensorily uncomfortable.

I have seen people with extreme emotional hypersensitivity being bombarded with 'rewards' of suffocatingly personal and directly confrontational emotional outpourings that they cannot tolerate nor process in the context in which these happen.

I have seen people with an information processing problem who are already trying their hardest to keep up with mechanically processing important information, being needlessly bombarded with 'rewarding' superfluous stimuli that pushes them into information overload and sensory hypersensitivity and sensory-system shutdowns.

I have seen people who rely highly on ritual to make processing connections, being 'rewarded' in uncomfortably unpredictable (and incomprehensible) ways.

I have seen 'punishments' such as non-inclusion being used with people who are suffering from information overload who seem relieved to be 'rewarded' with being left out.

I have seen 'punishments' of non-inclusion used with sensorily hypersensitive people who show obvious relief at being relieved of the expectation to be involved in sensorily discomforting activities.

I have seen people with emotional hypersensitivity being 'punished' with the (welcomed) retraction of praise and direct personal acknowledgement and its welcomed replacement with detachment and formality.

I have seen people 'punished' for indulgence in rituals by ritualistically placing them in a corner or 'scolding' them in a highly ritualistic and predictable way.

Sometimes, the links with rewards or punishments simply aren't made because of problems of connection and the whole behaviour modification program may feel like a senseless ritual of abuse, regardless of its 'good' intentions. What is more, when people display natural responses to 'rewards' that they find disturbing or confusing, or clearly mistake punishments for rewards because they are felt that way, they can infuriate their carers, sometimes resulting in even more confusing, unpredictable or disturbing responses from their carers.

Ultimately, for some people, the only message that may be getting through is, 'I am not meant to exist as myself'. Compliance is not learning, because you do not connect it with your own thoughts, feelings or intentions. Compliance is mindless. Compliance may appear to achieve things in the short term, but the arrest in the development of connections to thought, feelings and intention may not only create extreme (though generally compliantly repressed) chronic stress, but may ultimately result in physical, emotional or mental breakdown if the effects of pervasive compliance are not properly addressed.

Some behaviour modification programs are tougher than others. Some use a firm, detached approach that allows little room for the person with 'autism' to 'manipulate' or 'reason with' the professional or carer. Some professionals or carers are more intelligent and sensitive in working out punishments and rewards and do take account of what each person *actually* seems (rather than is assumed) to like or dislike in tailoring these rewards and punishments personally. Here the rewards and punishments used have a better chance of making personal sense to the person they are being used with.

Behaviour modification practices, however, generally take little account of identity or personality. This may be because it is assumed that the person either hasn't developed a 'healthy' identity yet and that it is too intertwined in the undesirable or problematic behaviours they seek to get rid of, or that identity and personality are irrelevant as far as the objectives of the 'treatment' are concerned.

Behaviour modification generally allows for little ownership over one's own behaviour, except where it adheres to what is desired by the professional or carer and their definition of 'normal', non-'autistic' behaviour. One of the side-effects of this may be that, if 'successful' in inhibiting unwanted behaviours or teaching new ones, it can also easily train people to be compliant and that can have its own dangers when people are taught not to defy or to follow their own judgements. In my view, compliance may teach people more about other people's power than about their own behaviour. Whilst behaviour modification may make for some success in the classroom and help achieve 'independence', it can set people up to be easy victims in life where there may be no-one there to correct the behaviour of those who would cash-in on someone else's easy compliance.

For those whose personalities and identities *are* intertwined with their 'autistic' behaviours, attempts to modify behaviour might be met with expressed or unexpressed defiance and counter-strategies, making it a long hard war that for some might be endless. One of the saddest consequences in a case like this is that where stringent attempts to modify behaviour are then abandoned, the 'autistic' person may feel they have won but be left with a much greater sense of distrust, invasion or persecution than they began with. When behaviour modifications do appear to work with these people, it might result in someone robotically or reluctantly compliant but basically seeming without a soul. In fact, they might have left their soul back with the behaviours they 'successfully' abandoned.

On the other hand, people whose identity or personality is at least partly not intertwined with their 'autistic' behaviours may have at least a part of them that feels suffocated, repressed, distorted or controlled by behaviours they mightn't be able to monitor or help. For some of these people, behaviour modification programmes may be taken on with less consistent aversion and defiance. They may even be taken on as some kind of joint venture between people who mutually recognise 'autism'-related problems as 'the enemy'.

'Hug' Therapy

'Hug therapy' was popular some time back but most people have come to think of both the practice and the ideas it is based upon as outdated. 'Hug therapy' involves showing the autistic person who is in control but is sometimes about trying to project messages of 'love'. This is a bit like trying to wave a magic wand over an 'autistic' person to take the evil spell away.

What 'hug' therapy overlooks is that 'love' is not about going through the motions of 'hugging' someone based on a theoretical awareness that you love them. This is like eating when you are not hungry merely because you have the idea that you like food.

Many people with 'autism' may not be able to read body language or facial expressions or understand the meaning carried by words or intonation in the context these things happen in. Nevertheless, they may still be able to smell out the inconsistency and incongruity of insincerity from miles away. It may be that at the moment that the parent puts him or herself into gear to hug on cue, he or she is actually feeling anxious or excited about the dinner party he or she is going to tonight or feeling uncomfortable or cold because he or she didn't wear a jumper today.

About the only thing that a very sensitive person with 'autism' might sense of all of this is that non-'autistic' people are surfacy, false and seem to pursue an assemblance of 'normality' not for the sake of the person with 'autism' but for the sake of their own insecurities.

As to whether 'autistic' people need to know they are loved, some already know, at least in theory and this may be all that delayed information processing may be capable of affording them. In those who don't know they are loved, no amount of forced demonstration is going to make neurological connections happen in context where the brain isn't equipped to do so.

In some people with perceptual problems or problems of systems integration, they may actually be cognitively unable to conceive of themselves and another person within the same context or be unable to quickly process any visual, auditory or tactile experience as a whole with meaning in the context it happens in. Both of these things might preclude anything more than a theoretical awareness of what 'love' is meant to feel like, no matter how much you try to force 'recognition' of the existence of that love.

Recognition is not only about what is demonstrated to you, it is about the ability neurologically to fully process the perception of that demonstration in a coherent way, in a short amount of time, within the context of the demonstration. For some people with 'autism', bombarding them with surfacy 'love' symbols they cannot process efficiently, may be like expecting a legless man to walk without artificial limbs. Trying to drum the experience into people who are impaired in their ability to process or perceive the experience in the context it happens in might only frustrate the hugger and the huggee and line the pockets of the therapist.

For some people with 'autism' for whom inherent emotional or sensory hypersensitivity makes life so overwhelming, hug therapy may only be seen as one more ignorant infliction that further demonstrates people's lack of empathy for their hypersensitivity.

If 'hug therapy' works at all in such cases to produce the expected or wanted compliance, it may only be because it has been incidentally used like an unintentional punishment, teaching people that if they give the desired responses quickly, they are set free. None of this makes for a well adjusted, nor 'normal' person, even if you may occasionally succeed in intimidating someone into better hiding their problems.

Holding Therapy

Some forms of holding therapy are about showing the person with 'autism' who is in control and that the person in control is the non-'autistic' person.

Many people with 'autism', if aware of nothing else, are sharply aware on some level that they live in a social, emotional, sensory and perceptual world that is not congruent with the non-autistic social, emotional, sensory and perceptual world around them. Most don't need to learn what type of people dominate their surroundings; it may be because of this very domination that so many of them avoid sharing in it with other people.

For some carers and professionals, holding therapy or hug therapy is like 'breaking-in' a horse. For some, all that might be produced is souless compliance. On the other hand, there may be some people who feel suffocated, repressed, controlled or distorted by avoidant behaviour they may not be able to help, but with which they do not identify. For these people, external control (relinquishing responsibility) may sometimes be welcomed.

It is reckless and destructive to attempt to employ this sort of technique upon anyone merely because they share the label 'autistic' and it might be more damaging than helpful when applied in the wrong cases. This is as reckless as giving medication to the wrong patient or one who may not be able to tolerate it. The problem to look at is how to identify those people with whom it is more likely to do no harm or even help, and to avoid further damaging those for whom it might be the wrong approach.

There is perhaps one case where I wonder if holding therapy may really have something to offer.

Self-abuse can be about getting a sensory buzz. It can be about expressing a displeasure with something and used to control the actions of others in an attempt to stop them doing whatever is causing sensory discomfort or information overload. It can also be merely an entirely uncontrollable, instinctive and unwelcome response to information over-load. It is in this third case that the self-abusive person may develop extreme mistrust of themselves in being unable to stop these unwelcome self-attacks.

Inability to trust oneself can be a huge force in motivating someone to indulge in repetitive self-stimulatory and compulsive behaviours which help them to lose awareness of their own existence ('disappearing'). In this case and this case only, sometimes finding that someone else will protect you from your own uncontrollable self-abuse can be a psychological tool to building trust of oneself and of others and some self-abusive people (myself included) have sought this external constraint voluntarily, finding themselves more able to get on with life in between these self-abusive urges. With such people, holding may be one non-violent and effective short-term means of helping some self-abusive people to develop eventually greater self-trust and perhaps also self-management skills in the eventual handling of their own self-abuse. Ultimately, however, these self-abusive urges very often have a biochemical origin much better dealt with, or at least backed up by, a nutritional approach.

The Options Approach

Few professionals seem to take an experience-based approach in 'treating' 'autism'. The options approach attempts to take, as its starting point, the experiences of the person with 'autism' and so to take account of things like identity and personality or, even more fluffily, the soul. It attempts to look beyond 'appear', to 'be'.

The options approach is one example of an experience-based approach which attempts to relate to the person with 'autism' along any lines which make sense to that person (even if it doesn't always make sense to the non-'autistic' person involved). This type of approach uses a relatively directly-confrontational approach which might make sense to people whose greatest obstacle to communication or involvement is that nobody will build the bridges between their reality and that of others.

On the other hand, it may have disadvantages in not addressing sensory or perceptual problems underlying 'autistic' difficulties in some people or in not helping people to control thoughts, feelings, communications, movements and behaviours they did not intend. For example, where the goal of the options approach is to accept, understand and use as a basis for interaction, certain perceptual and sensory 'differences', this does not necessarily mean that understanding will assist people in removing some of these things and, thereby, freeing these people to communicate and interact more easily in less 'autistic' ways. Also, where someone is com-pelled to communicate, interact and behave in ways that they do not intend, so frustrating themselves, the options approach, using any expres-sion as the basis for interaction, may potentially further frustrate and alienate those people who do not identify with or intend these expressions in the first place. The options approach may be able to encourage some emotionally hypersensitive people to dare self-exposure but there may be others in whom emotionally hypersensitivity is so intense that they may merely turn further inwards when approached using any directly confrontational form of interaction, and a less directly confrontational approach may be necessary.

Facilitated Communication

Another 'technique' that involves an experience-based approach is a communication 'technique' called facilitated communication. Facilitated communication (FC) is a technique of assistance which attempts to assist people in self-expression. So, for example, it may involve the use of word or picture 'grids' and involve physically assisting the person with autism in pointing to responses whilst simultaneously being sensitive to the direction taken by the person with autism. It can also involve physically assisted typing, again whilst remaining sensitive to indications of direction from the person with autism. FC can be used to assist those with intense exposure anxiety where the person with autism can be allowed to appear to delegate responsibility for his or her own expression to the physical support of the facilitator, or for whom typing is far less directly confrontational than speaking. A good facilitor will progressively 'fade out' the physical support, allowing the prson with autism gradually dare to more and more personal responsibility for his or her expression so, for example, hand support may fade out eventually to elbow support, then the mere touch of a shoulder, to eventually merely standing nearby.

FC may also be helpful for people with impulse-control problems (some of which are the result of compulsions to divert caused by intense exposure anxiety). A good facilitor will be able to accept that a person with autism may verbally spout what may seem utter nonsense but still be able to type out his or her felt reality. They may also be able to help the person with autism to weed out the intentional expression of typed letters from the sometimes jumbled invasion of unintended typed-in diversions. FC might also be used to help people discuss theoretically some of their problems regarding verbal communication, movement and self-control and to discuss their perceptual or sensory problems and come up with ways in which these things might be resolved. This all sounds great in theory but the problem is sometimes in actually putting what has been discussed into practice.

To go from a problem to a practical solution involves the ability to get information or help, to make a plan to solve the problem and then to make your way through the plan, not mentally or in writing, but through actions in the real world. Facilitation in the right hands may be a great approach if it is used correctly and the things it achieves are followed through. In inexperienced hands, however, it can produce more problems than it solves. A too easy-going approach with someone requiring a firm one, may lead not to the facilitator manipulating the typist, but in the typist intentionally or unintentionally manipulating, confusing or misleading the facilitator, with imaginable consequences. On the other hand, a too firm or too clinical approach used with someone who requires only encouragement and a gentle approach may result in freezing that person out of communication or even blocking their perception of themselves, which is at the basis of an ability to express with intention.

It is important to point out the role of stereotypes in contributing to some of the problems confronting facilitation. The residue of assumptions by facilitators that 'autistic people do not joke' or 'autistic people do not understand lies' can have its effect on the validity of what comes out in FC. Where an autistic person has written something as a private joke or for its shock value, to test a reaction or even in response to a perceived expectation to have experienced something, some facilitators may take these communications to be facts and truths and act upon them with unfortunate consequences. This is not to say that people with 'autism' lie or joke or attempt to shock or manipulate or meet expectations any more than any non-'autistic' person does. What it means is that many people with 'autism' are as capable of these things as non-'autistic' people are and that even if they don't express them verbally or through their actions, they may do so in their thoughts (if only subconsciously) and this, in the case of FC, just might come out on paper.

Ultimately, like any approach to autism, underlying causes must also be addressed. If someone has serious biochemical problems causing their problems, then writing about these might significantly help people psychologically and emotionally, but to have this translate into their actually becoming more 'high functioning', underlying biochemical problems should also be addressed and corrected.

Sensory Integration Techniques

Other experience-based approaches involve sensory integration of various types.

One such technique is multi-sensory integration which seeks to get people to use their vision, hearing, sense of touch, smell, taste, body sense and proprioperception in an integrated way. This approach acknowledges that some people with 'autism' are working in 'mono'. That is, that some people with 'autism' only use their eyes or their ears or their sense of touch or their sense of smell at one time, but don't use these things simultaneously like non-'autistic' people might. So, for example, some people with 'autism' might look away when listening to something or they might use their sense of touch rather than their eyes to orient them or identify things.

Multi-sensory integration programmes seek to get these people to use several systems at once. Although it is acknowledged that sensory integration problems are taking place, such programmes sometimes take no account of what may be causing the problems, that is, why sensory integration has not taken place naturally in the first place. This is a bit like finding someone who can't walk properly and training them to walk without taking account of the fact the person has got two broken legs.

There are several disadvantages to overlooking why sensory integration has not naturally taken place. I will take the example where sensory integration has not taken place because the brain is not able to filter out enough information on each sensory channel for it to be able to cope efficiently with all that information at once. In this case, not using certain sensory channels (like not using vision when listening, for example) may actually be a way of getting to process information more fully and quickly on the channel that is being used (hearing) rather than getting an overwhelming, confusing and overloading jumble when too much comes in through the eyes and ears at the same time, or slowing down processing so that nothing is understood in the context in which it happens. In this example, to assume that the problem is not using one's vision may result in worsening the person's difficulties.

If the therapist forces someone like this to look whilst they are listening, one of several things might happen. One is that the person might continue to process what he or she hears but might stare obliviously straight through what he or she is made to look at without registering its meaning or significance. Another is that his or her systems might switch and he or she might process what is seen but might no longer process what is heard. The third, and more disastrous and damaging consequence is that the person might continue to process what he or she hears, also process what he or she is looking at but, after a short amount of time the accumulative effects, or delayed processing caused by too much coming in at once from too many channels, might result in information overload. That overload, in turn, can result in a sharp attack of sensory hypersensitivity (with its resulting 'tantrums' and 'behaviour problems') or might go further to result in the vegetative oblivion I call 'total systems shutdown'. This example might be exchanged for any other combinations of systems, such as being unable to process what one hears whilst processing touch, unable to process what one sees whilst moving, and so on.

Another situation where the cause of the person's sensory integration problems may be overlooked is where the person with 'autism' has perceptual problems. If, for example, a person with autism has visual perceptual problems that result in processing the part but losing the whole or the context of what is being processed, then the person may find that using vision does not bring him or her meaning, and seriously compromises the ability to process more fully what is being heard. This person might avoid looking but still attend with their ears to what is going on. Forcing such a person to look as they listen might only compromise an otherwise fully functioning system of processing (hearing) and the person may actually end up learning or experiencing far less than they otherwise might.

Again, by addressing any underlying causes of impaired systems integration, half the job is already done and sensory integration programmes can then pick up the developmental pieces rather than merely work with the symptoms.

Auditory Training

Another sensory integration 'treatment' which uses an experience-based approach is auditory integration training. This technique seeks to reduce auditory hypersensitivity and improve the clarity of hearing by training people to readjust their perception of pitch.

However, whilst many people with 'autism' do suffer from auditory hypersensitivity (among other hypersensitivities) the underlying causes of this hypersensitivity may have nothing to do with the perception of pitch or volume. For example, many people with 'autism' have sensory hypersensitivity as a result of an information processing problem that leads to information overload and sensory integration problems. For these people, it is not the hypersensitivity which is the problem, but the overload that leads to the hypersensitivity.

The causes of information overload, on an auditory level, are, in my own experience and that of others like me, not to do with pitch and volume but to do with the number of simultaneous sound sources, the duration of the bombardment from those sound sources and the rate of that bombardment relative to processing capacity; in a nutshell, too much going on for processing to keep up. This is like boiling a kettle. Eventually, the whistle is going to sound.

Any apparent achievement by auditory training or auditory integration therapy in getting people to relate or communicate better may be due to establishing trust through acknowledging the pain of sensory hypersensitivity in a world that seems to ignore it and by raising refreshingly new expectations of recovery (that some might just try to live up to). If this is the case, it perhaps may help account for why success with this 'treatment' is often partial and not long lasting. There are much cheaper and longer lasting ways to establish trust and raise expectations.

Furthermore, the assumption that the communication or comprehension difficulties of people with autism are the result of problems with auditory clarity are as simplistic as the assumption that 'autistic' people don't attend to what they hear because they can't hear. Anyone who can echo back in your own accent what you have said but seems unable to comprehend the meaning of the words is *not* having a problem with the clarity of sound but with the processing of those adequately clear sounds for meaning. These problems have nothing to do with what the ears hear but with what the brain is or isn't doing with what the ears hear.

Asking people at Auditory Training Centers about whether their technique will improve how the brain makes meaning out of what the ears hear clearly may be like going to an optician and asking them if glasses will help the brain make meaning out of what the eyes can clearly and distinctly see. If you can't explain that you *can* clearly and distinctly see or hear, in spite of not making meaning out of what you see or hear, you may well be given glasses, or auditory training for that matter, just to see how you go. With everyone then expecting improvement, this just might be a big enough expectation to live up to, even one that one may have wished of oneself. But basically, this amounts to faith healing.

Some people with 'autism' who might not be able to pronounce things clearly may have a problem with hearing their own speech, not because they cannot hear clearly but because they have a systems integration problem. Such a person, for example, may be able to speak and may be able to hear properly with meaning, but not at the same time. This might mean that pronunciation problems in such a person may have nothing to do with how they perceive sound in their environment, but be because their brain may not be able adequately to monitor the sound of their own voice at the same time as their body is active in the physical mechanics of speaking.

It is true that the hearing acuity of people with 'autism' is often very good at pitches that non-autistic people often cannot hear. This, however, does not automatically equate to painful hypersensitivity. It may merely be that extreme or chronic stress results in painful sensory hypersensitivity and that under these circumstances senses are more acute than they normally would be. It does not follow that to train the ear out of the perception of some of these usually inaudible frequencies will remove the stress that caused it.

Using cotton wool to plug your ears whilst in a state of information overload leading to sensory hypersensitivity may reduce some of the sensory overload at that time but won't do anything to alter the same thing happening tomorrow. Training hearing out of perceiving certain frequencies may reduce some stress in the short term for some people but it may not directly improve the efficiency of information processing and subsequent overload. Also, sooner or later, hearing will generally readjust itself to the environment. You may have to have golden pockets to be able to afford to keep lining up every six months for the symptomatic relief that auditory training offers.

Information overload can result in a reactive sensory heightening and certain vitamin-mineral deficiencies and food and chemical allergies have also been implicated in sensory hypersensitivity. It may be possible to address both of these things by exploring underlying biochemical problems, such as hormone imbalances and their effects on enzyme production affecting digestion, the synthesis of vitamins and minerals and their interconnections with auto-immune problems such as food and chemical allergies and intolerances.

Special Tinted Lenses

Tinted lenses, specifically designed to combat visual-perceptual problems are another 'technique' that comes from an experience-based approach. The Irlen technique is a worldwide technique of assessing, fitting out and producing these lenses (which they refer to as Irlen Filters). Another technique being used by some specialists in the area of opthamology (the study of visual-perception) is the color-imitor technique. Both of these techniques use tinted lenses, or filters, to filter out certain light frequencies in order to reduce information overload through the eyes. Assessment for the correct tints within the Irlen Method involves looking through tinted lenses (through which one may look at the page or around at the environment or faces) and may be a more precise method of assessing when a tint is effective. The Color-imitor technique is primarily designed to deal with problems with the printed page and involves the shining of a colored light onto the printed page to assess which tint may be appropriate for lenses – a method which may be questionable in its accuracy. By reducing visual overload the brain can better process for meaning what the eyes see. These lenses can also have a secondary effect of reducing hypersensitivity to bright light and also in helping to reduce some of the 'interference' (the visual-perceptual equivalent of 'white noise') that can happen with visual hypersensitivity and visual-perceptual problems.

One of the other benefits of these tinted lenses, or 'filters', is that they may also improve functioning in other systems, such as processing for meaning, what is heard or tasted or smelled or improving tactile processing and processing of body messages. This is because it is sometimes the case that other systems are forced to compensate for an overloaded system.

Because visual processing counts for around 70 per cent of all information processing, if it is overloaded, the effects upon these other systems can be quite extreme. When the burden upon visual processing is removed the burden on these other systems may also be lessened quite significantly. In other cases, where compensation by other systems has not occurred, impairments in those other systems might remain independent and fundamentally unaffected.

There is a screening process for these lenses and only people who actually have this particular visual-perceptual problem are then fitted out for the particular tinted lenses that might help them. However, the procedure to ascertain the correct colour and shade requires some level of basic interaction and some feedback. Those with no observable form of reliable feedback, expression or communication may be unable to assist the diagnostician in their fitting of the appropriate colour or shade even though they might, in fact, benefit from the lenses. They may, therefore, be fitted with a colour or shade that does not properly or fully correct their visual-perceptual problems or not be able to be fitted for tinted lenses at all. Despite these limitations, it may be possible at least to ascertain a basic idea of the type of colour which might help them through keeping a diary of the 'autistic' person's responsiveness, awareness, self-control, motivation or relaxation under different brightly coloured light bulbs.

At present it might seem that this technique is limited in its fuller application to those who have some consistent and reliable form of verbal or non-verbal communication or feedback. Perhaps, in the future, electronic equipment may be developed to measure reliably responses to different colours and shades of lenses in a way that might not be dependent upon co-operation, feedback or interpersonal observation.

There are other implications that have to be handled properly when there is such a drastic change in what has been the visual-perceptual reality of people for five, ten, twenty or more years. Perception gets wound up in one's conception of the world and oneself and one's identity and how one feels about these things and what is familiar. Seriously altering, albeit restoring, any form of sensory perception can have a profound effect on a person's emotional and mental capacity to cope with the changes and what they might mean for them. Because of this, some people who are affected severely by visual-perceptual problems may need to get used to the lenses at their own pace. The experience can be like being meaning-blind and suddenly everything you see makes sense and has meaning and context. Although that may be welcomed, it can be emotionally and mentally overwhelming. The younger people get the help they need, the less adjustment they may have to make in coming to terms with the changes (and possible awareness and regrets) these changes may result in.

Also, as many people have a parallel perceptual problem in processing for meaning what they hear, it is hoped that a device may be developed to filter out permanently certain sound frequencies in order to allow the brain more fully to process with meaning what is heard. This, however, should not be confused with auditory training or auditory integration therapy which are currently used to train the ears to adjust their perception of pitch in order to combat hypersensitivity, rather than improve the processing of clearly heard words for meaning. It should also not be confused with techniques which attempt to speed up auditory thresholds by making the brain process more quickly what it hears. Ultimately, such mechanical speeding up in one system might not reduce a problem of information overload and so might only work in cases where the under-lying problem is generally slow processing rather than normal but over-loaded processing of too much, due to poor filtering. In the second case the result may likely be that other systems might compensate and process more poorly than they otherwise had.

Finally, it is important, in considering treating perceptual problems, that other developmental foundations for these perceptual problems also be considered. In some cases, there may be a problem in neuro-physiologi-cal development or biochemistry that may be at the basis of inefficient processing causing perceptual problems. In this case, it may make sense to address some of these problems first.

Chemical Intolerances

An intolerance to certain forms of a naturally occurring amino acid called phenol is an example of this. Phenol takes many forms. Two of those forms, gallic acid and malvin have been found associated with dyslexia (or SSS). Intolerance to gallic acid is also associated with hyperactivity and attention problems and intolerance to malvin has been found associated with autism, epilepsy and MS (Ber 1985).[1] According to Dr Ber's article, gallic acid is found in around 70 per cent of known foods and malvin is in about 35 different foods. Phenols also occur in tobacco, alcohol and many non-food substances, including petrochemicals, plastics, rubber and paper, making environmental avoidance of these substances extremely difficult if not impossible to manage.

Intolerance, sensitisation and allergy are words that are often used interchangeably. Basically, they mean that the body, for some reason or another, can't properly process certain food or chemical compounds. Recent studies have shown the presence of proteins in the urine specimens of a large percentage of autistic people, indicating that their bodies are unable to digest or metabolise certain food substances properly. These incompletely digested substances are not only toxic to the body but also wouldn't do much for brain functioning. Furthermore, when undigested food molecules are absorbed into the blood, they may act as allergy producing substances. People who may consider there to be no physical signs of food or chemical intolerance need to think again if the effects of these intolerances shows itself in brain function. 'Brain allergies' are well documented in literature in the field of alternative medicine and the brain depends on the endocrine system, digestive system, circulatory system, respiratory system and excretory system for the supply of nutrients and elimination of toxicity that keep it functioning to its maximum potential.

Neutralisation (desensitisation) to allergy producing substances is sometimes available but this should be done by a GP trained in complementary medicine. Many professionals pursue ideas about foods like wheat or dairy products, assuming a gluten or lactose intolerance when both are rich in the phenols, gallic acid and malvin, linked to dyslexia and autism (along with other very common foods such as sugar, corn, tomatoes, soy, chicken, citrus fruits, chocolate, coffee, tea or potatoes). Certainly, there have been good results for many people going off the heavily consumed foods of dairy products and/or wheat, but assuming this to be lactose or

---

1   1985, *Neutralisation of Phenolic Compounds in Holistic General Practice* by Dr Abram Ber, Phoenix Arizona, published in the *Journal of Orthomolecular Psychiatry*.

gluten intolerance may be building yourself a brick wall just when you may have glimpsed light at the end of the tunnel.

Food intolerance is a very new field and many practitioners may offer to help but be unqualified or only partially qualified or equipped to do so. As gallic acid and malvin intolerance involve such a wide group of foods and are implicated in autism and dyslexia, it could be a good place to start by finding a practitioner well aware of these phenol intolerances and how to treat them. Furthermore, the underlying causes of these intolerances is being explored and it may ultimately be that one day the way forward may not be through neutralisation but through finding and treating underlying organ or endocrine dysfunction or imbalances. For example, the liver and pancreas are responsible for enzyme production and digestion and excretion of food molecules, the synthesis of vitamins and minerals, regulation of blood sugar levels, blood detoxification and for ridding the body of excess amino acids. Sensitisation (intolerance) occurs when the body is consistently challenged with a substance it can't properly utilise or get rid of. It may be that intolerance to the amino acids, gallic acid and malvin, implicated in autism-related conditions, may one day be found to have its origins in treatable liver, pancreas or general endocrine dysfunction. Until then, dealing with the developmental results on perceptual development may be the best that can be done.

Inhibition of Infantile Reflexes

There are some places which look at the inhibition of infantile reflexes as an underlying cause of perceptual, sensory, learning, reading, movement, communication, emotional and behavioural difficulties. People are initially put through a rigorous repertoire of exercises to look for the presence of uninhibited infantile reflexes. (I was surprised to learn that most of these were still present and uninhibited in me at the age of almost thirty in spite of having learned to compensate for and cover them up. One which was still present was an infantile reflex that babies have to assist them in passing out of the womb! It was also found that I had different infantile reflexes present in different quarters of my body and that some were partially inhibited and some not at all.)

Infantile reflexes are meant to become inhibited naturally in early infancy through feedback to the brain regarding changes in growth and adaptations to the environment. As these infantile reflexes become inhibited new, more appropriate and more functional reflexes develop to take their places.

In spite of these redundant infantile reflexes not becoming naturally replaced by later ones, people can learn to behave as though they have been and to use actions that would naturally stem from newer, later reflexes that are not actually developed. For example, not having inhibited these infantile reflexes, I had instead gradually learned what can only be perceived by my body as the unnatural movements that 'normal' people use. This may appear functional but can have its disadvantages.

When huge amounts of energy are put into hiding and controlling redundant infantile reflexes and mechanically using 'normal' movements that feel unnatural, this may detract from the ability to process information efficiently through the senses. Furthermore, the unequal development of different infantile reflexes in different quarters of the body may pose an obstacle to the fuller and more complete integration of various systems of functioning (ie: seeing, hearing, smell, taste, touch, proprioperception). The chronic strain put on functioning as a whole could also have flow-on effects to many health-related problems.

After identifying uninhibited infantile reflexes a programme of exercises is written up which can be done at home to inhibit these and allow the body to develop more appropriate ones in their place. People are screened for the presence of these reflexes before any large costs are run up or any programmes started. Theoretically, this means that nobody should be treated who isn't in need of the programme. There are, however, a few things to consider.

One is that after ten, twenty or thirty years, people with systems integration problems, due to whatever reason, have pretty much developed adaptations to their difficulties which might be mentally and emotionally difficult to change. Also, in correcting an underlying problem someone has taken many years adapting to, the impact of these changes upon one's previous conception of the world and one's identity and personality may sometimes be more than the mind or emotions can handle in too big a dose. Because of this, this type of programme, whilst not excluding older people, is generally considered best employed with young children.

The second thing which needs to be considered is that the brain requires efficient feedback, in the context in which information happens in order to respond naturally to the fact that these infantile reflexes are no longer useful in the present environment. If there is a problem with the brain efficiently processing this feedback in the context in which it happens (such as processing delay) then those messages may not be *able* to be acted upon. If this is the case, then it may be that no amount of physical training would result in the inhibition of these reflexes.

Hemisphere Integration Programs

Some cases of 'dyslexia' and learning disabilities have been considered to be due to a problem with the integrated use of left and right brain hemispheres. The same problem may also be at the basis of certain feedback difficulties for some people with 'autism'. Examples of this might include:

- ○ problems in maintaining a simultaneous awareness of internal 'self' and external 'other' (rather than switching between awareness of only one or the other).

- ○ problems getting expression and understanding to work smoothly together (such as simultaneously monitoring one's speaking and also processing what one thinks about what someone else has just said).

- ○ problems with the interruption of subconscious automatic thinking, behaviour or expression into the place where conscious, intended and voluntary thought, behaviour or expression would normally be used (affecting conscious and voluntary access and control over thought, action or expression).

Left–right hemisphere integration programmes generally involve exercises to improve the ability of these hemispheres to work together. What is interesting is that some people with 'autism' employ, as if by instinct, some of the exercises which are known to help improve hemisphere integration.

One such exercise, the weaving in and out of one's hands in a sort of formation of an 'infinity' or sideways figure-eight sign in the air, is something that I, myself, was compelled to do for the reason that it made me 'feel right'. A number of people with 'autism' weave their bodies or heads in this way too.

It is just possible that behaviours like these are the result of the brain's instinctive attempts to establish order or balance. It may be that an information processing problem, causing inefficiency or delay in the relay of messages between the left and right hemispheres, is interfering with the establishment of a fixed pattern of left–right hemisphere integration. If this is the case, no amount of trying to train left–right hemisphere integration would help. Perhaps that is the very reason why some people who are instinctively driven to do these 'exercises', do them repetitively without actually achieving any of the sought-after permanent neurological changes. It may even be that one reason why some 'autistic' people seem compulsively to engage in behaviours that would normally aid in this integration is *because* their brain isn't able to achieve the integration that is sensed as lacking.

Other techniques which have been used to try to aid hemisphere integration include attempts to establish a dominant side (the use of left or right sides of the body). What this approach possibly overlooks is that if there is a problem in the efficiency of processing information in the context in which it happens, this may include the feedback of which side of the body was being used as the dominant side. In this case, no amount of trying to get a message through about the *significance* of a dominant side may have much effect.

Biochemical 'Treatments'

In some people with 'autism' significant improvements in their processing of information, sensory hypersensitivities, communication, mood and behaviour have been brought about through various diets and supplements that address biochemical, immune system and metabolic problems.

Some people have seen these problems as 'causes' when all signs of the person's 'autism' have disappeared. Others have seen these problems as 'aggravators' of the person's 'autism' and have found that although the condition did not disappear, it was significantly improved.

Basically, the way biochemical approaches work is by improving the efficiency of information processing. Some do this by increasing nutrients that assist in general brain functioning, some by giving supplements where nutrient deficiencies are found or by taking away the underlying causes of nutrient deficiencies. Some work by trying to correct excesses or imbalances in brain chemistry. In every case, it is very important that people seek professional advice on these things as, used wrongly, they can potentially do more harm than good. Some of the different biochemical 'treatments' that have been used with people with 'autism' include:

(1) Candida diets

The efficiency of information processing is affected by the supply of nutrients to the brain. One of the major causes of interference in the supply of those nutrients is immune and auto-immune system problems. One of the most commonly occurring underlying causes of immune and auto-immune system problems is candida albicans.

Candida albicans can affect general health (the immune system) as well as result in multiple food and chemical allergies (relating to the auto-immune system). It can also cause or aggravate a condition called reactive hypoglycemia which can cause extreme hormone fluctuations and imbalances as well as result in intermittent deprivation in the supply of oxygen and blood-glucose to the brain.

Candida albicans is a fungal infection. It occurs when the natural balance of flora in the intestinal tract becomes disturbed. Yeasts normally live within the intestinal tract and they multiply with the intake of things like refined sugars and die off naturally. Their multiplication is usually kept in check by the body's natural immunity (good germs) so that even on a high-sugar diet, their numbers can usually be kept down in most people.

When the natural immunity of the body is reduced, it usually corrects itself after some time as 'good germs' build up their numbers again. If, however, the body's natural immunity is constantly and chronically under attack, these are not replenished and yeasts are not kept in check. When this happens, they multiply at a rate that produces too much toxicity for the body to cope with.

Toxicity can make you feel yukky physically. It can also cause chronic aches and pains. Most important, like any kind of toxicity, it can affect your brain. That means it can affect your moods, your responsiveness and your ability to process information efficiently, just like alcohol can.

The causes of candida albicans are many. They can include inherited low immunity, a history of repeated treatment with antibiotics (which kill off not just the bad germs but the good ones too), the frequent use of steroid drugs (such as some for asthma, which also destroy the body's natural immunity) and the long-term use of certain other prescription drugs (which supress natural immunity). All of these contribute in a cumulative way to supress the body's general immunity, which allows yeasts to proliferate.

A chronically polluted environment (cigarette smoke, exhaust fumes, aerosols, perfume, factory pollution), a diet high in chemical additives such as colourings and flavourings and preservatives and bleach (which is used in most white sugar and white flour), alcohol, and lack of regular exercise (regular exercise helps the body rid itself of toxicity), can all contribute to the build up of toxicity in the body and make the effects of candida albicans worse and overburden the body to such a degree that it can do little to correct itself.

A diet high in *refined* carbohydrates assists in the already unchecked multiplication of yeasts in the intestinal tract. These refined carbohydrates include the added sugars found in most tinned and packaged commercial foods, confectionary, soft drinks and foods made from white flour.

Non-nutritional yeasty foods such as bakers yeast, which the body's natural yeasts thrive and multiply on, also contribute to this problem. In both the multiplication process as well as when they naturally die off, yeasts produce toxins into the bloodstream which the generally already over-stressed system has to to try to get rid of.

Candida albicans also upsets the body's auto-immune system and is, therefore, a major cause in the development of multiple food and chemical allergies. Allergies put a further strain on the body by using up most of the body's nutrients to counter allergic reactions. This means that severe multiple food and chemical allergies can reduce the oxygen in the blood as well as use up a whole range of vitamins and minerals that would otherwise be used for things like brain function, mood regulation and cell repair.

The effect of reducing the supply of nutrients to the brain, in terms of mood regulation and information processing, has been called 'brain allergies'. 'Brain allergies' are a combination of the effects of toxicity on the brain and the effect of allergies on both circulation and the supply of nutrients. In some people, 'brain allergies' make them manic and seemingly 'bouncing off the walls'. In others, they can make them unable to attend or comprehend.

Because these nutrients are used up elsewhere, this may not just reduce information processing efficiency and the ability to regulate moods but also mean that the body is less able to repair itself. This leaves it more open to infection and less able to fight infection once it takes hold. In some people this may result in allergic reactions such as asthma or eczema or infections such as chronic bronchitis, repeated ear infections, repeated eye infections or repeated bladder infections.

There are books available on candida albicans and information is also available from the Autism Research Institute in California in the USA (address at the back of this book). Treating candida albicans generally involves anti-fungal treatments such as high dose garlic capsules or high dose Caprylic acid (coconut palm oil) or there is an anti-fungal drug called Nystatin. The first two weeks of such a treatment sometimes sees symptoms worsen (due to dramatically raised frequency of yeast die-off) but not long after this, significant improvement is usually seen. In addition to this, dietary and environmental changes are sometimes also necessary to alleviate the condition. Dietary changes and anti-fungal treatment may be necessary for up to six months in mild cases or for two years or even longer where the problem is more severe.

The candida diet and anti-fungal supplements are not harmful if applied in cases where they are not needed. They should, however, preferably be used under the supervision of a sensitive nutritional therapist who is aware of the condition.

It may be very hard to find this kind of professional help from GPs. It may be easier to find help in the field of alternative or complementary medicine and your local health-food store may be able to advise you of a reputable and trained professional in this field.

(2) Amino acids

Studies have found that some people with 'autism' are deficient in certain amino acids. Amino acids form proteins and peptides responsible for enzymes which are used by the body to help break down or digest different types of food substances. Lacking certain amino acids might, therefore, mean that a food substance that is otherwise quite harmless may be indigestible and quite toxic to someone missing what is needed to digest it and make use of its nutrients.

The effects of amino acid imbalances or deficiencies might result in toxic effects upon the brain. It might also lead to vitamin-mineral imbalances or deficiencies where the vitamins or minerals a person might otherwise have got from digesting a particular food group is not derived from that food because it is not able to be properly digested and because essential nutrients are otherwise used up in ridding the body of toxicity.

Certain amino acids such as dimethylglycine (DMG derived from rice – details of how to order by mail are available through the Autism Research Institute), have had some remarkable effects in improving frustration tolerance, mood, interaction, communication, sleep disorders and information processing in quite a number of people with 'autism' as well as reducing the frequency of epilepsy episodes in a large number of people with this problem.

Other enzyme deficiencies, such as those responsible for the digestion of a group of food substance called phenol may also be the cause of a lot of difficulties in certain people with 'autism', and milk or wheat intolerance in a large number of people with 'autism' is also often due to a lack of the appropriate amino acids or enzymes to digest these foods. More research needs to be done in these areas, although amino acid supplements are available through many well-stocked health food shops.

Although these supplements are generally safe, it is still very important that an informed and qualified person ascertain the presence of an enzyme or amino acid deficiency before long-term treatment with these substances is undertaken. Persistent excess may actually lead to sensitisation (or allergy). It is also important first to address whether candida albicans could be contributing to any deficiencies in amino acids or digestive or vitamin-mineral deficiency problems.

(3) Vitamin-mineral supplements

There are certain physical and behavioural signs of vitamin-mineral deficiencies. Even in the absence of these signs, vitamin-mineral supplements can improve information processing and reduce anxiety (and its consequences) in some people with 'autism'. The dosages, however, which seem to show the best results, are high dosages, or mega dosages, and these should be taken *only* in an approved combined formula multivitamin-mineral tablets or capsules.

In particular, some people with attention deficit disorder and hyperactivity have improved with very high doses of vitamin B6 (preferably as part part of a B complex preparation) and magnesium (preferably combined with calcium) as well as high dose vitamin C (preferably as ascorbate). The B group vitamins seem to have an effect on improving information processing (thereby decreasing information overload and its devastating results). They also seem to help to reduce stress levels. Magnesium is known as the anti-anxiety mineral and can have beneficial effects on digestion, blood sugar regulation, circulation and mood. Vitamin C is a natural antihistamine important where food and chemical allergies are suspected. It is also a natural detoxifier and helps in the absorption of iron. Potassium is another mineral that it may be important to consider, especially where there is high sodium intake or hypoglycemia which may cause potassium deficiency, as potassium is important for the elimination of toxins and the transportation of oxygen to the brain.[2]

It is very important that people realise that they should not play chemist with vitamin-mineral supplements and that it might be dangerous to do so. Whilst the body will rid itself of any excess of most vitamins and minerals, there are a small number of these of which it cannot rid itself of an excess and where any excesses can build up in the body with sometimes health-threatening consequences. Furthermore, there are certain vitamins that, taken in isolation, can actually cause a deficiency in other vitamins. Certain B group vitamins work this way, so it is essential that if one of the B group vitamins is needed, for example Vitamin B6, a

---

2   Mindell, E. (1980) *The Vitamin Bible.* London: Arlington Books.

combination B complex vitamin (containing B6 and its other relatives) be taken rather than taking B6 on its own. A similar relationship exists between magnesium, calcium, phosphorus, sodium potassium and Vitamin C.

The safe solution is to take a high dose *approved* multivitamin-mineral tablet which contains combinations of vitamins and minerals in a safe and balanced dose and which should not result in imbalances. Recommended dosages are available through the Autism Research Institute.

Though vitamins and minerals are naturally occurring, they are still powerful and should not be abused or experimented with. My advice is that people take only approved dosages in approved combinations under the supervision of a sympathetic nutritional therapist who is aware of mega-vitamin treatment and 'autism' and is able to monitor such long term usage.

It is also important to point out that some people may be allergic or intolerant to certain substances or coatings in vitamin-mineral preparations and that any adverse reaction should be taken seriously and advice sought before continuing taking any preparations. It is also important to point out that not everybody will respond to vitamin-mineral supplements and that these things should be used initially on a trial basis only for a month or so and stopped if there are any adverse reactions whilst advice is sought.

Finally, as candida albicans, insufficient stomach acid, pancreas or liver dysfunction can all be a major cause of vitamin-mineral deficiencies or inability to synthesise vitamins and minerals properly, it is very important to have these possibilities checked out as you may otherwise be treating the symptoms instead of the cause.

(4) Complex Homeopathy

Various research in the field of autism has found the following:

- undigested protein molecules in the urine samples of the majority of people with autism.
- frequent findings of severe vitamin-mineral and/or enzyme deficiency.
- marked improvement with supplements such as mega doses of B6, vitamin C and Evening Primrose Oil as well as magnesium, calcium, zinc and enzyme supplements.

- ° frequent cases of candida albicans as an underlying cause of the sort of multiple food and chemical intolerance indicative of allergy-induced autism.

- ° suspicion that pancreas and/or liver dysfunction underly allergy to phenolic compounds (intolerance to the phenolic compound of gallic acid found associated with ADD, hyperactivity, dyslexia and intolerance to the phenolic compound of malvin found associated with autism, dyslexia and epilepsy).

In the book *21st Century Medicine*,[3] Dr Kenyon, a GP trained in complementary medicine, writes about a very treatable condition worth further consideration in view of the connection it may have with such research findings.

Dr Kenyon writes about dysbiosis, a condition affecting the permeability of the lining of the gut. The initial symptoms of dysbiosis are largely physical and Dr Kenyon includes signs such as flatulence, bloating, disordered bowel habits but also liver, gall bladder or pancreas dysfunction, acne, fungal infections, asthma, urticaria, excema, post-viral fatigue, and rheumatism and later mentions conditions such as chronic sinusitis, and repeated tonsilitis as indicators of toxic stress due to underlying disbiosis.

He suggests that the underlying causes of or contributors to dysbiosis include the effects of common antibiotic use upon the balance of the normal gut flora (the balance of naturally occurring bacteria which assist in digestion and immunity) as well as poor nutrition common to high intake of junk food, chronic stress and the effects of attacks of enteritis. Dr Kenyon writes:

> 'Most importantly, there seems to be a relationship between the permeability (a measure of the ability to filter substances through) of the gut mucous membrane (the internal gut lining) and normal bowel flora. If the flora is abnormal or imbalanced, then the gastro-intestinal mucous membrane becomes abnormally permeable, rather like a sieve in which the holes are too big, allowing the absorbtion of inadequately broken down proteins and the reabsorption of toxins from the bowel contents.'

On the connection of this with food intolerance, he writes:

---

3   Dr Julian Kenyon (1986) *21st Century Medicine.* London: Thorsons.

> 'This is often what happens in food sensitivity and, in my experience, dysbiosis is a major underlying cause of such sensitivity.'

He goes on to write about the effect of these toxins on the liver; one of the major organs involved in synthesis of vitamins and minerals as well as the regulation of sugar, fat and protein metabolism.

He goes on to make a link with vitamins and the effectiveness of mega-vitamin therapy, saying:

> 'Intestinal bacteria can synthesize vitamins, mostly of the B group but also vitamin K. In dysbiosis, the majority of vitamins taken by mouth, either in food or by vitamin replacements, will be taken up by the abnormal bacteria, resulting in vitamin deficiency. This may well be why large doses of vitamins are found to be effective, whereas low doses produce no result... My suggestion is that if the underlying dysbiosis was adequately treated then smaller doses of vitamins would be adequate.'

And on the connection between dysbiosis and candida albicans, he writes:

> '...its recognition [candida albicans] is often fundamental to the successful resolution of multiple food sensitivities in many patients. In my experience, if the dysbiosis is resolved successfully using complex homeopathy and appropriate supporting measures, then the candida albicans will then disappear with most, if not all, the food sensitivities.'

Dr Kenyon suggests the use of complex homeopathy which addresses the causes and involves the use of homeopathic preparations to stimulate the organs into ridding themselves of the burden of toxic loads and helping to restore the body's natural processes and immunity. Conventional medicine, unlike holistic medicine, tends to focus on the suppression of symptoms, much of which involves short term treatment at long term cost to the fine balances within the body, rather than dealing with the causes.

What makes people 'autistic'. in my view, is the range of complex and varying involuntary and voluntary adaptations to information overload caused by poor information filtering and processing. If dysbiosis, in particular, affects information processing via its effects upon toxicity, synthesis of vitamin-minerals and the supply of nutrients to the brain and if, as suggested, it is a major and correctible underlying cause of these problems, it is possible that a large percentage of cases of autism-related conditions are entirely treatable within the field of complementary medicine using the type of technology (advanced techniques of Vega testing and Segmental Electrogram Technology) and complex homeopathy used by trained professionals like Dr Kenyon. Of course, there will still be developmental setbacks due to long term developmental delays but the important thing is to remove the blocks to development so the person can go forward, whether at the age of five, fifteen or fifty.

(5) Hypoglycemia

Hypoglycemia is a metabolic condition of having sudden drops in blood sugar level. The sudden drops can produce stupor and an inability to process information, initiate action, reason, concentrate or pay attention.

Prior to these sudden drops there is often a sharp rise in blood sugar level, which can result in an inability to control behaviour and an extreme burst of emotion or activity. People suffering from this may sometimes seem to swing between two extremes. Some people with this condition have been misdiagnosed as having manic depression or mood disorders.

The cause of hypoglycemia can be inherited and passed on genetically. Signs of this might be the presence, in older family members, of mature age diabetes, sugar craving or a history of mood swings. Reactive hypo-glycemia, however, can be acquired as a result of candida albicans. In this case, attacks of reactive hypoglycemia may be not just based on the amount of time elapsed between meals, but on what was eaten throughout the day, exposure to cigarette smoke or airborne chemicals, medications taken and general stress level, including emotional extremes or extreme reactions to sensory stimuli.

The long term treatment of hypoglycemia, contrary to the impression given by the label, is NOT to give sugar. The regular consumption of sugar actually contributes to the seriousness of the condition over time. Untreated, those who have the condition and binge on sugary foods and drinks may take their condition from mild to severe.

There are certain vitamin-mineral supplements specific to helping manage hypoglycemia which can be found in most books on the subject (often available through health food stores) and if any other supplements are already being taken, seek advice from someone qualified in natural medicine about whether it is safe to double up on supplements or how to adjust dosages.

Other than supplements, regular, *but not excessive*, exercise can help. So can a diet that is free of all processed and refined foods, free of all *refined* carbohydrates and free of all added sugars. Refined sugars, refined carbohydrates and processed foods get used up too quickly by the overactive metabolism of someone with hypoglycemia, resulting in a severe blood sugar drop. This, in turn, triggers the release of adrenalin to send a message to the liver to release fat stores to be broken down for energy. This adrenalin rush produces the manic highs before the oblivious lows of the sugar drop itself.

Because hypoglycemia is like a see-saw, the aim is to stay in the middle as best as possible and for as long as possible. The way to do this is to eat foods that take time to digest, such as complex carbohydrates (such as wholemeal and wholegrain produce and brown rice). In mild cases of hypoglycemia the way to do this might entail eating at least every four hours. In moderate or severe cases this may be to eat substantially as regularly as every two hours.

Again, the possibility of candida albicans causing this condition should first be considered and addressed. As the pancreas and liver are also implicated in blood sugar regulation (as well as detoxification) it is also important to explore dysfunction in these organs and hormone imbalances (ie: secretin which is responsible for stimulation of enzyme production in the pancreas and liver). In the article, *Neutralisation of Phenolic Compounds in Holistic General Practice*, Dr Ber[4] also makes mention of intolerance to another phenolic compound, phloridizin (rich in such common foods as beef, cheese, sugar and soy among others) and found common to people with diabetes. He goes on to raise the question 'is it possible that phloridizin interferes not only with the endocrine function of the pancreas but with the enzymatic exocrine action?' Aside from the effects of food intolerance on reactive hypoglycemia, it may be worth exploring an intolerance to the phenol, phloridizin, not just as an effect but as a cause of hypoglycemia.

(6) Hormone-related drug treatments

Recent research has found too high or too low a presence of certain hormones in some people with 'autism'. Drugs have been developed to restore hormonal balances in people with these conditions. There are two things, however, that are important to point out here.

One is that some apparently hormone-related conditions may actually have other underlying causes. In these cases, treating a hormone imbalance might be merely addressing the symptoms.

---

4   The Journal of Orthomolecular Psychiatry, 1985.

Extreme, prolonged and chronic stress is one example of something that might act directly on hormone levels. Immune system disorders, such as candida albicans, are other causes of hormonal imbalances and should be addressed and ruled out by someone aware and knowledgeable about this condition before hormone-related drug treatments are undertaken.

Sleep disorders and eating disorders can be linked to hormone imbalances but sleep deprivation and eating behaviours can also result in hormone imbalances, as can certain kinds of hypnotic or self-abusive behaviours. Whilst these things may sometimes be the result of instinctive attempts to correct hormonal imbalances, in any cases where hormonal imbalances are found, repetitive behaviours as an aggravator of these imbalances should be considered before the behaviours are considered as the symptoms rather than cause. It may well be that the numbing or 'buzz' felt from the hormonal effect of behaviours like sleep deprivation, forced vomiting, self-starvation, self-hypnosis or self-abuse are actually what is being sought by the person using the behaviours rather than hormonal imbalances being the cause of these.

Amino acid or enzyme deficiencies can be the result of hormone imbalances (ie: secretin responsible for enzyme production and regulation) which might result in behavioural, processing or communication problems as well as sometimes resulting in hormone imbalances. One recently reported example is a deficiency in the enzyme needed to break down phenol-rich foods. When this enzyme was deficient it was shown to result in raised serotonin levels. It is not enough to address one hormonal imbalance without looking at it within the context of others that may have caused this in the first place.

(7) Wheat-free, milk-free, sugar-free and additive-free diets

Many people who have found wheat-free or milk free diets to be beneficial in improving information processing in people with autism have then assumed that they are looking at a gluten intolerance (as in the case of celiac disease) or a lactose intolerance. In some people with autism, wheat intolerance may actually have nothing to do with gluten, nor dairy intolerance anything to do with lactose. Gluten and lactose are only two properties of wheat and milk. Both wheat and milk are also rich in the phenolic compounds, gallic acid and malvin, implicated in dyslexia and autism. A person can be intolerant to these properties of the commonly eaten foods of wheat and milk without having any problem specifically to do with gluten or lactose.

Even where intolerance to wheat is found to be caused by gluten intolerance or the intolerance to milk found to be due to lactose intolerance, underlying causes should also be explored. For example, it may be that these intolerances have arisen as a result of treatable enzyme deficiencies due to treatable liver and/or pancreas dysfunction or a problem with the hormone secretin, responsible for enzyme production necessary to break down gluten and/or lactose. It may be that intolerance to wheat or milk may be merely a symptom of the yeast infection candida albicans which would also be treated.

Sugar not only aggravates the yeast infection candida albicans but it is also high in the phenolic compound, gallic acid, implicated in dyslexia, hyperactivity and attention deficit disorder and is also a major aggravator of hypoglycemia. Those considering a sugar-free diet might also consider exploring the possibilities of treatable underlying conditions such as candida albicans, intolerance to gallic acid and any underlying problem of pancreas or liver dysfunction.

An additive-free diet is a good idea for anyone with or without a problem in detoxifying the body (with the consequent effects on the brain) because, basically, most additives are foreign matter merely put into foods to give them longer shelf life and make them more attractive to the purchaser. Again, most additive-containing foods are high in Gallic Acid and as both candida albicans and liver dysfunction are involved in detoxification it may be an idea to explore what is going on in these areas too.

(8) Desensitisation

Desensitisation, also called neutralisation, is basically a homeopathic approach used to reduce allergic reaction to food or chemical substances. Generally, this involves ascertaining the tolerance threshold for any problem substance and then giving very carefully adjusted dilutions of the same substance in order to find the dilution at which the allergic reaction is neutralised. Progressively, as the system adjusts, the response to these dilutions is progressively and carefully monitored and the patient is eventually able to tolerate more concentrated dilutions as he or she becomes less sensitive to the substance in question, until eventually being able to again tolerate exposure to the allergy-causing substances in the environment or diet.

I've been through desensitisation for severe food and chemical allergies and can say that desensitisation did work for me short term. In some people, it can last up to two years. In me, it unfortunately lasted for only around six weeks of relative clarity. In Dr Ber's article, *Neutralisation Of Phenolic Compounds In Holistic General Practice*, he does suggest that maintaining the patient indefinitely on the final dilution rather than discontinuing treatment at that point has been found to be successful in some cases where sensitisation otherwise recurred.

The alternative to desensitisation is usually seen as avoidance diets but seeking underlying causes of food or chemical sensitisation or intolerance is another path to be trecked, particularly where desensitisation has failed.

One of the problems with desensitisation is that it is a lengthy procedure and can cost a lot of money. Also, there is only a tiny handful of trained professionals (often GPs who are also trained in complementary medicine) able to deal effectively with it.

In my view, desensitisation is still about treating symptoms and, if possible, one should look for the underlying causes of food and chemical sensitisation first and treat those first before returning to the option of desensitisation if still necessary.

(9) Herbal remedies

The importance of herbal remedies shouldn't be overlooked as possible alternatives to drug treatments and in treating problems underlying food and chemical sensitivities and chronic stress. Many of the herbs still available today formed the basis of the synthetic drugs now being prescribed.

Herbal remedies are likely to be handled more easily by the body than synthetic drugs, especially where a toxicity problem is involved. There are herbs used to detoxify the blood, to regulate hormone levels, promote digestion, reduce allergic reaction and restore and stabilise organ function. Herbal remedies are also less likely to have the sort of side effects that sometimes come with synthetic drugs.

On the down side, in spite of the fact that herbal remedies have been passed down for hundreds of years, it can be difficult to find good, reliable and informed help in the use and dosages of herbal remedies.

Psychotherapy

Although psychotherapy has its place more specifically in the treatment of people who have psychological problems or emotional disturbance, it has been included here because, whether it is applicable to 'autism' or not, it is still sometimes being used to 'treat' people with 'autism'.

Those using the technique see themselves as dealing with causes, rather than symptoms, but the use of psychotherapy with people with 'autism' is based upon the false assumption that 'autism' is a form of mental illness or psychological or emotional disturbance.

In my view, 'autism' causes a lot of mental and emotional problems in the carers. I also think that the inability of non-autistic people to understand people with 'autism', can also create a very high degree of mental and emotional stress in people with 'autism'. Neither of these things means that 'autism' is a form of mental illness or psychological or emotional disturbance.

Although there are probably 'autistic' people who *also* have mental illness or psychological or emotional disturbance, these are additional problems. On their own, these problems would not result in the spectrum of problems seen in 'autism'.

Although people with 'autism' may be subject to a much higher degree of stress than most people, an information processing problem may actually rob a person of meaning and personal significance, which are two of the key elements in becoming psychologically or emotionally ill or disturbed in any focused or complex way. Mental illness is primarily about attributing too much personal significance to things. That is the very problem that some people with 'autism' might wish they had.

Without the ability to process efficiently what has upset you in the context in which the upset happened, in my experience, it makes it less likely to have any particular focus to mental or emotional disturbance so the development of complex disturbance or illness would be a processing miracle for some people with 'autism'. Also, low thresholds for information overload can result in shutdowns in processing, happening so frequently that the meaningful impact of anything highly disturbing doesn't have a very prolonged effect. It may be that by being pushed over the edge many times a day, a person actually avoids being pushed over the edge in any sudden and big way. These things may, however, be different for some people with Asperger Syndrome, who, in spite of information processing problems, sometimes do process consistently what they see or hear and get some degree of consistent personal significance from these things.

Psychotherapy often assumes that the person's problems have been caused by the environment. Although the problems of some people with 'autism' are made significantly worse by non-autistic people not understanding their sensory, perceptual or processing problems or emotional hypersensitivity, this is usually not what the psychotherapist is trained to set right.

Certainly, the 'autistic' person's problems can be aggravated by environmental ignorance but this is not the same as saying that carers have not tried to be understanding, compassionate or supportive, only that nobody is informed enough, from an 'autistic' perspective, to assist them in how to show this understanding, compassion and support in a way that will make sense to the person with 'autism'. This isn't the job of a psychotherapist, it is the job of an expert in the nature of 'autism'.

Many parents, low in self-esteem and social support, too readily blame themselves in the absence of any other easily visible cause. This is sometimes what is exploited in the process of psychotherapy. This can stress parents who are often already mentally and emotionally stretched in trying to cope with their child's 'autism' and their own inability to help.

Psychotherapy sometimes assumes an inherent or acquired psychological or emotional fragility rather than a hypersensitivity caused by information overload. It also sometimes overlooks the fact that people do adjust and adapt to all sorts of circumstances, traumatic or otherwise, and that in the absence of efficient information processing in the context in which things happen, some people with 'autism' are actually far more resilient to the personal significance of experiences than most people. Psychotherapy has had some success in getting otherwise uncommunicative or non-interactive people to communicate and interact, but this may be coincidental.

Whilst a change of environment might bring out changes and abilities in someone, there are often cheaper ways to achieve this than a trip to the psychotherapist's office. On the other hand, informed counselling for parents may sometimes be a good idea in helping some of them to cope with the added stress of dealing with their child's 'autism' and the grief and guilt they too often feel.

Play therapy may be a better alternative in promoting interaction and communication where neither parents nor child need counselling. Furthermore, a good play therapist should be able to train a parent in techniques they can use at home. Such an approach would be a more empowering one for parents who sometimes feel very robbed of control by professionals as well as by the children they may feel helpless to assist.

Music, Art and Movement

Music, art and movement can also be used as media through which to build interaction and expression and as a place in which a carer or therapist can 'meet' the person with autism. They can be less directly confrontational than speech and so may be particularly useful with people who suffer from intense emotional hypersensitivity or exposure anxiety. These media can also have or bring a sense of balance and rhythm which can be soothing and levelling for some people with high anxiety levels or mood problems. Music, art and movement can be used flexibly in terms of the degree of structure and the degree of direct interaction/expression involved.

Like some forms of play therapy, puppetry and 'speaking through objects', they can be used in a 'Simply Be' way where the person with autism is encouraged to express freely through them.

Brushes need not be used in art and one can merely be encouraged to touch colour and join with it through covering oneself. For someone who generally finds initiation of action or choice in front of someone else too difficult to dare, even this may be a major achievement. Colour is also emotionally evoking and making peace with colour, even choosing to approach it by choice or making it part of you can be part of the process of making peace with emotion.

Music and movement can be meeting places on a more abstract level in which the conscious mind most responsible for the anxiety response to the realisation of exposure may be less on guard as bridges are very gradually but progressively built from the abstract and indirect to the more tangible and direct, first within these media and then beyond music to vocal patterns, beyond movement to touch patterns.

Expression through these media need not be 'viewed', praised or assessed in any way that may bring too much force-fed directly-confrontational self-reflection before the person is ready for it. This may be particularly important for those who are highly emotionally hypersensitive or whose exposure anxiety is too high to be able to endure the intense impact of self-reflection that can come of having someone attempt to share too directly in any expression that may have been allowed out.

Reflexology

Massage has recently been used to help people with 'autism' and even some people who can't cope much with social touching or who have very poor body connectedness, have been able to tolerate, and even appreciate, some forms of massage.

Foot massage has been used to generally alleviate stress but is also part of reflexology. Reflexology is part of ancient Eastern Medicine and relates to pressure points on the feet that are used in traditional acupuncture. Unlike traditional acupuncture, reflexology is non-invasive and is a form of acupressure. It has been used for centuries, and is still a major form of medical treatment in the East. The pressure points on the feet are considered to correspond to all sorts of body functions and stimulation of them is thought to be able to do things like improve circulation, digestion, mood regulation, cell repair and the elimination of toxins from the body.

It is thought to have the potential of improving immunity and assisting in the correction of auto-immune problems and generally reducing stress. If it did all the things it claimed to do, it could just about cure anything, even improve information processing in people with 'autism'. Whether it does so is a question that people need to consider if they are paying a lot of money for this service.

As a person with 'autism' who generally avoids touch, foot massage is one of the few forms of touch that I welcome from anyone willing, and many other people who don't cope well with touch have also responded enthusiastically to 'foot massage'.

Whether it cures things or not, it does seem to reduce stress for me quite drastically and could be a point of interaction and a key to establishing familiarity and some kind of relationship for some people with 'autism'. I would not, however, recommend that anyone persist with this 'treatment' if the cost outweighed the results or if, in the absence of results, 'foot massage' were unwelcomed by the person receiving it. There are reflexology courses people can take to do this themselves.

Cranial-Osteopathy/Craniosacral Therapy

Just as there are cardiovascular and respiratory rhythms, there is also another, less commonly known body rhythm – the craniosacral system. This system influences many body functions and an imbalance in this system can adversely effect the development of the brain and spinal cord which can result in sensory, motor and intellectual dysfunction.

Craniosacral therapy is a gentle non-invasive manipulative technique which involves the use of light touch to locate the source of the problems in the hydraulic forces inherent in the craniosacral system and to then stimulate the body's own natural self-corrective mechanism in order to improve the functioning of brain and spinal cord, to dissipate the negative effects of stress and to enhance your general health and resistance to disease.

Its relevance to the treatment of autism, in my view, may be twofold. First, as a large number of cases of 'autism' involve biochemical imbalances and auto-immune problems, a therapy like cranial-osteopathy may be able to complement allergy-related and nutritional approaches. Some examples of this may be in the reduction of toxicity and chronic stress as contributors to vitamin-mineral deficiencies and allergy conditions, both of which can severely impede more efficient information processing and sensory-perceptual integration. Second, for those who experience problems of body-connectedness or acute exposure anxiety, the purposeful/pragmatic, structured, less personally-confrontational, non-engulfing and empathic nature of the touch involved in cranial-osteopathy may be a relaxing, user-friendly introduction to touch and interaction for those who might otherwise find these things too jolting of consciousness or causing sudden and disturbing sensory-perceptual systems shifts. Having become accustomed to such treatment, cranial-osteopathy could be 'bridged' into other complementary forms of touch-interaction such as reflexology, aromatherapy and, perhaps later, shiatsu (any of which can also, if relevant, be used therapeutically with problems of auto-immunity, digestive disturbances and chronic anxiety).

CHAPTER 6

The Straws on the Camel's Back

If you've got a camel which is finding it hard to walk under the weight of all the straws on its back, the easiest way to make it easier for the camel to walk is to take as many straws off its back as possible. Management is about training the camel to walk or appear to walk whilst carrying the straws. Cure is about taking the straws off the camel's back. The two can work together.

Trying to make systems function when they are buckling under the weight of other burdens is a drain on everybody's energy and success, if any, will be slow. Too many 'autism' 'techniques', 'therapies' and 'treatments', spend their time building up the camel's muscles to carry what is more than his share of straws or to teach the camel to act as if he is carrying less than he actually is. It makes more sense to take these straws off and then the camel's job will be easier (and so will those caring for and working with the camel).

To take the straws off the camel's back, you have to do two things. One is to identify them and the second is to know how to remove them or where to go to find someone who can.

Identifying Those Straws

I have already talked about the different categories of problems;

- problems of control
- problems of tolerance
- problems of connection.

There are several things that can go wrong to cause each of these problems and there are solutions to some of these things or places to start looking for those solutions. What follows is a journey through causes to solutions.

The Role of Information Processing

All kinds of messages come into the brain via the senses, including the muscles, the joints and the balance centres involved in movement as well as body messages relating to emotional sensations. These are incoming messages.

Incoming messages are DECODED in order to make them possible to INTERPRET. To do this, the left and right brain hemispheres (and all their departments) have to be able to relay messages efficiently between different parts of the brain.

Information Overload

Information overload can happen if you are too slow to keep up with the rate at which information is coming in. This is like one train being late causing all the others to be late too. Information overload can happen because your brain doesn't filter out the same range of generally irrelevant information as other people's do. This is like having one whole jar of peanut butter but having one hundred sandwiches to spread.

In either case, information overload means that scarce resources get spread too thinly and that the brain calls a range of involuntary compensations into play in order to manage this; compensations that generally don't make much sense to non-autistic people whose brains have never required them.

What follows is my own simplified version of how I experience meaning and significance when in a state of overload, when my ability to process incoming information and respond to that information has become very slowed down and inefficient.

Making Literal Meaning

In order to make literal meaning of information that has come in through our senses, it has to be decoded and interpreted. So, for example, my eyes might pick up a whole load of light pulses that have bounced off things in the room around me (I don't experience this part with awareness). This raw information is relayed to areas of the brain which will decode it. The decoded information might now be something like 'white and flat and thin and square with a smooth surface'. At this point that means a lot more than nothing but it still doesn't mean much at all. It doesn't tell me what I'm looking at, just what it looks like. At this point, this decoded information needs to be interpreted.

The decoded information, 'white and flat and thin and square with a smooth surface' becomes interpreted into the recognition that what has been 'seen' is 'a sheet of paper'. At this point, I know what the thing looks like and what it is but there is still no interpretation of what, if anything, to do about it. Without processing further than this, there is little or no thought about what has been experienced.

From Meaning to Significance

At this point, I may know I have experienced 'a sheet of paper' but haven't yet understood the SIGNIFICANCE of this. I don't yet know what, if anything, to do about this experience. This deeper processing, for significance, requires further internal messages to be sorted and relayed. Significance tells me what to do about paper, ie: 'I need some of that to write on' or 'that's not what I'm looking for'.

When something is processed for significance, this would usually drive action and/or expression and again there are many more messages that need to be relayed efficiently for significance to result in action or expression. This is when realisations of significance go from 'I need some of that to write on' to my actually reaching for it and picking it up.

The relaying of information for processing can be inefficient in a whole variety of ways. The following are just some of these.

Types of Inefficient Processing

(1) 'Sorry, wrong address'

Messages can be sorted inefficiently so that they are relayed badly. This is like putting a call through to the wrong number or the next door neighbour's house instead of your house.

These are what I call 'misfires'. Some examples of these in my own life have been where I've come up with words or names that have a similar shape, pattern or rhythm to one I am trying to recall without being similar in meaning. I've had this trouble with names such as Margaret and Elizabeth because they seem to have the same feel and seem similar to me.

In the same way, I've said things like 'I want my shoes' when I meant 'I want my jacket' and been surprised to get the things I apparently asked for. Sentences like 'I'm trying very hard' have come out as 'I'm trying very difficult'.

I have known I'm having a problem to do with my body messages but find myself going off to the toilet because I felt cold or putting on a coat because I felt hungry or eating or drinking because I felt full.

I have also been the one to leave my own house because I knew someone was meant to be leaving but got it wrong about who it was and how to get them out.

I have meant to look at something but the message came out wrong and I've gawked suddenly into the opposite direction.

I am always pushing doors that I mean to pull open and pulling at the doors I meant to push.

I have felt glad to see someone but instantly ignored them.

Another experience that feels like a mixture between messages going to the wrong address and getting crossed lines is to do with 'fluffy people causing me lemons'. 'Fluffy' people (those who are are very self-exposed, without image or facade and emotionally vulnerable) 'cause me lemons'. Being around them or involved with them 'causes lemons' because it triggers a sensation that feels exactly how eating lemons makes me feel. Though the taste isn't there, the response in my mouth and neck and muscles is the same. These people cause a 'sour taste' that is as extreme and of the same type that lemons cause me when eaten (and it is not easy to put up with).

(2) 'Sorry it's late'

Messages can be sorted all right but take a long time to be relayed. This is like not putting birthday calls through until after the birthday has passed.

Non-firings are 'life with a rain-check'. For me, they are thieves of the ability to understand and feel the reward of interaction or emotions.

As a child, this was consistently how life was for me, so it appeared as though I didn't feel pain or discomfort, didn't want help, didn't know what I was saying, didn't listen or didn't watch. By the time some of these sensations, responses or comprehensions were decoded and processed for meaning and personal significance, and I'd accessed the means of responding, I was fifteen minutes, one day, a week, a month, even a year away from the context in which the experiences happened. At the same time, I was taught to act as though I *had* processed what had happened; to act like I had a 'life'. The first problem, of delayed processing, had robbed me. The second problem of being made to act as though I had no processing problems was like rubbing my nose in it.

At school, and later university, I sat for hours not understanding more than the occasional word and listening to what mostly sounded like gobbledeegook and watching meaningless face-pullings (facial expression) and actions. I'd scan volumes of largely meaningless print and my body generally seemed without hunger or tiredness, cold or discomfort.

In situations that should have caused affect, I generally registered none (even though I learned to display stored copies of what was 'normal' and expected). In situations I was meant to enjoy, I usually felt indifferent. In situations that were meant to provoke me, I generally thought nothing. Though all sorts of disembodied niggles were happening, I mostly didn't know where they were coming from or what they meant.

Sooner or later, I'd wake up with a sense of realisation without knowing what I'd realised. Information that I didn't know I'd processed would be triggered by questions and actions by others and I'd have no idea where the understanding had come from or how it got there and it would often be wholly disembodied from the context from which it had originated.

Unprocessed, indistinguishable sensations of pure unprocessed contextless emotions (that were probably meant to be connected to the information that was not yet fully processed) too would often suddenly flood me in a heap after their immediate context had gone, leaving me sensorily and/or emotionally overloaded to painful extremes. These felt almost like attacks or 'fits' after which there was often a time of growth, as through these 'exorcisms' were some kind of bulk processing.

The effect of these persistent severe processing delays on life made people respond to me as everything from stupid to disturbed, mad and eccentric and the local amusement. For me, the world seemed basically incomprehensible, unrewarding and purely a place in which to pass time. All the realisations, connections and affect that were meant to reward me for interaction and experience were so delayed and out of context that continuity was a shambles and a myth. The attachment that was meant to flow from it became nothing but a well-trained facade for which I had only theoretical and disembodied understanding which made me feel, 'under glass' and forever external.

(3) 'I think we have a crossed line'

Messages can be sorted all right and put through quickly, but redundant information insufficiently filtered out. This is like putting through a call complete with crossed lines and background static.

For much of my childhood, the air was full of charged air particles ('sparkles') that most people's brains filter out as meaningless information. Not only did my brain not do me this favour, but these 'sparkles' were much more active (they swirl about crazily in air currents) and abundant and in the foreground than anything else I was seeing. This made everything else not only irrelevant and background, but meant that it took a lot of conscious mental effort and energy to attend to. The same happened with my hearing and I was often more tuned in to the white noise that is the 'sound in silence' than I was to the sort of noises other people seem to easily tune in to and process quickly.

Similarly, because things that were meant to be tuned out weren't, these things were all competing for processing when they shouldn't have been. I was jumping between processing the white of the page as well as the print, the flicker of light and shadow as well as the objects themselves, the sounds of the people moving about in between syllables of words being said at the time, the rustle of clothing and the sound of my own voice.

(4) 'Sorry, your line's been disconnected'

Messages can be sorted all right, some of them put through quickly enough and redundant information sufficiently filtered out, but the relay of further connecting messages is inefficient. This is like putting calls through in gibberish, telling jokes but leaving the punchlines out, or putting through a call about something important but then jamming the phone lines so the recipient can't call anybody else to tell them the news.

I first started intentionally trying to squeeze meaning out of language when I was about ten. At this time I knew that words were theoretically meaningful based on previous experience, but as I heard them again, their meaning was as elusive as ever.

The clarity was fine and I would play about with their shapes and the spaces between syllables and words but it just didn't go anywhere. Later, the category the word belonged to would be triggered so I'd come up with all its opposites or its possible similes or all the words it rhymed with or that had a similar shape but the word or sentence that had triggered these responses basically remained gobbledeegook until the moment passed and it was all unimportant (then it sometimes eventually sunk in, by which time I generally didn't care, nor attended to its comprehension).

The same was true of touch, where I could describe the tactile sensation quite exactly and make all sorts of associations in memory with related textures or sensations, but what I actually felt in terms of personal pleasure or pain or how I should or wanted to respond to it or what it meant for any future experience, just didn't connect at the time (though its processing was often delayed and responses triggered later sometimes demonstrated that processing had occurred at a delayed, subconscious level).

These sort of experiences meant that the usual sort of curiosity didn't happen with me because I generally hadn't made enough connections in the context in which an experience happened for my mind to form questions, let alone drive actions to get answers. I also found life a sort of hit and miss thing because only a limited number of connections happened in a complete way (and those I generally repeated over and over). The rest seemed sort of like one-off 'accidents' or coincidence. This also made usual attachments more to do with whether other people wanted me about than whether I had formed any appreciation or in-context comprehension of the experiences I had with people. I did, however, learn to respond to certain cues where I was meant to have comprehended, been curious or formed attachments but these were mechanical and performed actions for which there was no internal feedback so they mostly seemed stilted, forced or repetitive.

In the following chapters I will talk about each of the types of problems; problems of connection, problems of tolerance and problems of control and give some advice about what can be done about these things.

CHAPTER 7

Problems of Connection

I looked in my head
for a sentence to say.
I found nothing but sawdust,
all thought gone astray.
Of the familiar,
there was not a trace,
no connection with name,
body, words, touch or face.

In my own experience, problems of connection, which I will generally refer to as information processing problems, are at the root of some kinds of problems of tolerance and problems of control.

It is important to point out that there are two distinct types of problems of connection. One is about delayed connections. These people find it hard to keep up with the flow of incoming information, or make inefficient connections with what would otherwise be outgoing, or are inefficient at consistently monitoring what is coming out. It is this problem that I will deal with in this chapter.

The other type of problem seems to be about making connections that are almost too fast. Some of these people find themselves almost too far ahead of the pace of incoming information. In my experience, some people with Asperger Syndrome come into this second group and, although this may seem to have its advantages, it can also have serious disadvantages. I will be talking about this later.

For me, problems of delayed connection fall into three basic categories:

- **PROCESSING** of information that comes in through the senses. This is about getting meaning and significance out of what you see, hear, feel, your movements and where your body is in space. Without efficient and consistent processing, it can become difficult or impossible to get personal significance, relative significance or even literal meaning or sense of location of experiences (even though processing may continue on a subconscious or preconscious level).

- **MONITORING** one's own expression in things like movement, body language, actions, facial expression, vocal intonation, pace, pitch, volume, word order, sentence structure and what words one is actually using. This monitoring problem is about keeping track of the connection between intention and expression. Without efficient and consistent monitoring, it becomes difficult or impossible to express yourself with intention in a way that appears socially comprehensible and purposeful to others.

○ **ACCESSING** the words and body connections one intends to use to express something or sustain a grip on the thoughts, feelings or experiences needed to make sense of or respond to new information, without these drifting into a subconscious and inaccessible (though sometimes still externally triggerable) state. This accessing problem is about connecting or linking and is the key to expression and self-'awareness' on a conscious level. Without efficient and consistent accessing, it becomes difficult or impossible to achieve conscious self-awareness or conscious and voluntary reflection (even though both may continue to happen on a – sometimes externally triggerable – subconscious level).

I will now look at each of these things individually to show the contrast between being mono, and multi-tracked information processing.

'Multi-Track' Versus 'Mono' Processing

Most people can efficiently and consistently process information through more than one sense at a time. This means that they can generally keep up consistently with the meaning and the point of what they are experiencing and what they are getting out of it and what they think about all of that.

Most people can use all of their senses simultaneously. When they tune in to the meaning of what they are hearing, they still continue to make sense of what they see and feel emotionally and physically. If they have been moving or walking whilst they've been interpreting what they've been watching, they still process where their movement has taken them. They generally don't suddenly tune back into their physical position when they stop processing what they are watching and then wonder 'how did I get to here?'. Most people can do all these things because they are 'multi-tracked'. They aren't one train or the other, they are the railway network itself. They are all the trains all at once on all the tracks.

People who work in 'mono' are like the trains rather than the network. They are this train or that train or the other train but they generally aren't all the trains all at once. For these people to process what they are watching whilst walking may mean that their body seems to arrive at places as if by magic. To process the meaning of what they are listening to whilst being touched may be to have no idea where they were being touched or what they thought or felt about it. To process the location or social significance of being touched whilst someone is showing them something may mean that they saw nothing but meaningless colour and form and movement.

'Multi-Track' Versus 'Mono' Monitoring

Most people know what their body is doing whilst they are speaking or what their face is doing whilst they are using their hands. They keep track of these things – they monitor them – because they are multi-tracked.

People who work in mono are not so efficient at this. Whilst speaking, they may have no idea of their movements or facial expression. Whilst monitoring facial expression, they may lose track of the volume of their speech or its intonation or pace. Whilst monitoring their volume, pace or intonation, they may lose track of their word order or even lose track of the words they are using and whether they are saying what they mean to be saying.

'Multi-Track' Versus 'Mono' Accessing

When something happens, most people not only process the literal meaning of what has happened but also instantly access information from past experiences, thoughts and feelings which direct them in knowing how they personally intend consciously and voluntarily to respond to what has happened. Because of this, most people learn from experience how to respond to new situations. They don't need rote learned rules about how to respond to things because their own learning gets accessed instantly in new situations. Furthermore, most people can access movements and thoughts and words and memories all at once. They can do all this because they are multi-tracked.

People who work in mono can't do all this so efficiently. They may have processed the meaning of what has happened but still not have accessed any information that would give them some idea of how to respond to what has happened, in spite of understanding it.

When new things happen they may not access any information from related past experiences and so may not respond at all.

They may respond by avoiding or running away from what they don't know how to respond to, even if they understand the meaning of what has happened.

Some people might have rote learned rules about how to respond to situations. In this way, they can recognise the components of the situation and respond according to the rule, without having to rely on inefficient accessing of past experiences that might have helped them to respond in a truly self-expressive way that came naturally and spontaneously from themselves (from personal feelings and experience at the time, as opposed to responding from stored learning).

People who are mono may also only be able to access one thing at a time. They may be able to access the thought of what they intended to do but once they access the movements to do it, they forget the thought that was driving the movements. Because of this, they may reach their destinations but then have no idea why they had been going there.

People who are mono may access the words they intended to say but then when they access the physical means to say what they had to say, they may lose the thought they intended to express. Even if they can recall the words they intended, they may not be able simultaneously to access the purpose or intent behind these words. The result of this may be that the motivation of speaking gets lost so nothing is said or what was to be said comes out but sounds personally detached, or even unintended.

In Summary

Most people can use all these functions, processing, monitoring and accessing, quite smoothly together in a consistent way. Most people can consistently and simultaneously access what they intend to express and monitor whether it is all coming out as they intended whilst they continue to process the response of the other person to what they are expressing. Most people know whether they are being understood or whether the other person is listening or watching or interested. They usually have some idea of what the other person feels about what has been expressed to them. These people have the mechanics of social communication and social interaction. They know the personal rewards of smooth, relatively work-free, two-way conversation. They know what it is to have consistently the social experience of 'with'. They can do this and have all this because they are multi-tracked.

People who are mono, on the other hand, may be unable to use processing, accessing and monitoring simultaneously with any consistency. They may be able to process incoming information but be unable at that time to access the connections necessary to respond or express anything or even know what they thought or felt about what they processed.

At another time, people who are mono may be able to access the connections to express something but whilst accessing a stream of what they intended to express, may have little or no monitoring of what is coming out or whether it is as they intended.

Whilst accessing the connections to what they intended to express, people who are mono may then have little or no ability to process simultaneously the listener's or viewer's response to them so they may have no idea if they are even comprehensible to others or whether others are interested in what they are saying (which can be shatteringly isolating, alienating and lead to an absence of reinforcement of interaction as a rewarding experience).

The worst part of all this is that the concept of 'social', which requires simultaneous ability to process and monitor and access, becomes a shattered and intangible one and, at best, an evasive, undependable and inconsistent one.

Involuntary Compensations

There are various involuntary compensations and adaptations that can make up for inefficiency in processing, accessing and monitoring. They include:

(1) Systems forfeiting and systems shutdowns

In my experience, systems forfeiting and systems shutdowns are a means by which my brain can more fully process information on one channel at a time rather than spreading my processing more thinly in trying to process on more than one channel at once. This can result in only being able to process information on one sensory channel at a time.

(2) Shifting between conscious voluntary processing, accessing and monitoring and doing these things on a subconscious, involuntary level

Systems shifts mean that only certain systems may be able to work on a conscious voluntary basis and that all else may still continue to work but only on a subconscious and involuntary, though triggerable basis.

(3) Shifting between self and other

Shifting between sense of self and sense of other is about switching between processing, accessing and monitoring but being unable to do more than one at once.

Processing is about doing something with sensory information that primarily comes from outside of oneself. It is a receptive process and, as such, involve what can be called 'sense of other'. Accessing of feelings, thoughts and the means of expression and the monitoring of that expression is about doing something with information that has already been taken on board. These are expressive processes and, as such, involve what can be called 'sense of self'.

When one is unable to maintain a consistent and simultaneous processing, accessing and monitoring, then one is unable to take simultaneous account of 'self' and 'other'. This is what I call having a self–other problem and it is, in my view, the cognitive problem underpinning most of the social and communication problems of people with autism.

The Relationship Between Involuntary Compensations and Mono and Multi-track

All three of these involuntary compensations are about being 'mono'.

'Mono' is a means of shutting down or switching between different 'departments' in order to keep the remaining ones going more efficiently. This is like having one employee working in a huge department store instead of having a whole staff. If a customer has a demand in the shoe department whilst the worker is presently dealing with a demand in the toy department, the customer in the shoe department wouldn't find anybody there.

'Mono' is an involuntary compensation which involves no conscious decision or choice and although one can learn to work with it or against it, it basically cannot be reasoned with, for we are not talking here about the mind over which the self has some control, but about the brain to which the whims of the mind and the wishes of the soul are seemingly inaudible, invisible and a world away.

The involuntary compensation of mono is an adaptation to information overload – it is a mechanism by which the time and energy that goes into processing, accessing and monitoring gets spread a little less thinly than it otherwise might. This is like the single worker only partially handling different enquiries and sometimes closing shop in different departments when she can't cope with the demand.

Information Overload, Shutdown, and the Involuntary Compensation of Accumulating Unknown Knowing

Just because someone can't keep up consciously with processing incoming information, doesn't mean that it doesn't get stored and gradually processed over time. For me, however, the time in which I might regurgitate this stored information is taken up with a whole load of new bombardment to have to wade through. That means two things.

One is that when my boiler is full and more is getting poured in, I can explode and purge myself of this build up, or cause the shutdown of any capacity to take anything else in. The other thing that can happen is that this information gets processed beyond the voluntary access of awareness of my conscious mind.

The disadvantages of this are that this sort of subconscious processing happens outside of conscious awareness so that one is not aware of what one knows nor able consciously or voluntarily to access that knowledge. Secondly, because this subconscious or preconscious processing usually takes place after overload has passed (such as during sleep), it happens outside of the context in which the information originally came from so it can be devoid of personal subjectivity and affect and is treated purely as logical-factual information, rather than personal information.

Some of the consolations of this compensation is that, even if this information can't be consciously and voluntarily accessed, it can sometimes still be triggered or cued by something outside of oneself (like post-hypnotic suggestion or cueing). For me, these external cues have included typing, music and art as well as automatically correcting misquotes and errors and filling in the gaps where people have left things out.

Even if this cannot replace the ability to think and respond on a conscious and voluntary level, it may still be an important part of building skills and being functionally able. Unfortunately, most education of people with 'autism' does not address this level of consciousness at all and addresses only conscious voluntary capacity which may be severely impaired in spite of an untapped, even exceptional, ability to function on 'autopilot', albeit without conscious awareness. Many teachers or parents may feel there's no point teaching 'at' people who appear to be blank. From my own experience, the accumulation of unknown knowing is still worth something, even if one has either to wait for when one has managed information overload enough to free up the processing, accessing and monitoring of information, or if one must also back up information accumulation with the development of triggering and cueing strategies in the absence of more usual interaction.

Implications of Mono-related Involuntary Compensations for the Idea of 'Retardation'

Some people appear to be only mildly affected by their problems because they have become masters at adaptation and managing compensations, but may actually have a greater degree of impairment than they seem to have. Some people, on the other hand, may appear severely affected by their 'autism' but actually have very low motivation to develop functional adaptations which would help them manage what may actually be only a mild degree of impairment.

Some people ARE exactly as they appear and some people are not. Mental retardation should never be assumed because, even if someone is functionally retarded and seemingly incomprehensible and uncomprehending, this says nothing about their intellectual capacity. It may merely be that an intelligent and potentially able person has had no form of self-feedback through which to discover all their knowing that is as yet unknown, blocked by problems of conscious processing, accessing and monitoring and exacerbated by a condition of information overload that an essentially multi-track environment has done little or nothing to alter.

What Can be Done

For me, there are seven basic types of approaches to dealing with problems of connection:

(1) Training people to behave as though their problems didn't exist.

(2) Rote learning.

(3) Improving efficiency of information processing by addressing any deficiencies, fluctuations or imbalances that effect the supply of nutrients going to the brain.

(4) Leaving things out to speed things up.

(5) Slowing down what's coming in to speed up what the brain does with it.

(6) Keeping things concrete, observable, tangible and more quickly able to be interpreted.

(7) Using an indirectly-confrontational approach.

(8) Adaptive and compensatory strategies that are

    (a) involuntary

    (b) voluntary.

I will deal with each of these individually except for (8) which I will leave for the next chapter.

(1) Training people to behave as though their problems didn't exist

Some people, in the absence of finding much else that seems to work, put their energy into encouraging and training people with problems of connection to appear to make connections 'normally' when they don't. I could argue that it would be immoral or mentally cruel to do this at any time but my experience has been that there are certainly times when being taught to 'act normal' has its advantages.

In my experience, being socially accepted in some way (whether I could efficiently process the experience, meaning or significance of that social acceptance consciously and *in context* or not) still meant that I was exposed to a greater range of information than I otherwise might have been and, even if I couldn't process this information at the time, I could still accumulate it for eventual preconscious or subconscious processing. The knowledge arising from that processing could then sometimes later, albeit haphazardly, be triggered or cued.

Being in mainstream schools meant that I accumulated lots of information about how people moved and spoke and what they said they liked or wanted or thought and how they responded to certain things. I accumulated information about people seeming like other people in certain ways when they said or did things in the same way someone else had.

Because I was mono, I was so busy trying to process everything coming in that I generally didn't get much time to access much of my own store of experiences. Because of this, I had virtually no curiosity in thought nor action nor expression about why other children did what they did or what they got out of it so I didn't learn these things. Nevertheless, the accumulation of facts about their behaviours and expressed wants and interests, gave me something I could model myself on in the absence of efficient connections to develop in any natural way to be like them.

If asked what I liked, wanted, was interested in, thought or did, I had theoretical information about what a person liked, wanted, was interested in, thought or did. If intending to move across a room to get something, I had accumulated information about how others did this and could do it as them. In the absence of body messages and other connections, if I'd never accumulated all this information, I'd probably never have been socially tolerant and tolerable enough to go to all the places I have been.

If I hadn't learned to act as if I could keep up with speech (or let some believe I could), I would not have been spoken to as much as I have been. No-one would have thought there was any point.

If I hadn't been exposed to all those words, the huge vocabulary that I accumulated subconsciously, which would often later be triggered externally by others, would never have been so broadly accumulated and I'd never have had the compliment of having been referred to as 'the walking dictionary'.

I would never have accumulated information about things people say (which I gradually learned to use, over decades, more and more purposefully). I may not have understood conversation, but I built up a bank of information and even if I couldn't draw on it easily myself, it could be triggered. For better or for worse, triggered language has been my wild horse that I gradually learned to ride. If I'd never used it, I may have had greater control over my life and intention but I think I'd have appeared more disabled and, on that basis, excluded from the wide range of experiences that, whether I wanted them or not, expanded my wealth of information even if it didn't directly expand understanding.

There are two final points I would like to make about teaching people to behave as though their problems didn't exist.

Sometimes the external expectation to control yourself and behave with apparent intention is better than having no internal or external expectation to control yourself and having inefficient connections to be aware of, or to express, intention. Because of this, placing severely disabled people in mainstream classrooms should perhaps be coupled with external expectations that these people must try to have control and behave with intention, even if it sometimes has to be copied intention, based on what (albeit multi-track and non-autistic) people appear to want, think, do and so forth.

Waiting for such people to be motivated to control themselves or interact or express or do with intention may not be enough, because motivation, if not driven externally by prompts and cues, comes from efficiently processing information for meaning and significance within the context it happens in. If that isn't happening, external expectation may be the only way to get some people to try rather than be carried.

My final point is that external expectation may improve functioning for some people but it does *not* mean that these people will necessarily be able to experience their own functioning. To experience your own actions consistently with meaning and significance requires efficient information processing in the context of your own expression and actions happening. Sometimes there has to be a choice. In the absence of 'want', is 'can' or 'should' good enough? For me, I look at what my life would have been if I'd waited for 'want' which never came. For me, that answer is yes, 'can' and 'should' are sometimes better than nothing. Life is not just how you, yourself, experience it, it is also about how you affect others and how they experience you through your doing, even if that doing is not truly self-expressive. For me, life is not just what you feel but also what you do. To be able to do, even if that doing is without 'want' or feeling or self, is still half a life and that may be better than none at all.

It is important to recognise the risks of chronic stress in training people to function in the absence of being able to feel for, identify with, or experience their own functioning. This can be like starvation of the soul.

It is important that people still know who they are inside, whether high or low functioning and it is important that people get to be who they are for at least some designated part of every day even if it means they sit there doing nothing, rock or play with buttons. Without this, it is my fear that a starved soul can be a candidate for physical or emotional breakdown (I don't mention mental breakdown, which I believe requires a developed ongoing capacity for some degree of conscious personal thought and the ability to process information efficiently enough to be consciously aware of complex social experiences as personally significant).

(2) Rote learning

In the absence of efficient accessing of what is already known, rote learned rules and responses can provide ways of responding constructively, even seemingly sociably, to situations.

Some people with autism are against 'programming' but so much of it happens indirectly from the media and advertising and for many of those who become so-called 'high functioning' it is often this programming that forms the basis of the actions, expressions and even stored reasoning, that they have in their repertoire. I got a lot of my life rules and responses from things like TV sit-coms and TV commercials where certain responses and phrases were repeated again and again in a highly predictable way.

In the old sit com, 'Gilligan's Island', the character of Mary-Anne uses three highly consistent and predictable postures and tones of voice for each time she is either asking Gilligan for something, giving him something or upset with him for doing something. The posture and facial expressions of the character Ginger, in the same programme, were also totally routine and predictable when asking one of the male characters to do something for her or when she was upset with one of the other characters.

The responses of the Skipper were also predictable. Unlike people in real life, the Skipper always asked for favours, looked for what was missing, or was upset with Gilligan in what seemed exactly the same way every time. The responses of most of the characters in the old programme, 'The Brady Bunch' were also very routine and predictable. These programmes have their modern equivalents today.

What they did for me was to serve as rote learning for standard responses in the absence of efficient accessing to find my own, inefficient monitoring to make consistently intentional and purposeful or even comprehensible responses.

Even in the absence of efficient processing by which to know the meaning of what was said or done or felt, I could still perceive pattern cues and respond to them according to rote learned responses. Rote learned rules and responses can also be formally taught, which I will raise again later.

The important thing, for me, about rote learned responses and rules is to know the difference between these things and true connected self-expression from personal thought, belief and emotion. The first is part of a sort of mechanically and constructed personality and identity. The second is an expressions of true personality or identity. It is probable that as long as problems such as information overload and emotional hypersensitivity are not addressed and managed, many people with autism may either never develop this second type of expression or may develop it internally but never display it publicly or in interaction with others.

Like teaching people to behave as though their problems don't exist, rote learned rules and responses have their place but I don't think it is healthy or moral to accept these things as 'success'. For me, they are compensatory strategies, nothing more. They shouldn't replace all attempts to find responses that come from self nor should they be pretended to be responses from self.

(3) Improving efficiency of connections through improving the supply of nutrients to the brain, reducing toxicity and addressing imbalances

Some of the things that can effect the efficiency of making connections through improving the supply of nutrients and reduction of toxicity are:

- ◦ treatment of the fungal infection, candida albicans
- ◦ treatment of vitamin-mineral/amino acid problems
- ◦ treatment of auto-immune problems
- ◦ treatment of hormonal problems
- ◦ sufficient exercise.

If you suspect problems of connection (processing, monitoring or accessing) one of the most constructive and energy saving things that can be done is to find out if these are being caused by a correctable problem affecting the supply of nutrients to the brain or causing toxicity that is messing with the efficiency with which connections are made.

MRI and PET scans have shown up abnormalities in the brains of some people with 'autism', particularly in the supply of oxygen to the brain. These scans, however, are expensive, time consuming, limited in what they can show and when they show it and generally don't tell you what is causing the problem or how to deal with it, just what you already know; that a problem is there. Even, for example, if a brain scan shows decreased or uneven oxygen or blood supply to different areas of the brain, that doesn't tell you what, of a huge range of things, may be causing that decreased or uneven supply.

THE FUNGAL INFECTION, CANDIDA ALBICANS

I mentioned the yeast infection, candida albicans, earlier as one of the most easily treatable causes of toxicity in the body (including in the blood supply going to the brain), metabolic disturbance (effecting hormone imbalance) and deficiencies in the supply of nutrients to the brain.

Studies have shown that candida albicans is a major contributor to 'autism'-related problems in a significantly large percentage of people, and (my other autism-related biochemistry problems aside) I am one of these people.[1]

VITAMIN-MINERAL/AMINO ACID PROBLEMS

It is important to eliminate candida albicans as a cause of vitamin-mineral or amino acid problems as this fungal infection can very seriously tax the body's supply of nutrients and disturb the body's ability to properly digest certain substances. But as we saw in a previous chapter, candida albicans is not the only possible underlying cause of vitamin-mineral and amino acid deficiencies where there is adequate diet. Liver and pancreas dysfunction and/or insufficient stomach acid may also play a part in the impaired synthesis of vitamins, minerals and amino acids and in resulting problems of toxicity.

AUTO-IMMUNE PROBLEMS

As so many auto-immune problems (such as multiple food and chemical allergies) are caused by candida albicans, it is best to eliminate the possibility of candida albicans before dealing directly with the auto-immune problems and, again, to explore possible underlying causes such as liver or pancreas dysfunction, insufficient stomach acid or hormone imbalances effecting digestion and the auto-immune system.

The absence of obvious allergy symptoms doesn't mean they aren't present. Allergies can be clearly recognisable or they can be masked. Allergies tax the body's supply of nutrients and contribute to toxicity in the body (and brain). A large percentage of 'autistic' people have food allergies that dramatically effect their moods, senses, comprehension, awareness and personality. The most common food allergies are to wheat and milk products, yeast, additives (colorings, flavourings, preservatives and MSG), Phenol (high in around 70% of all foods including chocolate, coffee, cocoa, carob, tea, dairy products, soy, eggs, wheat, corn, tomatoes, chicken, potatoes, citrus and stone fruits, bananas, many vegetables, artificial sweeteners, petro-chemicals, tobacco smoke, alcohol (which is also in perfume) and also, as the lining of tin cans is often sprayed with

---

1   To understand more about candida albicans the Autism Research Institute (ARI) has free information about it and there is an excellent book called *The Yeast Connection*, by Dr William Crook which explains just about everything you might want to know. One piece of advice. In Dr Crook's book, he recommends an anti-fungal agent called Nystatin. A number of people have found that high dose garlic capsules or caprylic acid may be a more natural and easily tolerated and equally effective alternative for some people who can't tolerate the Nystatin.

this, it is in most tinned foods) and salycilate (which is found in most processed foods such as sauces and soft drinks).

If you suspect food or chemical allergies, don't panic and don't starve anyone. Avoidance diets are one way forward and no matter how restictive a diet may at first appear, there are substitutes for most foods and even if these aren't in a tin or packet or in the frozen food section of your local supermarket, the ingredients and techniques for making some of these things at home can be found and used with imagination. You should get professional advice on how to deal with any dietary change from a qualified nutritional therapist aware of food and chemical sensitivities and remember that avoidance diets are not the only way forward, there may also be the possibility of desensitisation to allergens and the possibility of finding and treating the underlying causes of food or chemical sensitivities.

There are invasive and non-invasive forms of allergy testing (some of which can be done at home) and a reputable and qualified naturopath may be able to help. ARI (listed at the back of this book) has a lot of up to date information about auto-immune system problems and 'autism' and keeps up to date about new developments in solving these problems as well as having information about dietary measures to help counter some of the effects of some auto-immune problems.

To help the body and brain cope with food allergies, taking vitamin-mineral supplements is usually recommended. A list of those that have worked best for people with 'autism' can be obtained through ARI. The Allergy-Induced Autism Support Group (AIA) – also listed at the back of this book – may also be able to help.

HORMONAL PROBLEMS

An endocrinologist is an expert in how hormones work or don't work. Hormones are responsible for the regulation of many functions of the brain and the body which feeds it with its nutrients. Hormonal imbalances can be aggravated by metabolic conditions such as Reactive Hypoglycemia or candida albicans as well as various organ dysfunctions so again it is important to eliminate the possibility of underlying causes of hormone problems.

Some behaviours, such as sleep deprivation, eating disorders as well as some repetitive hypnotic or self-abusive behaviours can also cause hormone fluctuations so it is important to consider whether any observed hormonal imbalance is the cause or the effect (some people with 'autism' actually pursue certain behaviours for the chemical effect).

If these things have been considered and it seems that hormonal problems might be a cause rather than an effect, an endocrinologist may be able to test for hormone imbalances and may be able to suggest treatments to correct some of these. It may, however, be an idea to get a second opinion regarding such suggestions by approaching the Autism Research Institute (ARI) which keeps up to date regarding the effects of hormone treatments in people with 'autism'. It may be there are some things the endocrinologist might need to know, particularly with regards to these problems in people with 'autism'.

LACK OF SUFFICIENT EXERCISE

Regular applied structured exercise can help the body to rid itself of a build up of toxicity that might otherwise contribute to inefficiency in making connections.

Regular exercise improves circulation and digestion, both of which can both mean a greater supply of nutrients to the brain, including oxygen. The Higashi Method claims a high degree of success with people with autism and a large aspect of its program is an emphasis on applied exercise.

(4) Leaving things out to speed things up

Leaving things out to speed things up is about reducing the *number* (or rate) of incoming sensory information so that the brain has time to process what is left more efficiently, access what is needed to respond and monitor one's own responses.

This is a bit like having one worker who is being shouted at without warning from too many directions all at once. The worker is bound to be unable to meet all the demands sufficiently and will not have time to work out priorities. When the worker gets overloaded too much, she throws the job in. If only those jobs that need her to attend to them are presented and if they are presented one at a time, the worker will be able to cope for longer. That's how it can be for someone with a problem of overload.

Superfluous information is all the background stuff that isn't important. It also includes all that is more than what is needed for get information via your senses. Most people filter this irrelevant, or excessive, information out naturally. For 'autistic' people who don't, this can cause serious information overload, distraction, hypersensitivity and can significantly slow down information processing.

When people are putting all their time into struggling to keep up with even the literal meaning of what is coming in through their senses, there is very little capacity left to access the connections needed to respond or to monitor one's own responses. By cutting down on processing demand, some of this capacity is given back. Superfluous information can be mechanically cut down in two ways:

(a) Transportable ways that a person themselves can use to cut down irrelevant, excessive and distracting sensory information.

(b) Making the environment adapt to cut down irrelevant, excessive and distracting sensory information.

TRANSPORTABLE MEANS

Some of the transportable ways I have found to cut down on superfluous information include Irlen Filters to cut out an amount of visual information, ear plugs or ear muffs to cut out an amount of sound information and well padded clothing to cut down on the impact of touch information. These things can cut down on some background information that is not relevant without cutting out visual, sound or touch information entirely. This means that the messages still get through but may make it easier to tune in to what is relevant or excessive to a degree that is both comprehensible and tolerable without causing overload.

IRLEN FILTERS

Irlen Filters (discussed in an earlier chapter), in my own experience, are currently the most successful, transportable means of reducing the rate of incoming sensory information, though only visually. They are specially selected tinted lenses, worn as glasses and no one colour works for all people requiring them. The colour selected must be specific to the way each individual responds to particular light frequencies.

Irlen Filters are not a cure and they can't help everyone but they can help reduce information overload in some people with problems of connection and some people with sensory hypersensitivity. How they work is by cutting down on a particular light frequencies coming in through the eyes.

Visual information accounts for around 70 per cent of the incoming information that has to be processing and comes into the brain in the form of light frequencies. By using certain colours to block some of these frequencies, the brain has less visual information to process so it has time to work more efficiently on what is left to process. The results can be better filtering out of useless information, less processing delay and deeper and more accurate processing of information.

When the correct colour or combination of colours is worn, there is no noticeably significant disturbance in the ability to perceive the full spectrum of colour in the environment as others 'normally' do (even though someone else looking through the coloured lenses that are not for them will see a tinted world).

Because of improvements in things like depth perception and processing of the meaning of what is seen, there should only be improvement and enhancement of what is seen, rather than a lessening of it. However, because this improvement has actually come about by something being taken away (a light frequency) this enhancement does not result in information overload, but actually reduces it.

There are Irlen Centres all around the world and there is a contact at the back of this book through which readers can find their nearest centre. There is a preliminary screening to see if they are able to help and this avoids unecessary costs. There are also a handful of people who use a technique called a Color-imitor to assess and supply coloured tints to address the same sort of problems that Irlen lenses address. Whilst the service provided by the Irlen Centres is currently not covered by national health schemes, they generally don't have long waiting lists. Clinics using the Color-imitor technique have the advantage of being covered by national health schemes but may have the disadvantage of having very long waiting lists.

ENVIRONMENTAL ADAPTATIONS

Ways that environmental adaptations may assist in reducing information overload include the following:

ON THE SOUND CHANNEL

- Turning off or shutting the door on any background sources of sound, reducing all non-essential verbal intonation, and good turn taking in all communication can decrease the number of simultaneous sound sources, cutting down on sound distraction and overload.

- The reverberation of sound is one of the biggest contributors to sound information. Carpeting, cork flooring, ceiling tiles and large padded furniture can all help cut down the reverberation of sound, as can lowering the volume of speech, such as in whispering.

- Reducing non-relevant visual or touch information can improve the efficiency with which sound is processed.

ON THE VISUAL CHANNEL

- Light refraction (ie: 'shine') is the visual equivalent of sound reverberation and is the major source of visual overload. To someone sensitive to these things, the 'shine' (light refraction) can cause a visual effect of shooting out streams or 'sparks' of light. This distracts from paying attention to other things but this 'shine' also can have the effect of 'visually cutting up' people or objects up. Turning off any unnecessary lighting (especially fluorescent lighting) when there is adequate natural light, matt surfaces on walls, lamps rather than overhead lights and low wattage light bulbs all result in less light refraction bouncing off a lesser number of surfaces and reduce distraction and overload.

- Deep coloured light bulbs (ie: red, orange, purple, blue, green or yellow) used in place of clear or pearl ones can cut down on colour contrast in a room without dramatically altering the definition of objects created by light and shadow. Because colour contrast is another major source of visual information, certain deep coloured light bulbs can reduce visual overload for some people (from my experience, different colours work for different people).

- Keeping surrounding movement to a minimum can reduce sources of non-relevant visual distraction and decrease visual overload as can keeping rooms relatively tidy and orderly (though keeping things observable and accessible) and cutting down on all sources of unnecessary visual information including all non-essential body language.

- Consistency in the colour of wall or floor coverings especially within rooms, can mean there are fewer non-relevant visual changes to adapt to as one moves about. (Floors that are a distinctly different colour to walls can make for easy visual orientation) so there are fewer visual changes to have to process as one moves about.

- Plain, non-patterned, wall, floor and furniture coverings are less bombarding, less distracting, less disorienting and less 'fragmented' in terms of non-relevant visual information. Plain coverings are also less likely to contribute to some compulsion-related problems.

- Positioning furniture around the peripheries of the room can make it easier to navigate and mean that there is less need to keep constant visual account of where large obstacles are. If furniture is a plain colour that is distinct from floor or wall coverings, they are also easier to make sense of more quickly as whole objects and also where everything is in relation to everything else.

- Reducing non-relevant sound or touch information can help people attend to and process visual information as well as cut down on sources of distraction.

ON THE TOUCH CHANNEL

- Reducing all non-essential physical touching can cut down on touch distraction and touch overload.

- Overtly signalling the intention to touch and informing or indicating where you intend to touch can assist people in shifting focus so that touch is not so surprising, jolting, difficult to follow or without meaning or significance. In the same way, overtly signalling any change in the type of touch happening and informing or indicating the location and type of change in advance, can help people adjust.

- Reducing non-relevant visual or sound information when wanting someone to attend to and process touch information can improve their ability to make sense of touch.

(5) Slowing down what's coming in to speed up what the brain does with it
I talked about the role of NUMBER, now want to talk briefly about the role of PACE in slowing down the rate of incoming information.

If you have an old computer that doesn't work very quickly and you put a very quick typist typing information into it, the computer will fall further and further behind until it stops taking in any more information at all (or it blows up or shuts down or makes rude beeps at you or throws your information out). If you type in only what is absolutely necessary and type this information very slowly, the computer will be able to keep up for a longer time.

Having inefficient information processing works a lot like this for me. You can slow down the PACE at which you yabber away at me, slow down the PACE with which you show me something and slow down the pace with which you move around me or the suddenness with which you touch me. Provided you actually do not increase the amount of information you originally intended to get across, then I am usually able to process what I have heard or seen or felt more efficiently and sustain contact for longer. Furthermore, because the strain on processing is reduced, capacity for monitoring one's own actions, utterances, volume, pace and so forth and capacity for accessing one's thoughts or feelings about something or word retrieval or the connection to body that is the key to intentional expression are also improved. Some important points about reducing pace are:

- ◦ SLOW DOWN
- ◦ reduce all non-relevant and non-essential sources of information overload.
- ◦ give REAL breaks (this does *not* mean trying to start up chit chat or burbling over with praise for how well someone has done. REAL breaks also do not mean giving sensorily bombarding 'rewards'. For people with an information processing problem like mine, the saying 'a change is as good as a holiday' does *not* apply).

(6) Keeping things concrete, observable, tangible and more quickly able to be interpreted

I talked about the role of NUMBER and PACE in slowing down the rate of incoming information. Now, I want to talk about ways to help improve the efficiency with which sensory information gets interpreted.

A foreigner in a strange country with gestures and expressions and language he doesn't understand will still try his best to make as much sense as possible of what other people are saying and showing and doing. If those other people all say and show and do too many things at once, the percentage of sense he makes out of everything will be less than it could be if they only said and showed and did things one at a time.

If those people do everything very quickly and go on and on for too long without providing a break for him to 'catch his breath', he will be less likely to keep up as well as he otherwise might have.

If those other people give a whole load of context, long winded description, 'labour the point', waffle on and on, or use actions or expressions that are highly symbolic, intangible, unobservable and not CONCRETE, the foreigner will take longer to make sense of what is going on. He may fall so far behind and be distracted by so many unnecessary tangents, that he will make sense of far less than he otherwise might have and will be less able to sustain comprehensible contact with these people for any length of time.

From my experience, having an information processing problem is a lot like this. Many people go down the wrong track at this point. So many people have no idea at all of what *real* simplification is all about. Speaking in baby talk doesn't make anything more concrete. Adding exaggerated body language and intonation do not make anything more concrete. Giving verbal context before getting to the point of a message, does not make the message more concrete. Giving more information than is necessary, does not make a message more concrete. It is all these things that have taught me that, unfortunately, telling people you need things kept simple, doesn't mean they will *really* understand what simplicity is.

Simplicity is not about talking in fairy tales and using boggledee pretentious facial expressions. Simplicity is *not* about aiming below someone's intellectual level (which has nothing necessarily to do with their level of functioning).

In my view, many people with 'autism' may appear intellectually retarded because they have information processing problems (or flow-on monitoring or accessing problems, because they put so much energy into just keeping up with what's coming in that they don't get to do much with what's coming out).

Information processing problems can easily cause *functional* retardation. This is to do with how a person *functions* in the world. Functional retardation, however, is *not* the same thing as intellectual retardation. The first is about capacity to act upon information in the context in which it happens. The second is about the capacity to accumulate knowledge. You can have an unimpaired capacity to accumulate knowledge (no or little intellectual retardation) and still have a severe impairment in the ability to access or act upon that knowledge by yourself or monitor your own expression (functional retardation).

In a court, one is innocent until proven guilty. So it should be for people with 'autism'. When people with 'autism' are spoken to or shown things as though they were intellectually retarded until they demonstrate that they are not, this is like judging them guilty until they prove themselves innocent.

One man with 'autism' who I know of was taught the ABC and given soft play in place of regular classes until he was in his teens, when he began communicating. He then let people know how he was not only sick of soft play but had learned ABC back when he was three years old.

I know of another 'autistic' man who was diagnosed as severely intellectually retarded and recommended for institutionalisation who 'outgrew' his 'autism' two years later at the age of five and is now a very able and social person with good communication skills who is working as an engineer.

I am not suggesting that people with 'autism' should be assumed to be intellectual geniuses. I *am* suggesting that people with 'autism', regardless of level of functioning, should not be *assumed* to have intellectual retardation. I am suggesting that they be spoken to and shown things that anyone of their age would be, but spoken to and shown these things in language that is concrete, concise and to the point and in language that is slow and clear with a minimum of unnecessary, excessive or distracting information.

Here are some points based upon what has helped me better to make sense more fully and efficiently of incoming information (and, therefore, monitor and access what is necessary to respond comprehensibly):

- be concrete in language used.

- make what is being seen or heard clearly observable or tangible if possible or even able to be easily replayed if needed.

- be concise and to the point.

- be clear in your intentions and message.

- don't give any unnecessary setting of context.

- give REAL breaks regularly to allow time for the processing of chunks of information.

- present new information in a format or style that has come to be predictable (if successful).

- clearly and concretely indicate starts and finishes.

(7) Using an indirectly-confrontational approach

I have talked about overload relating to vision, sound and touch but body messages are also part of sensory information and emotions, which are perceived initially as body messages, are part of sensory information.

With visual overload, you can close your eyes. With auditory overload you can cover your ears. With tactile overload you can pull away or hide. With body messages, you can attempt to ignore them. When, however, emotions are provoked, and particularly if these are as unfiltered as other forms of sensory information, they may be the most powerfully bombarding, incomprehensible and inescapable form of information overload that there is. You cannot fight the sudden control-robbing onslaught of an invasive trespassing invisible enemy when you don't know what it is, how it got there or where it comes from.

Not knowing where these onslaughts have come from can cause some people to attempt to run away from the only place they may be able to locate; their own body. This may cause some to run manically, others to attack the body back as though it were some foreign and external attacker, others to realise it is inescapable and voluntarily or involuntarily tune out or dissociate from it. Others may come to realise that these sensations were provoked by watching, listening to or interacting with others or by the exposure of self-expression as oneself and they may come to actively and instinctively avoid these things.

Avoidance can be voluntary and can take the form of physically distancing oneself from these things and refusing interaction. Avoidance can also be involuntary and can take the form of cutting off from one's sense of self so that the responses of others are made into a façade and affect is successfully kept at arm's length. Over time, it is the second of these responses to emotional overload that can sometimes result in identity and personality problems.

One of the ways of reducing the information overload caused by emotion, is to assist people in managing its provocation. Emotive body language and intonation may not only be visually and auditorily distracting, superfluous and overloading but may also provoke emotional responses that someone may be unable to process or cope with.

Compliments or praise may make people consciously and rawly aware of their self-expression (and what it produces). The provocation of overloading emotional sensations that this awareness causes may result in someone responding violently or negatively to these attempts at praise. They may, for example, destroying the products of their expression as though these were the enemies that caused the sudden and unwelcome onslaught of control-robbing incomprehensible sensations that happen to be emotions.

One of the strategies that can be used to avoid triggering overload caused by emotion is to keep interaction and communication impersonal, formal and detached. For someone with these problems, this would not be an absence of love, but a demonstration of what love truly is; understanding, acceptance and empathy.

Most people relate to each other in an emotive and directly-confrontational way. When giving someone something, they walk straight up to them, look at them, address them verbally and personally and hand them what they had to give. When they speak, they attempt to make eye contact and use the person's name to address their attention. When they show interest in what someone is doing, they look directly at the person and walk straight over to them. When they wish to show pride or appreciation, they pour out praise and emotional expression and generally don't keep it to themselves.

An indirectly-confrontational approach to interaction and communication is about what I call 'Simply Be'. Some people find direct confrontation to be too jolting of self-consciousness and, therefore, emotionally provoking and painfully raw and exposing. For these people, being indirectly-confrontational in giving, might mean leaving what you had to give in a place where someone would know that what was left was for them. Another example of indirectly-confrontational giving might involve going near to the person without directly looking at or addressing them emotively and merely pushing what is being given in their direction with the impersonal statement, 'this is yours now' (or, for example, if it was given to me, saying, 'this is Donna's now').

Indirectly-confrontational communication can mean that if something needs explaining or showing, the person explaining or showing can do so as if out loud to themselves, addressing the wall or the floor, or one's shoes if necessary. More appropriately, explanations/demonstrations can be addressed towards the objects or items relating to the demonstration. This can mean that if you are explaining about light switches, for example, you address it to the light switch within the observable and audible range of the person you hope is attending. You can also talk 'via objects' which is about setting up objects through which to do role plays; a bit like impromptu purpose-specific 'puppet shows'. Even praise, if considered an essential part of feedback, can be given indirectly either by expressing these things impersonally and out loud to yourself in the presence of the person they concern or by doing so through representational objects.

The person with a problem of overload due to emotions or expression-exposure can also be prompted to respond in an equally indirectly-confrontational way by pushing objects in their direction through which they might respond or allowing this person to, similarly, address and interact with you through speaking out loud to themselves with you 'in mind'. Gradually, bridges can be built from indirectly to more directly confrontational interaction and communication.

Typing can be used in place of handwriting, as the personal hallmarks of observable physical contact upon the world can be much less with typing than with other forms of expression such as handwriting or speaking. With typing, it can be much easier to tune out the anxiety that comes with the conscious realisation one is expressing oneself in a way over which others can take some control. With typing, the movements, a simple, quite abstract moving of fingers can be much more easily dissociated from consciousness than the complex movements involved in handwriting or the multitude of physical connections, monitoring and modulation involved in speech. If conscious realisation triggers the automatic cut off to thought or the daring of expression due to intense and sudden exposure anxiety, then the tuning out of conscious awareness is the key. Sometimes this dissociation may be the only way to free up the thought or the expression.

Typing and handwriting are both indirectly-confrontational forms of communication. One can do these things after the events and people they relate to are past, in one's own time, in a place of one's own choosing. One does not have to be at the ready with a verbal response, nor is one necessarily so immediately held accountable, nor even responded to or praised for one's expression as when expression is verbal. With written or typed expression one is face to paper, in the company of oneself, not face to face as with speech, in the company of another person.

Speaking through songs and advertisements are forms of indirectly-confrontational speech, but it can be difficult to tell when these are being used purposefully and when they are just sensory or obsessional indulgences or diversions to avoid the exposure of real felt self-expression. Nevertheless, they can have their part in progressively and gradually building bridges from the indirectly-confrontational to the directly confrontational.

Art, music and movement, like typing, can be dissociated from conscious awareness. The more abstract the use of these media and the more indirectly confrontational they are in the way they are employed as a basis for interaction and communication, the easier they may be for someone with exposure anxiety to dare use. Here again, bridges can progressively be made from abstract and indirect to more tangible and direct at doses designed to expand on growth without triggering withdrawal and aversion to the medium as a 'meeting place' and means of communication. The use of colour can eventually combine with form to create image and story. The use of rhythm and sound can eventually combine with vocal sound pattern and flow into abstract and then progressively meaningful word patterns without jolting consciousness into avoidance. The use of creative abstract movement can lead into abstract patterns of touch and later more purposeful patterns of touch and movement can progressively incorporate the use of the abstract use of face and body that forms the basis of facial expression and body language.

'Non-Firings', 'Over-Firings' and 'Mis-Firings'

Lots of people with 'autism' have trouble processing physical sensations and how these are or are not connected to emotions. Knowing how to process information about what feelings mean is only one part of this and is something that learning can sometimes make up for in part. What follows is a description of some of the mental mechanics involved when this 'autistic' person (me) processes emotion. I describe these mechanics with the terms, 'non-firings', 'over-firings', 'mis-firings'.

'Non-firings'

'Non-firings' are one type of emotion-related connection (or lack of connection) made in the brain. There are two parts to 'non-firings'.

One is about not getting feedback. Here one is effectively unaware of feeling and this can be a temporary and partial state due to a systems shutdown caused by overload at a particular time or it can be part of a systems compensation involving relatively extended and total forfeiting of the processing of emotion in favour of diverting energy towards other types of processing, more efficient accessing or monitoring of expression.

Emotional 'non-firings' relate to what I call being 'feeling-dead' which have their sensory equivalents in 'meaning-blindness', 'meaning-deafness', 'touch-deadness' and dissociation from body. The other form of emotional 'non-firing' is where physical feedback for emotional meaning fails to be processed (so one may have something going on but not have a name for it or know what it means).

Temporary emotional 'non-firings' can take work to live with and form adaptations to and compensations for. If, however, emotional 'non-firings' are a relatively permanent state, then one may not really miss what one doesn't perceive. The biggest problem for some people with emotional 'non-firing' may be the expectations of non-autistic people for them to perceive a whole lot of identifiable emotional sensations they generally don't connect with.

Being in a permanent state of emotional 'non-firing' (not aware of feeling or not processing what you are feeling) can be much easier to live with than having connection to emotions switch on and off or overload and shutdown continually. This can be like being able to feel one moment and the next moment becoming *completely* 'feeling-dead'. This can make life feel 2D, artificial, futile, unpredictable and scary and could, in my view, easily lead to depression. This is why, for one person with a permanent state of emotional 'non-firing' it might be just a matter of development, yet for another in whom the functioning of this mechanism is always fluctuating, it might be a battle to handle their 'autism'.

'Over-firings'

'Over-firings' can happen on a sensory, cognitive or physical level as well as an emotional one. Hypersensitive touch, hearing or vision are examples of sensory 'over-firings'. The thought 'explosions' of some people with 'autism' who talk of anxiety, compulsion or obsession-driven mental 'playing out' or compulsion-driven mental repetitions, may be having a cognitive version of 'over-firings', as might those having overwhelming sense of self or overwhelming sense of other. Physical over-firings involve doing something in what may have been an intentional way but being unable to modulate the action. Crushing someone's hand when you intended only to hold it, shouting or whispering when you intended to speak, walking when you intended to run or running when you intended to walk may all be 'over-firings'.

Emotional 'over-firings' are just like any other form of information to the brain. The effect of an emotional 'over-firing' can make 'caution' feel like 'terror', 'like' feel like 'falling in love', 'irritation' feel like 'rage', 'happy' feel like 'manic', 'feeling low' feel like 'depression' or 'sadness' feel like 'mourning'. It can also make 'love' feel so big that rather than being comforting, it feels emotionally too overwhelming to endure.

With emotional 'over-firings', one may know what one has felt, but one's brain may turn up the sensation 'volume' to a level that can make having emotions physically very difficult to endure. This can lead to learning to be socially avoidant in order to avoid being affected.

In my experience, these are brain 'firings' that I must fight and manage because otherwise the discomfort they cause can (instinctually) come to dictate the terms of my life and it would do so so narrowly that I would be able to express and share very little of who I am.

Paul has both emotional 'non-firings' and 'over-firings' happening together. This means that he often has an exaggerated emotional response together with little awareness of what that response is.

'Mis-firings'

I have emotional 'mis-firings' (as well as 'non-firings' and 'over-firings'). Yet, for me, these generally don't happen at the same time. In my case, I either feel too much, feel nothing, have no idea what I am feeling or know what I'm feeling but find my brain telling my body to respond in a way that is totally out of line with what I am feeling. It is this last response that is an emotional 'mis-firing'.

'Mis-firings' are where the brain gets the message messed up. This may happen because the brain hasn't processed the context of the emotion that has been felt (so it doesn't distinguish between different emotions properly). In this case, if I felt deep affection for someone I was seeing, my body might respond with increased heart rate, deep breathing etc. If, however, my brain has stored the formula that 'increased heart rate + deep breathing etc = terror' and that 'terror is to be responded to by actions of avoidance' then my brain may drive me to instinctively, but mistakenly, respond as though I am in danger and may give all the messages to body parts, eyes, face and voice to avoid the source of the feelings or run or attack.

Imagine seeing someone who you are really glad to see and really feel affected by and secure with, but you are driven to look away from them, run away from them, busy yourself in every other distraction, be overly formal or push them away from you. Now, if what you are feeling is deep affection, or excitement, gladness or empathy, for example, these sort of emotional 'mis-firings' can make life incredibly frustrating and can challenge the motivation to have any deep or sustained involvement with anyone.

I fight my own brain 'mis-firings', not because 'the world' dictates that I should in order to 'act normal', but because I want to live my life and make ongoing deep connections in accordance with what I understand of my feelings and not what my brain, according to stored definitions, makes of them. In this way, I fight my 'autism'.

Fighting autism or letting it fight you

Some 'high functioning' 'autistic' people come out of the closet, being publicly proud to be 'autistic'. Some people just 'come out'. I do both. I am proud to be an 'autistic' person, but I will not willingly and passively allow my 'autism' to dictate the terms of my life and how I live it.

Anyone who is helping someone with 'autism' to understand feelings should be aware of the variations of emotion-processing that may exist for these people. Just because these people may share a label doesn't mean that their mechanics will always be the same as one another.

For me, for example, if I am happy to see someone, my heart will pound and my blood may rush in my ears but then my body may overreact so much that my brain sends messages to my limbs to run and my eyes to avert their gaze. Now if I am happy and I am getting feedback from my brain to run away, I listen to what shouts loudest. If I don't shout back mentally to my body's faulty messages, then I do what it drives me to do which is generally not what I wanted or truly felt. For someone else, they may have an emotional 'non-firing' whereby they may be happy but have no idea what they are feeling and may think their physical sensation means they are feeling sick.

Any one 'autistic' person who doesn't have extreme fluctuations between 'non-firings', 'over-firings' and 'mis-firings' (or combinations of them) may wonder why I might say that I fight my 'autism'.

'Autism' effects different combinations of functions within all people with the condition. In my case, my brain *does* have a lot of difficulty with emotional information (and its physical feedback). Someone else's 'autistic' brain may have trouble with language or sound or light or sense of body in space. Or they might have some of these and not others.

No person deserves guilt or shame for 'mis-firings', 'over-firings' or 'non-firings' just as no person should be made to feel guilty or shame for any involuntary response. If anyone should make such a person feel guilty or shameful for it, that guilt or shame should be put back into their ignorant, arrogant, hands.

People should have the right to be proud of who and what they are – 'autistic' or otherwise. But if someone is frustrated by their own 'mis-firings', 'over-firings' or 'non-firings' this is theirs to deal with and they may have to fight back against their 'autism' if it is fighting them and they may have to learn to ask for help if they cannot help themselves.

CHAPTER 8

Revisiting Adaptations
and Compensations

Many people with 'autism' have never consciously learned how to reduce the rate or pace of incoming information for the very good reason that nobody else ever demonstrated how to do it (because most people don't need it) and most people ('autistic' or non-autistic) don't have it in them to 'invent the wheel'. Nevertheless, adaptations and compensations are not always conscious. The brain does most of them for you, instinctively seeming to be aware of things that are either missing, not working or need closing out.

Adaptations and compensations can be *involuntary* or *voluntary*. When they are involuntary, you don't 'mean' to do them or usually even know why you do them unless you ever become directed towards focusing on them, recognising the patterns or environments in which they occur, and analysing this in order to understand why your brain might be making them happen. On the other hand, when they are voluntary, you usually 'mean' them (at some level) and you may be more capable of knowing what you get out of it or more able to work it out with less effort.

I have found that there are basically two types of involuntary adaptations and compensations: minor ones and major ones.

Minor Involuntary Adaptations and Compensations

Sometimes without even knowing why or if I want to, my brain has just driven me to do (and re-do and re-do) certain instinctive actions. Though these might look purposeless to someone who doesn't do these things, they do seem to occur in a pattern and often come up in response to particular kinds of situations. In these cases it seems to me that they are meant to correct or assist functions that are missing, aren't working efficiently or in order to close out something that can't be dealt with at that time.

These actions are involuntary but, because they sometimes just 'feel right', as a young child I voluntarily chose not to fight these instinctive drives. Similarly, these drives can be so extreme that sometimes no amount of wanting to stop them enables you to stop them. What follows are some examples of these instinctive and involuntary compensations and adaptations and why I think they may have happened in me:

INSTINCTIVE ATTEMPTS TO STORE THE COGNITIVE FOUNDATION SKILLS NECESSARY TO PROCESS INFORMATION

For me, some of these things might be compulsions to disassemble, put things in order, categorise, form contrasts. I think it is possible that these might happen, not because I have not learned these skills, but because my brain confuses an access problem (of retrieving these skills to make sense of new information) with a storage one (of not having stored the skills) and responds (wrongly) as though the skills weren't learned and need relearning (again and again and again). Perhaps it is that these skills were not properly stored or stored in a way they weren't meant to be. It may be that my brain sometimes responds as though these skills need constant consolidation so as not to be lost.

INSTINCTIVE ATTEMPTS TO GET LEFT AND RIGHT HEMISPHERES WORKING IN AN ONGOING INTEGRATED WAY

This may be at the root of compulsive repetitious physical left–right 'weaving' such as that done with hands, head or body. Side-to-side body rocking may also fit this purpose.

INSTINCTIVE ATTEMPTS TO ESTABLISH DEPTH PERCEPTION

Compulsive repetitive hand, head or body movements that fluctuate between near and far might be attempts to correct or establish depth perception that is missing because of visual information overload.

INSTINCTIVE ATTEMPTS TO BREAK UP THE FLOW OF VISUAL OR AUDITORY INFORMATION SO AS TO PROCESS IT MORE EFFICIENTLY

For me, some of the actions that I think did this were repetitive blinking and head bobbing and the repetitive contraction of the muscles of the inner ear (causing a 'clicking' sound) which provided a rhythm by which to somehow aide the flow of processing.

INSTINCTIVE ATTEMPTS TO SIGNAL THE NEED OF A SHIFT
OF FOCUS OF ATTENTION

For me, things like a sudden single clap seemed to be used like this.

INSTINCTIVE ATTEMPTS TO CLOSE OUT SENSORY DISTRACTION

One of the things that I think did this was running fast in repeated circles.

INSTINCTIVE ATTEMPTS TO ASSIST IN THE STORAGE AND ACCESS
OF INFORMATION

The rhythm of repetitive jumping when used in association with rote-learned information seemed to assist in these things for me.

INSTINCTIVE ATTEMPTS TO CORRECT A FEELING OF HAVING
BEEN 'ENGULFED'.

Being mono, in my case, affected what I call 'sense of self and other' so that I swung extremely between the two. When my sense of 'self-existence' became too intense I got swept up and lost in it. When my sense of 'existence of other' (such as another person, animal or object) became too intense, I felt equally swept up and lost in it but also suffocated. For me, repetitive self-tapping seemed to consolidate my own body separateness (from the world around me) and was a sort of instinctual and self-calming statement of 'I'm here'. Holding a button was sometimes a lesser version of the same.

INSTINCTIVE ATTEMPTS TO CORRECT A FEELING OF BEING
OUT OF CONTROL BY CLOSING OUT

For me, some instinctive closing out behaviours include clenching my fists or gripping my clothing, pursing my lips tightly and intense 'frozen' staring. A form of instinctual closing out of visual information is the involuntary turning in of one eye or staring through things which has the effect of putting visual information temporarily out of focus and, therefore, decreases visual information overload.

INSTINCTIVE ATTEMPTS TO CORRECT AN INABILITY TO SWITCH OFF
WHEN CONTINUING TO TAKE IN SENSORY INFORMATION IN A STATE
OF INFORMATION OVERLOAD

For me, sudden outbursts of self-abuse worked this way because the attack usually caused a welcome 'numbing' and sensory shutdown. Though it provoked intense insecurity to be attacked uncontrollably by my own body, it may have been this very external threat to personal security that was needed to cause the required information cut off.

INSTINCTIVE (THOUGH UNPRODUCTIVE) ATTEMPTS TO DESENSITISE THE BODY TO CHEMICAL AND SENSORY SENSITIVITIES

For me, this may have been behind craving the very foods I was allergic to but did not have the equipment to digest. This may also have been the reason I was so illogically attracted to so many sources of sensory arousal to which I was hypersensitive.

INSTINCTIVE ATTEMPTS TO RID THE BODY OF TOXICITY.

This may have been responsible for compulsive and seemingly excessive water-drinking binges that preoccupied me during childhood.

INSTINCTIVE ATTEMPTS TO DEVELOP THE VESTIBULAR SYSTEM (ABOUT GRAVITY AND MOVEMENT – SENSE OF BODY IN SPACE)

For me, compulsive and repetitive spinning, jumping from heights, climbing to great heights and throwing myself backwards onto things and falling through space may all have been attempts to develop a vestibular system that wasn't able to work consistently or efficiently.

INSTINCTIVE ATTEMPTS TO RESTORE ORDER IN A STATE OF CHAOS

I think that tuning in auditorily to rhythms, making them vocally or mentally when there were none or making them physically through movement were ways I was driven to do this.

How Constructive or Self-Expressive are Involuntary Compensations?

A word about involuntary adaptations. Just because my brain perceives something is missing and needed doesn't necessarily mean that its instinctive attempts to correct the problem can do so in any long term or ongoing way. If the mechanic doesn't have the tools, good intentions won't get her very far.

. Many high functioning people with 'autism' support the 'autistic' person's 'right' to indulge these involuntary responses rather than control them. These involuntary responses generally seem to be the result of a faulty interpretation by the brain regarding what is wrong and repetitive attempts to develop or correct something that it cannot. Because of this, encouraging indulgence in these involuntary responses may only waste time that could be spent more valuably developing what can be developed and building bridges to self-initiated, voluntary, self-expression instead of wrongly confusing instinctive brain responses with personality or identity.

Furthermore, there are many people who do *not* appreciate these involuntary responses happening and feel robbed of control by them. Instinctual responses by my brain are not the same as intended self-expression that comes from choice (though I certainly took a long time to get to the stage where I could see it this way). My brain, alone, is not my mind. For all these reasons, I do not agree in indulging the unintentional responses and behaviours driven by my brain even though I feel there are more constructive ways of limiting these than suppression.

I do not think that the removal of unintentional responses and behaviours signals an end to my identity. At the same time, because some of these instinctual responses feel so 'right', allowing limited indulgence in these things may sometimes be a source of reward and pleasure to some people *at all levels of functioning* whose processing problems already close out too many sources of experienceable pleasure.

In my view, it is important that people learn the difference between involuntary responses and behaviours and true, intentional, self-expression and identity. Life should be more than compliance, and actions and expression should be more than training and a means to an end. Life should, at some point, be a rewarding end in itself. I've had glimpses of that, but I continue to hope that it may one day be a consistent experienceable reality and not just a theoretical one that I know exists.

In my view, there are far more constructive ways to reduce the frequency of these involuntary responses than simply training people to put all their much needed energies into suppressing them. If involuntary attempts to correct problems is consistently interfering with the ability to interact, communicate or learn, it is more constructive and important to *real* development (as opposed to a well trained circus act of 'normality') to try to decrease overload. In my experience, having people put all their energies into suppressing their involuntary responses (rather than dealing with their causes) makes the perceived necessity for these behaviours even greater.

In my experience, addressing problems of toxicity, the supply of nutrients to the brain and biochemical imbalances and by decreasing the rate and pace of incoming information and keeping it concrete and easy to interpret, information overload can be significantly decreased. Then the burden upon the brain to employ instinctive compensatory strategies may be significantly reduced. The beneficial consequences of this, in my view, are not about improved 'social presentability', it is about being able to find out who you are beyond involuntary responses and behaviours.

Major Involuntary Adaptations and Compensations

In a state of information overload, the brain not only may instinctively employ strategies to try to correct things, but also signal a range of shutdowns and put certain systems of functioning temporarily off limits to improve the level of functioning in others.

This is like having a traffic cop directing traffic around the scene of a major calamity or gridlock in the city centre. She may block off traffic going in one or more directions until gridlock or the calamity is cleared away. She may let traffic leave the city centre but allow no more in. She may get confused in all the chaos and let more traffic into the city centre but stop any leaving. These are some of the things that the brain can do in a state of information overload. Unlike the calamity or gridlock, however, overload is sometimes chronic and doesn't go away. As a result, certain streets and directions can stay blocked off for a long, long time.

In my experience, there are three basic forms of these major involuntary compensations:

(1) Shutdown in the ability to maintain simultaneous processing of 'self' and 'other' (shutdown in the ability to simultaneously process incoming sensory information – 'other' – and thought, feeling, body sensation or the accessing and monitoring involved in intentional and voluntary expression – 'self').

(2) Temporary or extended shutdown in the ability to process sensory information simultaneously on several channels, in order to allow for the continuous efficient processing on remaining channels.

(3) Temporary or extended shutdown in the ability to maintain conscious and voluntary processing, accessing and monitoring on one or more channels even though automatic and subconscious processing (the knowing that is unknown) and externally triggered accessing may still occur.

I will look at each of these individually:

(1) Shutdown in the ability to simultaneously process self and other
If you are talking on a telephone to someone and they put you on 'speak', you may no longer be able to hear the person on the other end of the phone, even though, if you speak, the whole room can hear you. When you finish speaking, they may press 'speak' again and you can then hear

them. If you then press 'speak' on your phone whilst they are speaking, everyone in your house will be able to hear them but none of them will be able to hear you. This is a bit like what it is like to have a shutdown in the ability to simultaneously process self and other. When one is tuned in, the other gets tuned out. Here, concepts like 'us' and 'we' and 'company' and 'social' can become very cloudy if not non-existent.

All processing capacity may be diverted to processing incoming sensory information and few or no connections may be made to *responding* to that information in any outgoing way nor even thinking about it. This is a state I call 'ALL OTHER, NO SELF'. When this happens to me, it is as if there is only the world, and I do not personally and perceptually (only theoretically in memory and logic) experience my existence whilst experiencing that of someone or something else that is external.

On the other hand, incoming information, which has previously been processed, may be responded to at the expense of being able to further process any more new incoming information at this time. This is a state I call, 'ALL SELF, NO OTHER'. When this happens to me, it is as though there is only me and I only experience my own existence whilst the world, though observable sensorily, is meaningless and insignificant and feels as though it only exists theoretically – like it's all in a book that I can return to when I've finished living.

This adaptation has serious drawbacks which, in my experience, include the following:

- limited or no ability to feel 'social' in spite of the appearance of interaction.

- appearing to be egocentric purely because of a processing problem that restricts the ability to take account of 'other' at the same time as 'self'.

- appearing to be a mindless follower purely because of a processing problem that restricts the ability to connect with 'self' when processing 'other'.

- having to rely upon unconnected (and generally unfelt and unintended) stored responses in the absence of connections that others expect to have been made.

- limited ability to build up real, felt, closeness or trust (as opposed to the displayed role of closeness or trust) in interpersonal relationships in the way others can.

- increased chances of social danger though having limited idea of the intentions or motivations of others in the context in which their actions occur.

Yet aside from the drawbacks, there are, in my experience, advantages of:

- sometimes being able to appear relatively able and have the inclusion and opportunities that go with that.

- sometimes being able to appease some of the more major social expectations to appear interested, involved and aware which keeps people from far more basic and invasive expectations that may lead them to persist in provoking my recognition and having me demonstrate my intelligence.

- sometimes being able to accumulate knowledge through exposure, even if it only processed in a delayed and subconscious way. It may not be able to be voluntarily accessed, but may be able to be triggered by cues that comes from outside of myself. This increase in accumulated knowledge then ensures the appearance of an even higher level of functioning and increased access to more opportunities (or the blocking of fewer of them).

- sometimes provides the ability to live relatively independently, which ensures some degree of freedom to be who you are.

(2) Shutdown in the ability to simultaneously process sensory information on several 'channels' at once.

TEMPORARY PARTIAL SYSTEMS SHUTDOWNS

If your TV has ever been out of order where you get a picture but the sound is gone or you get the sound but the picture goes, this is a bit like what sensory systems shutdowns are like. These affect the ability to process sensory information on several channels at once.

The main difference between how temporary partial systems shutdowns work and this example, is that it isn't the sound or picture that goes away, it is the meaning and significance of the sound or the meaning and significance of the picture. Also, these temporary 'systems shutdowns' affect more than two channels. Systems shutdowns can affect the processing and monitoring of body awareness, touch, taste, smell, vision or hearing and can also effect the ability to process, monitor or access your own thoughts or feelings or connection to action or expression.

When information overload is constant and extreme, the flow-on effects of overload upon systems shutdown can mean the difference between appearing so-called 'high' or 'low' functioning.

Temporary systems shutdowns work by shutting down the ability to process information on a number of channels so you can more fully and efficiently process information on whatever channel or channels are remaining. So, for example, the meaning and significance of what is heard might be shut down (meaning deafness) whilst continuing to process the meaning and significance of where one's body is in space, what one is feeling, seeing or whilst accessing the means of expression. On the other hand, all systems but one might be shut down in order to divert processing to one single channel that requires intense focus or complex processing.

Temporary systems shutdowns can be partial or almost total for any one sense depending on the information processing requirements at the time. What this means is that only a percentage of processing may fall out of a particular sense (partial meaning deafness, partial meaning blindness, partial touch deadness, partial physical dissociation, partial ability to access thought or the mechanics of expression, partial monitoring of expression).

A partial temporary shutdown in the processing of visual information, for example, may mean that you might process the meaning of what you see but process none of the significance of what you see (as significance requires a deeper than purely literal level of processing). A greater percentage of loss might mean that you might process the meaning of familiar things only (which require less processing) and not process the meaning of anything unfamiliar and still process nothing for significance. My experience of a total temporary systems shutdown on a visual channel means that even though the eyes continue to see form, colour, pattern and movement clearly, the brain does not process any meaning or significance of anything that is being seen (ie: people, faces, objects, places, even parts of one's own body). The main difference between partial and total systems shutdowns is that whilst these are partial, there is still a sense of having some connection to the affected sense. When the shutdown of a particular system is total, however, all experienceable connection with the affected sense is severed and can feel permanent.

If information overload is not too high, processing might stop on only one channel. If overload is very high, processing on more than one channel may go. If overload is extremely high, processing on all or almost all channels may go. If this happens, the person may be entirely unable to respond consciously and intentionally or communicate meaningfully in response to what is said, seen, felt or experienced, regardless of the level of provocation. What is important to remember is that even though someone in total temporary shutdown may be unable to make any kind of intentional or conscious connections, and may not respond in any way to provocation, they may still be able to be cued, triggered or prompted on a subconscious and automatic level even though response will be without intention. This was how I lived a large part of my first twenty-five years – an involuntary sleepwalker-sleeptalker.

The disadvantages of temporary systems shutdown, for me, include:

- limited ability to consistently gather information in an integrated way
- limited ability to experience the world or your own perceptions in a consistently meaningful and reliable way.
- increased anxiety caused by constant unpredictable and unintentional perceptual shifts.
- increased anxiety caused by constant unpredictability regarding consistent access to thoughts, feelings and the connections to intentional action and expression.
- increased anxiety and depression caused by feeling consistently robbed of self-control and the experience of inclusion (as when meaning drops out suddenly it can feel like exclusion from meaning rather than a shutdown in the ability to process meaning).
- increased insecurity and lack of confidence regarding the inability to be consistently self-reliant and independent.
- a greater degree of social danger due to not processing important information on shutdown channels and being cued and triggered on a subconscious, automatic level.

The advantages of systems shutdowns are:

- improvement in the capacity to process information efficiently on one or more channels as opposed to efficiently processing information on none of these channels if they all contributed to overload.
- increased ability to experience the meaning of at least some information in the context it happens in rather than all information being delayed and processed out of the context it

happened in (so associated emotions are experienced and understood better).

○ a decrease in sensory hypersensitivity due to extreme pervasive information overload.

EXTENDED SYSTEMS SHUTDOWNS

These aren't permanent, even though they may feel like they are and even come to look like they are. Extended shutdowns are where a particular total systems shutdown is taken to be the most manageable way to handle information overload over an extended amount of time.

Though this is not the same as having permanent neurological damage that is interfering with the efficient functioning of a particular system, it may look like it. It may, however, merely be that the brain has found the extended shutdown of a particular system (or systems) of functioning to be the least chaotic and most easily managed way to continue to process, monitor and access information more consistently and fully on the channels which remain functional.

Though this is a bit like cutting off one of your legs because it keeps getting in the way, the brain, in my own experience, doesn't view things with this subjectivity (even if the mind does) and the brain doesn't care if its adaptations disturb the person socially or personally. What my brain is concerned about is keeping me as an organism (not a person) functioning in the most manageable way available and to its knowledge.

Whether I like it or not (mostly not), my brain has sometimes found it functionally useful or practical to shut down certain systems of functioning for prolonged amounts of time.

One of the most disturbing things about this is that when such a total systems shutdown happens, I actually don't remember what it felt like to have had the system working or how it all worked. Any connection to how it felt when working is severed when the function is totally shut down. In these circumstances, all I retained of the function that I had had is a flat, video-like, personally detached, logic-based serial memory which I can only trust to be accurate.

Extended total systems shutdowns happened to me at various times throughout my childhood and early adolescence. Fortunately for me, the most long lasting of these only lasted days, weeks and, very occasionally, a few months, although these have lasted a lot longer for other people, even years. Some extended shutdowns can, in my experience, include:

- extended shutdown in the monitoring of my own speech
- extended shutdown in the ability to consciously and voluntarily access my own personal thought. *Note:* this is quite different from the subconscious and automatic external triggering of stored knowledge/responses.
- extended shutdown in the ability to process emotion.
- extended shutdown in the ability to monitor and process body connectedness.
- extended shutdown in the ability to monitor and process connection to intentional conscious action and expression
- extended shutdown in the ability to process sound for meaning.
- extended shutdown in the ability to process what is seen for meaning.

The disadvantages of extended shutdowns, in my experience, are:

- decreased opportunities and increased risk of institutionalisation where shutdowns significantly effect the appearance of functional ability.
- limited ability to gather meaningful information on a particular channel.
- limits identity in terms of loss (like identifying yourself as the person who can't understand what she hears, can't say what she means, can't understand her emotions, etc) as well as alters conception of the world (ie: the place where people make meaningless noise, the place where people touch you for no apparent reason, etc).
- increased anxiety caused by personal limitations due to systems loss.
- increased anxiety caused by living in a world that interacts according to a system that doesn't function for you and defines 'reality' by something you cannot experience.
- increased anxiety and depression caused by feeling consistently robbed of inclusion where systems loss leads to being left out.

- ○ increased insecurity and lack of confidence regarding the inability to be self-reliant and independent because of systems loss.

- ○ a greater degree of social danger due to being limited in the number of functional systems available for use.

The consolations, in my experience, are:

- ○ much less unpredictability due to systems shifts as one or two extended systems shutdowns means less juggling of other systems with its associated turmoil in terms of meaning constantly falling out, shutting down and coming back again.

- ○ a greater stability of identity and relationships as other systems are not in such a great a state of constant shift.

- ○ a greater capacity to develop interests and abilities as shifts from one systems shutdown to the next don't interfere so much with ongoing interests and abilities.

- ○ a greater degree of calm in the environment which comes from living with a more predictable (and, therefore, comprehensible) person.

- ○ a greater ability to more fully and consistently develop functional ability of other systems that are still working, and which are not in a constant state of shift.

(3) Temporary or extended shutdown in the ability to maintain conscious and voluntary processing, accessing and monitoring on one or more channels

When information overload occurs, processing on one or more channels may cease for the duration of the information overload. Even though processing of incoming information ceases, however, the accumulation of those sounds and images and sensations can still continue to come in. In my experience, what sometimes happens to these is that they get stored in big unprocessed chunks.

When there is a shutdown in the ability to process what is going on, the sensory information that continues to accumulate is not understood, used or responded to on a conscious level. Furthermore, even once information overload decreases, there is no conscious awareness or under-standing relating to all that unprocessed information that has been stored.

Life goes on and as it goes on it is not the unprocessed and stored information that gets processed or responded to, it is new information that continues to flood in through the senses in a waking state. The unprocessed information that has been stored, however, is not lost. From my experience, it does get processed over time, well outside of the context in which it originated.

In my experience, this stored information is processed and stored in a subconscious way, a bit like in a state of hypnosis. It becomes part of the huge collection of knowing that is unknown.

I have found that although I cannot consciously and voluntarily access any of it (because I haven't been aware it is there) I have learned of its existence through it being externally cued and triggered. In this way, I have had externally cued and triggered thought and expression that has nothing at all to do with conscious voluntary wondering, curiosity or drive to respond. This is comparable to a hypnotic subject being triggered into responding with no awareness of what the response means or why it came out.

For me, I discovered the mechanics of how all this unknown knowing got there through its externally cued and triggered expression and also through the automatic and sort of preconscious expression I found through art, music and writing. I also found that, in place of dreams my subconscious mind seemed to use this processing time to work through some of these huge stored unprocessed chunks.

Just as one can sometimes be dreaming and vaguely aware of dreaming, I have had this with words and images and sensations. As I have slept, my mind has occasionally been aware of the replay of long strings of conversation and actions, feelings and sensations, perceptions of relative size and duration or things and events exactly as they had happened. In these states, there is no imposed thought or feeling about these things, no omission or focusing on some things over other based on personal significance. These replays are full of the most mundane and meaningless components of these experiences and seem played back with the personal detachment of a video.

It has been my assumption that these replays are like some kind of purge and that they serve to process the literal meaning of these experiences in a way that was not possible in a waking state under the conditions of information overload at the time. This subconsciously processed information still cannot be consciously and voluntarily accessed but it still remains a major involuntary compensation. If cued or triggered, this information can give a sense of identity and inclusion and a level of functioning higher than it otherwise would be, if left dormant.

Unfortunately, it is too often assumed that, if things are not understood or responded to in the context in which they happen, there has been no understanding nor wish to respond. I am often unaware of having conscious understanding or any conscious wish to respond. Yet I have been very glad to experience self-expressive responses that are the triggered products of my own unknown knowing, even if I can't access these responses for myself.

Voluntary Adaptations and Compensations

Even though the brain can dictate which systems are going to go, I have found that, if I can read the warning signs of overload and impending systems shutdown, I can quickly either alter my environment or remove myself from it to avoid or minimise the impending shutdowns.

Unfortunately, many 'autistic' people (myself included) are trained out of this kind of self-management with the result that we become (at least in such environments) less able to manage our own overload and the consequences of shutdowns. Not only are we often trained out of avoiding overload and managing systems shutdowns, we are also not trained in any way to monitor our own states of overload. On the contrary, my experience is that people are trained to ignore the signs and *keep paying sustained attention* to overloading incoming stimuli.

A handful of 'high functioning' people with 'autism' have been able to manage their systems shutdowns to the point of being able to use psychological aversion as a means of influencing which systems will be shutdown before others (rather than leaving it purely for the brain, as opposed to the mind, to dictate). This is where what was 'shutdown' is more like 'forfeiting'.

Some people (myself included) have psychologically found touch or emotion or conscious body connectedness disposable and so processing energies get put into every other system but these. Others have put their energies into comprehension rather than expression and some have put their energies into expression rather than comprehension. This is like deciding which limbs to sever when you'd rather keep them all. Though it is depressing, it is my reality, and I have found that it is possible to adapt to the necessary brutality of these 'choices'.

Psychological aversion is not the same as conscious choice but it is still better than nothing. Though the logic of the brain seems to find conscious choice to be irrelevant, it does seem to take some account of psychological aversion. I'd rather that some part of what is 'I' dictates the terms than my brain do so in the absence of 'I'. I am soul (which I do not confuse with ego). My brain is grey matter (tangible mush and a few neurons and arcs). It may not listen to my conscious choices but my aversions also speak at some level, of preferences according to 'I'.

So far, I have outlined these voluntary compensations and adaptations:

- voluntary systems forfeits or shifts.

- voluntary environmental avoidance of information overload and control.

- voluntary attempts to alter the environment in its capacity to overload.

There are a whole range of other specific voluntary strategies that can be used to compensate for or adapt to problems of connection. What follows is an outline of some of those things and some suggestions of how the people in the environment of a person with 'autism' can assist.

CHAPTER 9

Artificial Limbs

Voluntary strategies can be stumbled upon by chance and found to work. These are like artificial limbs in place of non-autistic functions that either aren't there or don't work efficiently.

If you are dealing with someone who has problems of tolerance or problems of control as well as problems of connection, it isn't going to be so easy to help people to attend to, or easily remain in the environment of the information they have to process and make connections with.

This doesn't necessarily mean people should be forced to attend to things, or remain in environments they clearly cannot stand. To do this would be to consolidate lessons too many have already learned; that a world which does not comprehend must be fought physically, psychologically or emotionally wherever possible in order to maintain self-regulation and what can feel like self-preservation. Because of this dilemma, I believe that the most successful way to get willing and aware (not mindlessly compliant) co-operation dealing with problems of connection, is first to take as many straws off the camel's back as possible.

I mentioned earlier how looking into improving the efficiency of processing is one way of removing some of those straws. The next thing to do is to remove as many of the straws that are causing the camel not to be able to attend to things and not to be able to tolerate things.

Once you have done everything possible to improve the efficiency of processing and reduce overload, I believe that the path of trying to help people connect will become easier to walk down. The next step is to build strategies to help people mechanically to make the connections that would usually have taken place naturally but didn't. What follows are some of these strategies:

Interpreting

First, a story.

Once upon a time, there was a tailor. When she wanted to make a garment, she started with the ideas she had about what sort of sleeves it will have, what sort of collar, and everything else. She'd make a pattern or design from these ideas and then she'd make a garment using this pattern and the pattern would tell her what to do with the material and how to cut it out and sew it. She was very successful because she had built up quite a collection of patterns and designs and could just alter them a little here and there to incorporate any new ideas. This was really good for her because she didn't have to go through the tedious and concentrated task of making whole new patterns and designs every time she wanted to make a new garment. Because she could whip up new garments so fast and without the clumsy trial and error that went into the very first garments that she had made from her designs, she became very efficient at what she did and was successful. This tailor never had to make apologies to her customers because everything she made was on time and almost always flawless.

Across the street from her tailor shop, was another tailor. This tailor made patterns and designs too, but his tailor shop was so cluttered that he could never seem to find his patterns and designs. This meant that whenever he had to make up a new garment, he just took one he had already made and copied it. This took time and often had a few errors.

If he could have found his designs, he could have laid one out and cut out the pattern and made each new garment more quickly and professionally; almost without conscious thought. If he could have quickly found his huge collection of designs, he could have just made minor alterations to them and produced a huge range of new designs. Sometimes he did find them, but that was usually after the new garment had already been painstakingly (and sometimes shabbily) made.

This tailor had to make constant apologies and excuses to his customers. When they wanted something on time, it was usually not what they'd asked for. When they occasionally got what they asked for, the event they'd wanted the garment for had already come and gone. They also often had to bring their garments back because buttons and things were missing and the seams came apart. Nevertheless, because the tailor was cheerful, friendly, so eager to please and seemed so hard working, some of his customers still came to his shop (though a lot didn't and some shopped across the road instead).

Making Meaning

For the brain to make meaning from a new sensory experience, it decodes that sensory information and interprets this decoded information. Decoding is like a computer program that tells the computer what bits of things tell you what information.

Our brains are not computers, but this is very roughly how what we see and hear and feel are usually made sense of. It all gets decoded and that decoded information is then interpreted.

What is really special about this process is that the brain knows that if it stores this sort of decoding pattern or design, it doesn't have to go through all that again and again (constantly reprograming itself). Instead of it having to be input every time there is new information, a pattern can just be grabbed really quickly from storage and used to help interpret the new experience. If the new experience doesn't fit with the old decoding pattern exactly, that's all right, because it is just a matter of minor editing to make it fit. That minor editing takes far less time than it would to input a whole new decoding pattern right from the start again. What is more, the pattern for these new edited changes also gets stored. This means that with time you can store patterns that help to process quickly and efficiently and make meaningful sense out of even very unusual new information. This process is like fine tuning an aerial but is also like updating your aerial every so often for a more sophisticated one.

This is one of the things that creates familiarity. Familiarity happens because that decoding is stored in long term memory like a sort of pattern that is used again and again to make sense of new information quickly and easily. This is how people can look and see someone they know and see more than just meaningless form, colour and pattern. Almost instantly, they know they have seen a living human being and they know if they know them or not and if they know them they know who they are, what their name is (if it is known) and what the personal significance of seeing this person is.

Someone like me does these things but I am like that second tailor who couldn't find his patterns in time. I am delayed in making these connections on every sensory channel. The result is that it takes me time to make meaning of, or label, or find personal significance to do with what I experience.

The ability to store and recall decoding information properly means not only does future processing of related information become quicker and quicker, but that information also becomes filtered better. This is like being able to pick up TV stations more quickly and clearly the bigger your aerial (or satellite dish) is and the better your TV aerial (or satellite) is tuned in. If there is something amiss or delayed with the storage or access of decoding patterns then there may be several consequences for the decoding and interpretation of new, similar, information.

One of these consequences, for me, has been that new experiences, sometimes no matter how similar to previous experiences, get perceived as 'new', 'unfamiliar' and 'unpredictable'. This is like being trapped in an infant's perception yet with the capacity of a grown mind.

Another consequence is that the amount of time needed to process each new experience often remains slow (or delayed), regardless of having had similar experiences in the past. In other words, things generally don't get easier with time or learning. Without being able to process efficiently what is experienced or access efficiently what has already been experienced or learned, learning sometimes doesn't make much difference at all in every day life. With a university degree, I would still have days when I had considerable difficulty consciously accessing things like the name of the thing that water came out of or which way to put my jumper on or how to fry an egg or how to respond to a full bladder.

For most people, where processing may have been slow the first time something was experienced, a similar experience is more usually more immediately comprehensible, recognisable and able to be responded to a second time. For me, because this generally doesn't happen, the experience often remains equally incomprehensible, unrecognisable and the responses to it poor regardless of the number of times that I experience the same thing. This has extreme repercussions for the building of closeness and relationships and trust. The result has been that in the absence of the mechanics to truly develop these things, I have alternately followed stored rules of 'a person should be close to and trust others' (and so done so indiscriminately) or followed the stored rule of 'trust nobody and let nobody in' (which I followed equally indiscriminately).

Furthermore, as patterns accumulate, the filtering process of recognising relevant from irrelevant becomes more developed and efficient. This doesn't happen efficiently for me. Too often everything I seem to learn from in one moment still gets responded in the next moment as though no lesson had been learned (yet if actually asked if I'd learned a lesson, I could repeat what I'd learned even if that learning didn't translate into action). The same is true of acknowledging the irrelevance of some piece of information. The next time it comes up, I too often have to go through the whole discovery of its irrelevance all over again. The result of this is that I put up with and respond to a whole load of things that I shouldn't and fail to respond to a whole load of other things that I should.

There are several mechanical strategies I developed to get around these problems. I learned to make 'sensory maps' of people, places and things. I learned to use 'serial memory' in place of learning. I learned to use 'stored theoretical definitions' in place of access to my own learning about experiences. I learned to respond to 'sensory cues' and pattern instead of comprehension in order to give the appearance of recognition and relationship. I will talk about each of these things in action.

(1) 'Sensory mapping'

The system of sensing precedes the system of interpretation. Even with major information processing problems interfering with the most basic literal interpretation, so long as the senses are functional, the system of sensing is intact.

The system of sensing is something most people probably begin to outgrow very early, as soon as the system of interpretation becomes the most comprehensible and reliable system for making sense of the world beyond one's own entity. In people with problems of connection where processing is difficult, fluctuating, inconsistent and unreliable, the 'natural' (?!) progression from the system of sensing to the system of interpretation would be difficult to achieve not just functionally but in terms of trust and how one may come to identify oneself with the predominant system of functioning. Where sensing is the predominant and most consistent and primary system, brain governs and mind may not even yet be consciously born (although it may be on a preconscious level). Where the system of interpretation becomes consistent, dependable and one comes to identify 'self' with it, the conscious mind becomes born at the level of minimal literal processing. This progresses to the development of a sort of socially constructed sense of 'ego' as processing becomes deeper and more complex and moves from merely literal interpretation to processing for personal and relative significance.

Before the senses are used in any direct way, there is still 'body mapping': the sense of one's own entity in relation to the space around it. In this state one can still, at some level, sense a degree of relative distance between one's own entity and anything which approaches it, be it a wall, an object or a person. Perhaps this is something to do with one's own energy field, but my own vague recollection of this state in very early infancy is that I could physically sense 'openings' and 'closings' in the wider space around me, such as walls and doorways, could sense when my body was being progressively approached by object or person, and had some sense of how permeable or resilient these other 'surfaces' were. It is a very difficult thing to describe to people who have only ever known the system of interpretation and especially because it came from a time before any conscious interpretation was known – even before the senses were used purposefully to gather information. This may actually be a stage some infants grow out of in the first weeks or earlier. This stage was still present in me up to around six months of age and, perhaps because it had been so delayed and 'known', perhaps even identified with, I still experienced it on and off throughout my life when I had total systems shutdowns and all interpretation was halted. I call this state one of 'non-physical-based' sensing and it becomes replaced by 'physical-based' sensing in which the senses are used in a directed manner to map out the environment.

The next stage of sensing involves the use of the senses but, again, this started up in me before and separate from interpretation. The result was that instead of using my senses to making MEANING of what I saw, heard, felt, etc., I used my senses to confirm my non-physical sensing. I tapped things to test out their already perceived permeability and resilience, traced their 'openings' and 'closings', used vision and touch to confirm a sense of relative distance and to explore the boundaries of objects.

Language as most people know it is born of the system of interpretation; the system of sensing is also not devoid of language, but it is a quite different language. The sensory experience of objects, people and places, define themselves. 'Rih' was the word for comb and for fence, not assigned by me to these things but given to me by them in response to the sensory experience of running my hand or teeth across the teeth of the comb or the pickets of a fence in which these objects 'said' 'rih'. The work for the experience of what others would call cat was, instead, 'foosh' for this was the word the sensory experience spoke when my hand stroked the fur of this thing. It said, very lightly, 'foosh'. Later, cat became 'brroook' (with a rolled 'r') because this was the noise which came from the object when stroked (many people think it says 'purr' but it certainly spoke 'brroook' to me). Space and shape also had its own language. The shape of the inside of a concave bowl was 'whoodelly' for this was what it said when one ran one's hand continually around and around within the concave inner shape of the bowl.

Within the system of sensing, things were also defined by their 'feel'. This wasn't their tactile feel. It was more 'a felt sense' of a material, an object, a creature, a person or even a place. I called this feel 'edges'.

Edges are like a fingerprint which remains the fingerprint regardless of the colour of the finger or how it moves or gesticulates. Edges are carried on the pattern of any footstep regardless of mood or changes in mood. They are carried on the slightest expressive sound, even something as involuntary as a cough, a sneeze or a laugh. They are carried on the pattern of any movement or the way any object is picked up or put down, quite irrelevant of changes in emotion or learnt overlaid behaviours. 'Edges' aren't seen or heard or felt with interpretation. Body language, facial expression and touch can be about interpretation and changing meanings; 'edges' aren't known with mind and involve no meanings or interpretation. They are senses, purely sensed. One can use one's senses with which to perceive the 'fingerprint' patterning of 'edges' but, even without using the senses, one can still somehow 'pick up' 'edges' through the body, or the body's energy field alone.

There are distinct types of edges and certain forms of interaction or changes in biochemistry (like when people are affected by chemical substances or 'in rage' or 'in love') can result in the shifting of edges and this is quite distinct from mood or behaviour. Fluffy edged people have few boundaries to their emotional self or (spiritual?) energy and are essentially empathic, unable to block out easily the feelings of others. The flow is unrestricted and when fluffy they are never defensive or reactive. Yet they are so easy to 'merge' with and can cause such 'resonance' in me that they bring out my anxiety exposure, resulting in 'lemons' (I offer no translations here as that would take a whole other book). Hard edged people can be deeply understanding and gentle but this doesn't change their hard edgedness. Hard edged people have some degree of control over the flow of their energy and the boundaries of their emotional self is more solid and doesn't escape so easily without will. These people have the feeling of 'owning themselves'. The definition to their energy boundaries means they don't tend so much to merge with others. In their presence, I feel stable and my own fluffy boundaries are less disturbed. Sharp edged people can be caring and loving people but they have a spikey and reactive feel. Their energy seems to build up and then spike out, released in a staccato-like way, often reactively or defensively. I sense them as unpredictable even to themselves and I don't feel very safe around them.

I feel these are systems animals have and still use, especially wild animals who aren't so domesticated as those which become indoctrinated with the system of interpretation and are considered 'clever'. The system of sensing has its own logic and the whole issue of 'intelligence' has no relevance within this system for 'intelligence' is a concept of mind and part of the system of interpretation. The system of sensing can be a whole and reliable system, but it is not a functional system within a world in which all interaction and communication is based on a shared system of interpretation, and in which the system of sensing became redundant long before most people can even remember or before it evolved into something valuable or into a reliable whole system. Yet, for those in whom the system of interpretation remains inconsistent, unreliable and not identified with, the system of sensing lends itself to the strategy of sensory mapping, one which it might be helpful for non-autistic carers and professionals to attempt to understand and use as a meeting place and a bridge towards gradually and progressively building the autistic's interest and trust in the system of interpretation.

The use of 'sensory mapping' as a compensation, is to create a sort of triggerable 'sense memory'. By touching the walls of a room or the textures in it, I have created a 'sense memory' of the experience of the room itself, even if I couldn't store the personal experience of BEING in the room. By returning to that room, I may still have felt no personal familiarity of experience relating to having BEEN in that room, but by running my hand over the walls or touching the objects in it again, I could re-experience the room in a way that registered as sensorily familiar. Sensory mapping can also be done visually by visually scanning the room. It can be done auditorily by clapping or tapping things as means of mapping out the sounds of the room and the things in it. It can be done with smell.

Sensory mapping can be done for rooms, for streets, for objects and for faces and for people. It can't be done for social experiences. I can't sensorily map out a social experience because the social experience itself is not an entity that is there to be sensorily tested out again in any comparable way.

Sensory mapping can be used to reassure myself that something is familiar but that familiarity is about the places, people or things as physical entities and not about the experiences had in those places or with those people or things. It is something and something is so much better than nothing.

One of the most unfortunate things is that I, and many others like me, are so actively trained out of using our senses to map out places, people and objects. By training people out of these things, in the ignorant pursuit of non-autistic 'normality', it is my opinion that these people may also be trained out of the ability to form felt familiarity, felt trust and felt recognition (as opposed to learning to perform the expression of these things in the absence of their experience).

(2) 'Serial memory'

Serial memory is also a kind of sensory mapping device. It can be triggered in a variety of ways including through sensory mapping. So, for example, touching the doorway to a room may trigger the serial memory of touching the same doorway of the same room another time and the events that happened after this. Serial memory can work for what was heard or seen or through movement but is linked to the time sequence in which events took place or the spaces they occurred in. So, for example, if I try consciously and voluntarily to remember what was said to me, it may all be floating about and I may remember a few keywords but may have little idea how they are linked or what the significance of that linking is. If a mental replay of a serial memory relating to a certain time or place is triggered, however, I will re-experience the placement of people in different parts of the room and replay a kind of mental audiotape of what was said as it related to where people were in relation to the objects around them when they said things.

By having a key point of a serial memory triggered, I can 'let the scene run' and I might find a string of things said in a certain order in relation to the order of other things done. I may even be able to repeat these strings, even if I hadn't processed them for meaning. This was how I impressed my primary school teachers that I had understood what they said. If I was asked what they said, in their attempt to prove I 'wasn't listening', I could play back the audiotape, speaking it as them. Those last words are the keywords here. It wasn't that I'd taken this information on as me, with the interpretation and understanding of significance that this entails, I had taken it on as the sources of this information. This is not like being someone in your own home movie, it is like being the whole movie. I have also been able to trigger serial memories by mentally replaying a physical movement or physical impact upon me.

As a compensation, the main use of serial memory is the ability to freeze experiences and replay them when the need for a response is perceived (consciously or unconsciously as required). Most information actually doesn't require processing at the time it happens, it merely requires *responding* to. If nobody checks you've understood or remembered, you can nod your head all day, throw in some impressive stored lines you've used elsewhere before, and pass for having kept up. If you are about to be discovered as not having kept up, you can change the subject or escape the situation. It is only when information is important *to yourself* that you need to access other related information.

If I was presented with a situation that triggered some sense of significance, it is very likely that something stored in a serial way will be triggered, not to make sense of the situation, but to offer up ways of automatically responding to it. This has often happened, in particular with songs and commercials, and I am constantly finding these triggered by someone using a related product, saying a keyword, using a key-rhythm or a key-pattern.

Although I have outgrown the use of these as language (songs and commercials can be used to give a rough impression of what you want or to acknowledge you've understood someone's topic), I still use many of their phrases to make my speech more fluent at times. An example of this is the line of a commercial for a cleaning fluid, 'Jif Micro Liquid, where are you?'. This has the useful phrase 'where are you' in it. If I want to know where someone is and want them to appear (like the detergent does on the TV commercial in response to the question) it is sometimes difficult to recall what I need to say or to regulate volume or intonation to get someone to respond or remember how to connect physically in forming those words at that moment. If the need for someone to appear triggers, by comparison, this line from the commercial, it can be much easier to call out the tail end of that commercial and the words, volume and intonation are all there without effort. Even if I regurgitated the whole commercial ('Jif Microliquid, where are you?'), someone like my husband (who is 'like me' so understands how I use these things) might consider the possibility that I'm looking for something and perhaps clarify it with, 'Are you looking for me?' to which I'd reply without much effort to this cue (his question) with 'yes'.

These songs and jingles can also be very annoying because they often can't be cut off halfway through so they continue to run mentally, even if I try to ignore my mind's occupation with them.

Sometimes, these things can be helpful. If you are faced with a situation where someone goes to attack you and you have no inner access to personal memories of previous experience, then it is virtually impossible to connect with messages of how to respond. If the attack, however, triggers a serial replay of the response of a TV character to the same type of behaviour then you may well play out the rest of the serial and defend yourself almost by accident rather than intention. Of course, the triggers usually have to be too precise and most of the time they don't happen when you need them most, although they are better than nothing at all.

The other thing is that the serial memory that gets triggered and played out in words or actions is specific to the context it originally occurred in and that can be anything from comical to non-sensical. So many of my triggered serial memory responses were from cartoons. In a serious situation, that can look anything from crazy to even more unintentionally provoking. Triggered serial memory responses can also come from very badly adjusted situations where the stored copied behaviour or language was inappropriate in the first place.

Triggered serial memory responses can also be used in less dramatic situations. They can be used to build the semblance of language (for it is not true language as, no matter how impressive as it appears, it is not used with *intention* nor true interaction).

Triggered serial memory responses can be used to build living skills. For example, when a plate is put in front of someone this can cue all sorts of triggerable serial memories (this can be hard if what is stored are serial memories of animals eating or TV characters with really bad habits). Even so, no matter how lacking in etiquette, some ability to function is better than none. Not being able to connect quickly or efficiently enough to consistently eat of your own accord at all means that if you can eat as someone else, you still fill up your body even if you don't process the meaning of what you are seeing or tasting – like the significance of seeing food in front of you, whether you like it or not, or what it tastes like. In a state of visual shutdown I have stared blankly at the round smooth circle in front of me with the shapes and colors sitting on it, without knowing it is food, or knowing it is food but not processing the significance of that which should have driven me to eat. In situations like this, responding to triggered serial memories can sometimes assist independence more than force feeding ever will.

Triggered serial memory responses can be used to create a semblance of affection or relationships where the processing of the complex social information or body messages might otherwise not happen. This can make some people feel like they fit in, although it can make others feel exploited and out of control. It can also sometimes please the non-autistic 'normality' seekers which can keep them from being more recklessly intrusive than they otherwise might be.

Triggered serial memory responses can be used to save oneself from danger such as in the case of fire or to do first aid. They can also be used to respond to needs for repair and help.

Triggered serial memory responses are usually idiosyncratic so they are limited in use. When they work, however, they may become routinised as successful and practical strategies and can compensate for an inability to store and access efficiently what is, for other people, learned from experiences. Catchy and concise, advertisement-length, home-video learning can play a large part in constructively controlling the type of behaviours and practical responses you wish to be triggered.

(3) Stored definitions

Without being able to rely on recognising the meaning of things, I have been able to learn response cues which are triggered by pattern rather than meaning. I call these 'stored definitions'.

I used stored definitions to build up a useable vocabulary and these also gave me some tools to break words down into their composite meanings.

By reading the dictionary, including all its prefixes, suffixes, affixes, similes and opposites, I accumulated a huge volume of factual information (although each definition was often stored in serial form). As I heard some of these words spoken, instead of just hearing meaningless blah-blah, the definitions were triggered because the meaningless sound pattern I heard triggered a match with a pattern I had stored along with its dictionary definition.

Someone could, for example, say 'hardy'. Instead of hearing the pattern of sounds in that word and still not being able to process it quickly for meaning, the pattern of sounds could trigger the definitions I'd stored in memory with that same pattern. So, for example, the thought 'robust, capable of enduring difficult circumstances' might be triggered. I may still not have been able to process the meaning of my own stored definition, but I could make word matches and by blurting these out they often passed for an indication of understanding. More important, I could often later replay long strings of conversation and use my stored definitions to analyse consciously a rough literal meaning of most of what was said.

Stored dictionary definitions also helped me to break words down into their component parts and define each part. Then I'd put these things back together to come up with a composite meaning. It still took a long time to process the meaning of words, too long for real 'conversation', but I now had some tools to speed it up a little mechanically.

I also developed exceptional fill-the-gap abilities so that if someone was looking for a word with a particular definition, they had only to give the definition for me to blurt out the word automatically. This made me feel part of things and gave the impression of listening and having interest.

Stored definitions don't just come from the dictionary. They can be used mechanically to read some facial expressions, aspects of body language, actions and what certain things are used for.

Looking at a piece of wood, I may not have processed the personal significance of what I was looking at (ie: what did I want this for?) but I had stored definitions of 'what a person does with wood'. The same was true of what a person did with other types of materials, containers and objects, what a person would find in cupboards, boxes and bottles, where shoes were meant to go on a person's body, when a person is meant to look happy, how a person is meant to look when they are (meant to be) happy, and even when a person is meant to enjoy touch and the noises meant to be associated with this. Again, advertisement-length home-video learning could be used to help people store these 'definitions'.

These strategies can, however, be exploited for the wrong reasons and it is very important to watch out for this in people who rely highly on stored definitions. Storing a definition, for example, that 'people have sex with people who like them' is one that is advertised repetitively. Used for the wrong reasons, stored definitions can be used to the detriment of vulnerable people.

It is also important that people respect the fact that some people *must* rely on stored definitions where they cannot efficiently access personal information about the things they intend to do or where to find things they need or how to respond in certain situations. Stored definitions are generally about 'can' and 'can' can be better than nothing at all, even if it isn't 'want'. So, for example, if you had needed to write on a piece of paper but couldn't access your own personal information of what you needed it for on seeing the stimulus (paper), it is sometimes better to do something with the paper than nothing at all, especially if your life consists of stimuli that don't connect with personal significance because they don't get processed beyond the concrete level. If the world were full of paper, would it not be better to fold it and wrap things in it and make things from it and use it to keep paint off the floor, than never to do anything with anything at all?

Finally, as a person who relies heavily on stored definitions, jokes can be a confusing luxury that I prefer to do without. I may have a sense of humour and I sometimes even realise someone else is being cheeky or silly, but jokes to someone like me is like moving the furniture on a blind person. I move in a literal world and jokes are a chaos that my processing is generally too inefficient to see until I trip over them. Jokes require processing at a level beyond the literal require some processing for significance. There is no point frustrating people with things they don't have the equipment to deal with. It doesn't make sense to give gloves to someone without hands.

(4) 'Rules'

Rules work a bit like stored definitions but rules say things like 'a person MUST eat vegetables' or 'a person MUST NOT fart in company' or 'a person MUST NOT touch electricals with wet hands'.

I don't easily connect to my own personal feelings about whether I like or want what I eat or whether I care if people are put off by what I do or whether something is dangerous. Because of this, for me, rules can take the place of these missing connections.

In accumulating rules, what is important for me is that I get to rehearse my rules through my own words, in my own thoughts or by having a rehearsal of them through actions. Being told rules is not enough. Unless I repeat them or act them through, I don't store them together with what they are meant to relate to. What that means is that when what they relate to comes up (such as the light switch and my wet hands), unless I've actually acted the rule through or spoken it out loud with meaning in the context of the stimulus that the rule relates to, the rule doesn't mentally fire and nothing stops me. If I've rehearsed the rule through in action whilst facing (or picturing, if possible, what I will face) then the next time I face the same stimulus, the rule often fires even if common sense is nowhere to be found.

These rules can be extended too far sometimes, but rules can be refined by being replaced with new or more detailed rules that talks about 'when'. So, 'a person must eat vegetables', might mean that every time you see a vegetable you must eat it, regardless of whose it is or why it's there. You can refine the rule with a new rule, 'a person must eat the vegetables on their own plate' or even 'a person must eat some of the vegetables on their own plate'.

Many non-autistic people senselessly play havoc with the strategies that some 'autistic' people have created to manage their processing problems. They don't seem to realise that they may actually be causing some 'autistic' people to be lower functioning than they might otherwise be if they were able to develop and rely upon this compensatory strategy.

A Little Detour Down Memory Lane

Something to consider. None of the strategies of 'serial memory', 'stored definitions' and 'rules' have to do with long-term memory. If long-term memory is to do with the storage of decoding-information that is used to help process the meaning of new, but related or similar, situations and also to do with the storage of *personally significant* events, it may be time that researchers looked into the role of long-term memory problems in people with 'autism' who have these types of problems of connection. It may be no coincidence that mega doses of vitamin B6 have had such huge success in helping a large percentage of people with 'autism'. One of the major functions of B6, and B complex vitamins in general, is in improving the function of long-term memory.

Too many non-autistic people are fooled into thinking that people with 'autism' don't have long-term memory problems because of their use of things like serial memory. Like a number of people with 'autism', I can remember events from when I was only six months old. The thing is, those old memories are from long chunks of serial memory and are most often to do with mundane events which held no feelings of personal significance for me, nor are those memories accessed, as they should be, to help learn how to respond to new situations.

Labelling

Having consistent trouble recalling the words that are used to describe things significantly slows down the rest of my information processing and this can be a great obstacle to interaction or communication. Among other things, one strategy that can replace the reliance on labelling is reading.

Reading

By labelling objects with single-word labels, problems with recall or labelling can be lessened as well as exercised in a way that may bring a sense of achievement. When you go to recall a word and it doesn't get there, all you have to do is look for that object in the room and read its label out loud.

When I learned other languages (I can speak four altogether) I labelled everything around me. I labelled the crockery itself. I labelled my clothes. I labelled food containers. I labelled door handles and drawers and the wall and the floor and the roof. Later I wrote the words for the colours written in the colours themselves and placed these labels on things that were those colours. I did this for materials that things were made from, labelling wood, metal, plastic, paper, fabric, leather, china and glass and stuck these labels on things made from these materials. I did the same for size and shape, sticking labels of long, short, big, small, round, square, thin, thick. I did it for containers, labelling all bottles with the word 'bottle', packets with 'packet' and boxes with 'box'. I labelled what the things were for, highlighting their use. The label on the door said 'for opening and closing'. The label on my shoes said, 'for wearing'. The label on the handbasin said, 'for washing'.

There are tear-off stick-on memo notes that can be used without much mess or bother and can be easily reused if they have to be removed and put back.

The reliance upon labels can eventually be weaned. Some people come to be able to visualise mentally the labels they would read as associated with the objects they read them on. In this way, the object or person requiring labelling can trigger a serial memory in which these were once linked to the labels. This can be like climbing into your mind, running a video and reading off the subtitles. I often do this with spelling words, so I somehow read them off my mind. I also used to be able to do it with written text and sometimes mentally 'looked to' a part of my serial memory to see what page number I was on at the time. For some people, the recall of labels will not be linked to serial memory (photographic memory) but to particular sensory experiences associated with particular words. One can be weaned from reliance on labels in this case once sensory triggers are established and working.

Larger stick-on labels can be replaced for smaller ones and their use faded once it appears they are no longer relied upon and the serial memory or sensory experience is now used to read off or trigger the associated word.

Sensory triggers

I learned the meaning of words long after I accumulated a huge collection of them as sound patterns and strings of sound patterns. I came to develop a very impressive and passable repertoire of triggered sentences and responses, even in the absence of having any related thoughts or feelings about what I was saying. At that point, I was highly cued, but these cues didn't have a lot of connection with meaning, only pattern. I learned meaning, and my own personal relationship to that meaning of words, through experiencing the words as more than patterns.

I couldn't do this by extracting meaning of words from the jumble of blah-blah. Blah-blah is not directly linked to any meaningful sensation that connects a word to its experience-context (especially if your processing of sound for meaning is severely delayed). The mechanical technique I used to teach myself may work with some people far more successfully that the 'learn as you go' techniques that frustrate therapists, parents and people with problems of connection, alike.

The touching or smelling or tasting or producing noise from the things that are labelled can become triggers to meaningfully identify things. Because of this, it makes good sense to me to combine sensory experience with the reading of labels. The memory of the touch, taste, smell or sound of the labelled objects may eventually become triggered by the thought of looking for the object itself.

The linking of words with sensory experience means that if I hear the word 'shoe', I link this with the sound it makes being thwacked on the floor. If I hear the words 'patent leather', I link this with cold shiny smoothness. If I hear the word 'silk', I link this with its feather-like flow, its sheen and the whisper of a 'whitt' sound that happens when I run my hand over its stretched surface quickly. If I hear 'picture', I re-experience running my fingers around its frame, the cold of its glass and the sound it makes being tapped. If I hear the word 'printer', I re-experience the sound pattern of my own printer printing out. If I hear the word 'biscuit', I re-experience the crunch and the feeling of it as I eat it. If I hear the word 'tree', I re-experience my own body-mapping of how it branches out. If I hear the word 'Paul', I re-experience the predictability of dinners on the table and scalp massages. I have built word searching skills through sensory triggers and as a result been more quickly able to make personal meaning out of the sound patterns that are words.

For a long time there were many words that didn't connect so I used whichever ones I could find in their places. These were often phrases I'd heard or jingles or bits of songs and that doesn't make for saying what you really intended even though it can be sculpted to sound all right. By touching, smelling, crumpling, feeling, jingling and tasting things, I came to be able to better recall what I *intended* to say. The word 'paper' was recalled often by its sound (when crumpled) and texture and visual impression and use so, for example, I would ask for the 'flat, square, white, cr-cr-cr, writing thing' instead of asking for 'paper'. By having contact with the object and commanding myself to name it (which is not the same as trying to recall its name), I could sometimes tap the thing and the word would come out.

The body as a sensory trigger

When I taught English to a Chinese girl who spoke none, I relearned how I learned language. If I wanted to teach her the word 'jump', I got her to jump. If I wanted to teach her the word 'run', I got her to run. If I wanted to teach her the word 'take', I got her to take. If I wanted to teach her the term 'look for', I got her to look for.

I sometimes use sign (overtly or mentally) as I listen or speak, as I make sense of and access a lot of words through the movements and other sensory experiences that they are connected with.

I have seen language being taught through action-songs. I have also seen conventional highly symbolic sign language used with people with 'autism'. For me, there is no point signing the squeezing of cow teats to ask for milk. For me, with only a literal level of processing, this would be more likely to be interpreted as, 'do you want to see a cow being milked?' When I see milk go into a cup, there are no cow teats in sight. It makes far greater sense to me to use sign that is closer to mime than signs that are highly symbolic and removed from the thing you are referring to. Mime is also something that is much more widely understood by non-autistic people who do not sign, so it can be used in a wider variety of environments than conventional sign language.

I personally prefer mime to using spoken language alone. It is less physically exhausting for me and I feel better connected to drawing my words through my hands than connecting to something so far removed and abstract as a collection of throat and lung exercises that are called speech. I have basically little trust of speech. I always keep checking to see whether I'm being understood. I can't actually SEE how other people can interpret the meaning of these sounds. With sign, I can see they have seen my meaning and I trust that more and can keep better track of my own expression. I also find the physical connections easier, quicker and more concise.

With me, mime, like spoken language, should be used slowly, clearly and without any unnecessary information added. Mime as signing can be used as one simple single action per word and those single actions can be used to make linear sentences. If I wanted to sign, 'I want to go and watch the TV', for example, I might tap my finger to my chest for 'I' then place my closed fist over my heart for 'want' (or 'feel'), then quickly move my flattened down-facing palm outward and away from my body for 'go', bring my two pointer fingers up to the sides of my eyes and quickly move them outwards away from my body for 'watch' (or 'see') and then use these same fingers to draw a box in the air for 'tv'. This is, for me, as quick to sign as conventional signing but more concrete and less abstract. It is also much quicker than finger spelling and, most important, *quicker to process for meaning* and I can trust the other person has observed my meaning. I can sign that this was something that I want now by beginning with a quick downward action with my cupped fingers of one hand coming down to strike the palm of my other hand, meaning 'now'. If I were talking about having watched gone to watch TV in the past, I would start with using the same cupped fingers in an action that looks like tapping something off over my shoulder which means the event is behind me or, 'before' (I use a different sign for the placement of objects being 'behind'). If I want to say I will want to go and watch the TV some time in the future, then I use my hand angled to the side across the front of my body and make a circle with it as though it was a hoop rolling and this signifies for me the days that are coming in the future (as days seem to roll on and on).

I have not consciously learned sign language (even though I taught myself the fingerspelt alphabet) and I don't know if these signs coincide with the sign language used by people with deafness. I know some of their signs are more symbolic than others. I know that the signing I use is more concrete than symbolic and quicker to process for meaning than more symbolic signing and that even if the signing vocabulary for the deaf is much wider than it can be with concrete mime-signing, mime-signing has an advantage over things like picture pointing because it is more transportable, widely understood and can, like sign language for the deaf, be used to form simple sentences and to hold simple conversation.

Visual language

'Compic' is a system of using picture diagram-cards to express needs, wants and interests. This makes sense but is limited when it comes to complex requests and sentences so it has to be combined with other language aides. It is also not as transportable as mime-signing because you have to have access to materials, whereas with mime-signing you only need access to your own body. The other limitation I've seen with Compic is that non-autistic people involved in Compic communication generally don't use the same system themselves to convey what *they* mean.

For some people like me, for whom the translation of blah-blah is very hard and tiring, something like Compic might have made me feel both better understood and less exhausted in keeping up as well as helped me use language with *intention* rather than just saying what I could instead of what I meant or wanted to say. It might have given me more energy to put into understanding things that I could process more easily. This would have made better sense than spending all my time mechanically plodding through the translation and retranslation of the same old words. That never built up my skills of understanding. Only cutting down on the causes and sources of information overload ever contributed to real development.

In spite of its limitations, Compic could be more successful with people who have trouble with fine motor skills than mime-signing. In one deaf–blind school I visited, there were 'autistic' children using a Compic system who had made their own cards to expand on what the usual collection could offer them. Instead of using Compic to communicate in single words, they were able to use the cards they'd made to communicate in sentences. There is no reason why this shouldn't be so for people with 'autism' in autistic schools, except that their intelligence to do so is possibly more often under-estimated than the intelligence of the same type of children in schools where their perceptual problems were recognised and not confused with intellectual handicap.

Diagrammatical representations

I learned emotions by drawing how some of them looked and getting names put to them. I learned the names for different body sensations by locating what words went with feelings from what place. To do this I had people help me place emotion-words and actions along illustrated scales and diagrams to show me variations of intensity such as the difference between pleased, happy and excited or tired, niggly, agitated, angry or furious. I did the same to show degree of familiarity, (such as stranger, acquaintance and friend) and closeness of relationships (such as hate, dislike, like, love) and the sorts of behaviours that are associated with each of these. I then kept these diagrams for my own reference as related confusion came up again in practice.

Pattern and rhythm

Another tool that I use to identify words, but particularly sentences, because I don't process their meaning quickly enough, is to recognise them by pattern. By tapping out common words and sentences, I have established an ability to identify many of these without the need to process the meaning of the words themselves. I have tapped this rhythm openly or 'bobbed' my head up and down to the 'beat' or the sentence or word. This is really just experiencing a word through another sense – my body.

Sentences like 'do you want a biscuit' translate into the rhythm 'ta-te, ta-te, taa, taa'. My name, Donna, when spoken translated into 'ta-te'. This use of rhythm can also help identify the different use of the same word. So, for example, I came to identify when I was being called, not by hearing the same word (my name), nor even by the volume (which was usually shouted), but by the distinctive pattern used to draw that word out

Don-Naa, which translated into the rhythm, 'taa, taa-aa-aa' which was quite distinctly different from the usual rhythm with which my name was spoken.

There are, of course, disadvantages to this. For example, 'have you seen the dishcloth' can have the same rhythm as 'do you want a biscuit' and you might want a biscuit, have no idea where the dishcloth is but answer 'yes'. All sorts of machine noises make rhythms too and if something makes the same rhythm as your name being called, you can find yourself coming to the call of the washing machine. Still, this strategy is better than none at all and can add to an arsenal through which to wage war against incomprehension and lack of response.

Which labels first?

Words to do with the names of objects are probably the most important ones to connect with as it is hard to ask for help if you haven't got these. If someone can only say 'book', at least you can work out what they might want done with it. If they just say 'look' but haven't connected with 'book', you have a whole house full of things that can be 'looked' (at or for).

Words to do with what things are contained in (box, bottle, bag, packet), made of (wood, metal, cloth, leather, glass, plastic, powder, goo) or what is done with them (eating, drinking, closing, warming, sleeping) are also really important to learn. Much later, less tangible, less directly observable words such as those to do with feelings (had enough, hurt, good, angry) or body sensations (tired, full, cold, thirsty) are really important to connect with.

Words to do with pronouns, such as 'I', 'you', 'he', 'she', 'we' or 'they', aren't so important. Too many people make a ridiculous big hoo-ha about these things, because they want to eradicate this 'symptom of autism', or for the sake of 'manners' or impressiveness. Pronouns are 'relative' to who is being referred to, where you are and where they are in space and who you are telling all this to. That's a lot of connections and far more than ever have to be made to correctly access, use and interpret most other words. Pronouns are, in my experience, the hardest words to connect with experienceable meaning because they are always changing, because they are so relative. In my experience, they require far more connections, monitoring and feedback than in the learning of so many other words.

Too often so much energy is put into teaching pronouns and the person being drilled experiences so little consistent success in using them that it can really strongly detract from any interest in learning all the words that *can* be easily connected with. I got through most of my life using general terms like 'a person' and 'one', calling people by name or by gender with terms like 'the woman' or 'the man' or by age with terms like 'the boy'. It didn't make a great deal of difference to my ability to be comprehended whether I referred to these people's relationship to me or in space or not. These things might have their time and place but there are a lot of more important things to learn which come easier and can build a sense of achievement before building too great a sense of failure.

Sequencing

Having trouble sequencing things efficiently makes it hard to learn to dress or wash easily or plan effectively or play in any non-ritualistic, complex, interactive way.

When I was young washing meant getting into water and then getting out. The order in which the clothes went on or off didn't always happen and I occasionally got into the shower with my clothes on (I then put this mistake to use a few times and washed the clothes that were on me, peeling them off and getting to the body underneath). The towel and the soap often didn't get used. After a bath, my dry clothes were usually unravelled back onto a wet but unwashed body.

The same has been true for me of dressing. Growing up I often had trouble with the order of over-clothes and under-clothes and was often leaving something out or putting it on too late. One major aspect of these problems is, in my opinion, poor sequencing.

Like labelling, sequencing relates to having delayed processing and inadequate flexibility in long-term memory recall skills (not to be confused with serial memory). Both involve being able to extract information (about labels or sequence) in the usual course of life. I think it is because my processing is delayed or partial that I don't get to extract those lessons like I should. I might extract all the component parts, like water, towel, body, soap, clothes and bath, but without ritual to go by, how all these bits relate to each other can remain fragmented and disconnected.

Numbering and rote learning

For me, numbering steps is one mechanical way of doing the sequencing that my brain should have worked out how to do (and which I should have been able to access quickly, but generally can't). I can learn the steps of things by rote but I've found that sometimes different things learned by rote can become entangled with each other. I can get things happening in the right order by writing out numbered steps but that can still involve having to process complex written instructions and my ability to process words meaningfully as I read them depends on my level of overload. Reading one line with meaning doesn't guarantee that my processing at the time is efficient enough to connect one sentence with the one that follows it in following through instructions.

Charting

For me, one of the best ways to draw up a chart with numbered steps is to do this diagrammatically using simple pictures that are easy to relate to personally and involve no distracting, non-relevant information (such as objects in the background on a picture, a particular patterned towel by the bath, etc). If the pictures used are too simple, I might know what things are involved but not connect to how I am involved in using those things. If the pictures have too many distracting, irrelevant details I may be distracted from the step itself and it may also be harder to transfer the step to some other environment (so if the picture has a particular towel in it and I go to have a bath somewhere where this towel isn't there, the triggering of the steps may not happen or may not feel like they 'fit').

Once these steps can be relied upon, they can gradually be made progressively more symbolic. So, for example, instead of a picture showing me drying myself, it may just show the towel. Once this move is made to symbols, a piece of towel, itself can be used and felt or a piece of soap can be felt or be smelled or tasted (if it isn't going to seriously hurt to do so) and these sensory experiences (that should not hold any sensory discomfort) may eventually come to trigger the action associated with them.

The same thing can be done with dressing. At the symbolic stage, articles of clothing or samples of the fabrics they are made from may be used to trigger the learned step.

This technique can be used for setting the table, clearing away, getting breakfast, making snacks, simple meals, doing dishes, making the bed, doing washing, catching transport, serving people, social skills (where these are absolutely necessary and there is no serious sensory or emotional aversion and where they do not invite information overload) or a whole load of other things.

At a more complex level, charts can be used to check through possible body messages to tell what one is feeling or needs. Without proper processing of body messages, for example, I have found it hard to tell if I needed the toilet or needed a jumper or needed to eat. Pressing on my stomach could tell me if I needed to urinate when I didn't process the usual messages naturally. Feeling my fingers, toes and nose for cold could tell me whether I needed food if I didn't process hunger properly. Checking for goosebumps or sweat could tell me if I needed a jumper on or off. Swallowing or feeling if my mouth was dry could tell me if I needed a drink. All of these things can be taught by charting out sequences for checking. Such a chart can be hung up on the exit door and everything can be checked and dealt with before leaving the house. In this way, overload and other crises that could occur outside of home can be minimised and, if necessary, a checking card can be made and carried about in a pocket.

Checking for emotional responses can be used like this too. I have found that having a want for something can sometimes be checked by taking something and holding it, then putting it back and then taking it again and learning to 'read' my own facial expressions and body language externally in response to these things (according to theoretical learning of what expressions theoretically usually go with what feelings). Charts can be designed to teach this sequence of checking too.

I have found that checking for feelings of attraction and aversion, by learning to read my own body language and facial expression externally, have also been a really important part of learning how to tell when I felt safe or not. The mechanical sequences for this skill, too, could be taught through step-by-step charts.

Planning skills could also be taught by putting the logical sequence involved into a step-by-step chart. This could cover what gets done in the morning (washing, dressing, breakfast), to going to work/school, what is done at work/school, what is done at lunchtime, what is done leading up to dinner, what is done after dinner, getting ready for bed, and what is done on weekends or public holidays. Charts could be made for packing to travel, how to make travel arrangements, how to ask for help, how to call attention to oneself and when it is needed, how to do simple repairs, when to call someone to fix something... just about any skill that involves a sequence of events.

Charts can be put up on the kitchen door, the bedroom wall, the bathroom wall (they can be laminated to be kept waterproof), they can be put onto long strips of cardboard, turned into transportable rolls or cards or carried in a flip-through card-wallet. They can be stuck to the dashboard of the car, stuck on the table, stuck on the dishwasher or the washing machine or on the front door or back door. They can be on cupboard doors, wardrobe doors, refrigerator doors, bin lids or even stuck to the roof or floor if it makes good logical sense for them to be there.

Laying things out in logical sequence

The laying out of clothes in order of progression is another really important thing. As a child, I sometimes got these things on in the wrong order, getting the outer clothes on before the underwear, the shoes before the socks and even now I am still struggling to remember the sequence in which I put my glasses on in relation to my clothes. By laying things out in a logical order, it can be as simple as walking along a sort of conveyor belt and sampling the wares.

One important thing, however, is that things need to be laid out in a way that will make them approached from the right direction. If, after washing, a person comes in through a certain door, I think things should be laid out in the direction of approach. If the person approaches clothes after getting up or after washing and coming through the door, the bed can be placed on the way to the clothes from the same direction as the doorway so that each time the clothes are approached from the same direction.

A step-by-step simple chart can even be made to lay out your own clothes in a logical sequence the night before. If the pictures on such a chart show a distinct end at which the row of clothes starts and finishes, this would be more successful. One way this could be done is by laying them out on an easily accessible bench that has numbered sections for each clothing article. This could be on a piece of cardboard that is placed on the bench and can be taken to some other environment if the person has to stay overnight somewhere else. Eventually, the person may simply be able to recite (out loud or to themselves) the progression of numbers and this might trigger which type of article they need to put on next.

If clothes have to be hung up or kept in drawers, you could put underwear in the top drawer, socks in the second, tops in the third and trousers or skirts in the fourth and even shoes in the fifth because this is the order in which they usually get put on. The sequence can be made easy by just going progressively down the chest of drawers.

The same thing could be done with clothes hung in the wardrobe so that shirts come first, then trousers or skirts, then cardigans or jumpers, then coats. In this way, you can just go the chest of drawers and get underwear and socks on and then work your way through the wardrobe. For some people, though, this might offer too much choice and it might be easier to have a set of clothes laid out.

Kitchen cupboards and shelves can be sequenced like this too so that if you take out crackers, spread them with margarine, then spread them with peanut butter, you can move along in conveyor belt fashion and not have to dart all over the room getting things out of sequence, becoming distracted, becoming frustrated and deciding you weren't THAT hungry after all.

Logical progression can also be used to put things away or to remember things on the way out the door. Things that have to go upstairs, for example, can be placed along that route. This is pretty much how I keep our house reasonably tidy. A cut out arrow that points in the direction things are meant to go could also help some people.

Lists of things that have to be bought or letters that have to be posted that day or rubbish that has to be taken out or a coat that should be worn, can all be placed in front of the exiting door so they have actually to be attended to on the way out in order to get out. Commands of things to do can be written or illustrated boldly on a page or poster and placed either on the door itself that will be faced on the way out, or on the floor in front of the door. These can even be checklists that include turning off any appliances, turning lights out, checking to see you have keys, checking to see you have money, making sure you have enough clothes on and taking something to eat with you, and so on.

Recording

For me, a problem with sequencing is also about sense of time and the continuity (or lack of it) in my sense of personal history. For me, this affects my sense of identity and self.

Labelling clocks with symbols for the sort of things that happen when the hands get to different points can be one way of keeping track of time and how it relates to things that get done at different times. If the minute hand is confusing, it can be removed so that the clock has only got an hour hand.

Albums with the day's events, keywords, objects collected through that day to do with smells and tastes and textures experienced and pictures or photos that capture things that happened that day, can all be put together in a way that can make up month by month accessible libraries. These can be kept year after year so that a person can look through them at any time and get some sort of composite sense of who they are, what they do, what they like, where they've been and who they spend their time around and where they spend it. This is very important for someone who doesn't have a consistent access to personally significant memories, by which one would usually get a sense of personal ownership over one's own life and form self-awareness and identity.

This is what I got in the reading back of my first book. I had stored, in a kind of serial memory, all the things I experienced but I couldn't access that serial memory with the same kind of personal affect that most people might feel in recalling something in long-term memory. Also, the recall of things from what I know as serial-memory is generally unable to be cut away from the string of everything else it is attached to. When I read my autobiography back I was able to experience the effect of the continuity of my life's events and to feel for them in a personal way that my information processing usually makes very difficult, if not impossible, most of the time.

Visualising

For me, not being able to visualise quickly something described to me, or mentally hold visualisation together well in any continuous or detailed way, means that verbal descriptions are very hard to make much sense of. Even when I do make sense of them, it is hard to hold their component parts together in some sort of whole picture in my mind and I keep losing bits like someone carrying too much shopping in flimsy split bags.

For me, having trouble visualising also means that it is very hard to alter a mental image once I've achieved one, so the effect of new information in altering old information doesn't happen so smoothly.

Also, partial information processing, for me, means that I don't generally perceive with meaning much of the social or emotional context in which events happen. This happens even if I am sensorily familiar with things in that context and know theoretically who things belong to or where they belong. I think that trouble visualising can affect imagination and curiosity too.

For me, the demonstration of things in 'real life' works so much better than verbal description. Re-enactments, mime and role play can bring descriptions to life in an observable way that doesn't require as much of a battle with interpretation as verbal description does. Demonstrations, however, need to be done very slowly and with all unnecessary information cut out. It is not always possible to do this, such as when talking about something that will happen in the future or elsewhere or something theoretical. Talking through objects may help someone understand what is coming up and to ask questions when they have poor visualisation skills.

Talking via objects

Talking through objects is one way in which visualising can be done externally and mechanically. You can start this by taking representations of the people or objects or environments involved and 'playing out' what you are talking about.

At first, these representations should be as similar as possible to the real things, rather than symbolic. At first, for example, there is no use using a toy bear to stand for a person or a drawn square to stand for a room. If you are talking about a bear, use a bear. If you are talking about a person, use a doll that reasonably well represents the person it stands for and put it in some of the fabric from something very familiar to the person it represents. An illustrated floor-plan with painted carpet or tiles of the room it represents, can be used as the platform for 'playing out' actions in that room. Doll's house furniture can also be used if it is an important part of what is being told (but should not be used otherwise as it may distract from what is important to attend to).

If you are talking about oranges, use oranges, not apples or balls. If you are talking about plates, don't mime them or use paper, use them the real thing to demonstrate.

If you are talking about two or more people where their relative size, age or gender are significant features, use dolls appropriate to this. If someone's glasses or beard or hair or jewellery are a meaningful, identifiable feature to the people concerned, add these things in miniature if possible.

Most important, start with the demonstration of very simple things and single instructions, *not* multi-faceted things or complex instructions and demonstrate all things slowly and methodically without any unnecessary information (such as intonation, excessive facial expression or body language, praise or chit-chat). If you are moving to complex instructions, it might help to make up a chart of what you have demonstrated.

It is also very important that talking via objects is free to be used as two way communication so that it is used not just for receptive language (what is going in) but for expressive language too (what is coming out). Speaking through objects should be empowering to *all* participants, not yet one more thing that non-'autistic' people impose upon 'autistic' people to 'get through to them' their own non-autistic version of reality and perception.

Speaking through objects can get fluent speech going with an observable context to make it more successfully comprehensible. It can be good training to limit redundant speech and to give the person with 'autism' some idea of what knowledge is being shared by themselves and another person. It can also be good for people who have no speech or sign-language at all to express themselves in a complex way.

Once speaking through objects has become a developed skill, it can gradually be used more and more symbolically so that a more flexible range of objects can be used to facilitate communication. My father would use matchboxes or knives and forks as symbols of interactive speakers and at a certain stage, this can work. Moving to using more symbolic objects will also make this technique more transportable to other environments where the availability of objects through which to speak will vary.

Using scales

Another of the skills to do with visualisation is to do with being able to visualise quantity; the concepts like 'more' or 'less', 'lots' or 'some' or 'not much'. This is something that can be done through objects but should also involve comparison. The same concepts should also be shown with a variety of objects so that these concepts don't get linked with one type of thing only. The other thing that may be important is to measure these things along some kind of a scale. One way of doing this is to line up these collections of objects, showing concepts of quantity.

The concept of intensity is another one that may need to be experienced to be understood. One way this can be done is by putting things along a diagrammatic scale. This can also be done with emotions to tell things like 'niggly' from 'furious', 'glad' from 'excited', 'disappointed' from 'grieving', 'tolerance' from 'love' or 'dislike' from 'hatred'. It can also be used to understand body messages such as the difference between 'peckish' and 'starving', 'sleepy' from 'exhausted', 'uncomfortable' from 'painful' and 'could do with the toilet' versus 'bursting'. Once you have put these kind of things on a scale you can also put illustrations of corresponding expressions or actions that usually go with these things.

Scales can also be used to describe different sorts of relationships between people and concepts like 'relatedness', 'similarity', 'familiarity' and 'closeness'. These are things that can be essential to developing good social skills and communication about social skills.

Making things observable

Having trouble visualising can also mean that you don't look for things that aren't immediately evident. If you see a cupboard door, or a container you can't see through, you don't get to wondering what is behind it or in it. All it is is a cupboard door or a container. If it is a glass cupboard door or a clear container you can see what is behind or in it and that seeing can trigger the reaching for it, which is part of self-help skills.

The same is true of what is in the cupboard or the drawers. If things are stacked on top of each other or behind each other, having trouble visualising can mean that hidden objects, effectively, 'disappear'. In the case of what's in the cupboard, this can mean that unless you establish a rule to look through these things, you will probably just take what is in the front. The same is true of drawers and only the clothes on top will be chosen and rechosen because it is as though the others don't exist.

Having see-through food containers, perspex (which is safer) cupboard or even wardrobe doors, perspex laundry baskets or perspex shoe boxes, are just some of the things that would make accessing easier for someone with this problem.

Keeping doors open is another, as too many rooms, including the bathroom, can just 'disappear' when there are just doors and no view of the rooms or their contents. If you need to keep doors like the bathroom door closed, you could always put a perspex inlay into them with a curtain that can be drawn across if the bathroom is occupied.

People, too, can 'disappear' if you can't visualise where people are and the doors are closed. If you need the doors closed, perspex door windows can be one way to decrease anxiety and decrease the need to keep persistently checking where everyone is or staying with them so they don't 'disappear'.

With the layout of food in the cupboard, ours look like library shelves. Things are next to each other or on top of each other so that each product can usually clearly be seen and easily accessed.

My clothes used to 'disappear' in the cupboard because I couldn't see the whole garment. One of the things that didn't make my clothes 'disappear' was to put nails along one wall and hang my clothes onto them so they laid flat and observable and there was more to choose from than grabbing the first thing I recognised. The same can be done for clothes kept in drawers. Having folded clothes laid out on easily accessible, even tiered, shelves, not only can be a way to categorise different clothes into type and order of putting them on, but can be a way to stop them seeming to 'disappear' into the drawers or under piles.

Linking

If your brain has trouble linking things up as one coherent and meaning-fully connected string of events then 'playing out' via objects is one way of seeing these links. With other problems of conceiving of connectedness, some of the biggest problems are the sense of unpredictability and problems of self-awareness.

Replaying

For some people (like me) experiencing things via the senses is difficult to process for meaning and significance *unless* you have already experi-enced the events once and, thereby, have an 'internal context' for that information. The problem is how to make use of this 'internal context' to make sense of *new* information coming in. If the new information coming in is actually a replay of old information for which you now have 'internal context', the processing of that information will be easier. One way to replay old information as though it were new information is with videotaping.

By videotaping important things you can play the events back if they weren't made sense of in their context the first time around. In this way, you can capture the linking of those events and the context is already mapped out internally from the last time the events occurred so things don't take so much processing the next time, provided they are *exactly* as they were the first time around. Videotapes can't capture an experience as fully as it was already experienced but they get as close as might be possible. What is more, they can be replayed over and over.

For many years, I had no interest in anything done by anyone else. I was only moved by music I'd composed. I was only moved by paintings I'd painted. I was only moved by reading books I'd written. I was only really thrilled to listen to regurgitations of what I'd already said. I could only keep up with the voices and movements of people I'd already 'mapped out'. It wasn't that I was inflexible or self-centred. It was that I had established 'internal context' for these things. Things that came from me had their context intact. Things I had mapped out the pattern of, had been 'formatted'. The context of ever-changing information evaded me.

Hearing and watching videotapes of what you've already done can help with 'realisation' of what you know but don't know you know. They can help you 'reflect' and can reinforce the links between cause and effect that delayed processing usually messes up in 'real life'. The experience of all of these things can help some people to inhibit behaviours they can now see didn't work for them or weren't intentional. They can reinforce the success of behaviours that did work where otherwise this 'realisation' may not have happened and the person might have continued in a hit and miss fashion as always (losing a skill they might otherwise have 'realised' worked for them). The usual experience of things as unpredictable and 'forever new' can also begin to be altered this way and a sense that life *can* be predictable can be experienced. Psychologically and emotionally, this can be really important in feeling like the world isn't as bad as it sometimes feels.

Mirrors

Another problem of linking is body-connectedness. Mirrors can help here as can tracing the linking of body parts (which can be done in front of the mirror). If you are looking at your shoulder and someone wants you to look at your hand but you don't perceive its connectedness, looking where you are meant to can be trial and error. By slowly tracing the line (through touch if there is not tolerance problem with that) from where you are already looking to where you are meant to be looking, the links can be made. Again, something like this should be done without any unnecessary information (such as praise or 'reassuring' patting or blah-blah etc).

'Have to' commands and triggering

If you have trouble processing information in a connected way or retrieving it in a connected or linked way, you can become disconnected physically. This is like being disembodied. When this happens, external cues are needed to make those physical connections or links happen. Sometimes the problem is with voluntarily and consciously accessing the information about connections. If this is the problem and you can't always move when you want, having something outside of yourself that *commands* you to move, can get around the whole problem of accessing this information – it is *triggered* and can happen automatically and uncon-sciously.

I have this problem and often get 'stuck'. Sometimes it is just a few seconds, sometimes it is minutes. Occasionally it is longer. It is almost always a suffocating and frightening experience of helplessness and it has one of the most unfortunate psychological side-effects which is that you sometimes can give up 'wanting'. If you give up 'wanting' or the realisation of 'wants', then you don't feel so suffocated or cheated. Sometimes, giving up the wants can even free up the processing of other information, such as the links between intention and your body.

There are lots of strategies I have learnt over the years to get 'unstuck'. Because 'want' (intention) is not enough, I have come to use cues. Cues are not wants or intentions. They are triggers.

One of those cues is to use the 'have to' commands relating to an object across the room. 'Have tos' are rules that are not learned but stored. They are picked up on a literal level without any processing for personal or relative significance, involve no questioning, nor real choice or discrimination in terms of belief. Because of this they are picked up in abundance and often remain unchallengeable because they weren't taken on by choice or understanding in the first place.

The acquisition of 'have tos' can be as simple as watching a TV sitcom in which someone says 'you shouldn't have eaten that pie' (actually a line from Gilligan's Island' said by the character Maryann to the character Gilligan upon his eating a coconut-cream pie). It could be as simple as a TV commercial which says 'brush your teeth with Colgate'. Stored 'have tos' aren't extracted through analysis. They are 'on the surface' and involve no digging, no reflection, no sense of I or you, or Gilligan for that matter.

'Have tos' can have all manner of triggers. A pie, or toothpaste might trigger the examples above, even a phrase said in the context of the 'have to' or a similar movement or garment to one involved in the original context. However, these cues can be put to use.

If something that triggers a stored rule of 'have to' is in the direction you were intending to go, all the better to get one going in that direction. If not, sometimes some movement is better than none at all and it can free up the connections. The good thing about 'have tos' is that they *command* you against your will (or you can try to relax your will and allow them to command you).

I have, for example, meant to go to the bathroom and been physically 'stuck'. I have focused on a piece of laundry which commands me to 'have to' pick it up. My body moves automatically to the piece of washing and follows through with the learned ritual of putting this in the washing basket. That has got me up the stairs where the bathroom is (I even pass it on the way but generally can't stop the ritual that is running on autopilot). Once I've dropped off the laundry, I am usually freed up to go where I meant.

Sometimes, even your visual focus gets stuck and it is hard to tear your eyes away from wherever they are, even if you aren't interested in or thinking about what you are visually focused on. 'Have tos' can still work to tear you away if you can visualise something that is not where you are visually focused. This can be something in the room you are in or something in the room you mean to be going into.

If you imagine the dishes piled on the sink, for example, your legs can often just carry you there on autopilot and your eyes will follow with your body. This can mean, however, that these 'have tos' trigger when you don't need them and I have a hell of a time making breakfast if the dishes are there because I am driven by my established (and functionally useful) 'have to' and can't get to make my breakfast until the 'have to' is taken care of.

The success of a 'have to' is the established commitment to it. You can't turn them on or off or they lose their potency to *command* you when you *do* need to use them as tools to get to other places and activities that *are* intentional. Sometimes the best you can do is establish useful 'have tos'.

One of the biggest obstacles most 'autistic' people with this problem face is the interference of non-autistic people in their 'have tos'. They may think they are 'helping' the person to break with them and they don't recognise what is sometimes their very important interconnectedness with so many other functions. This is what I mean when I talk about dentists taking out teeth with garden tools. People need to be extremely cautious, non-arrogant, non-ignorant and non-assuming when trying to alter a system they do not understand and do not, themselves, use nor need.

Linking or connecting lines

Some people use the perception of lines like a 'have to' command. They latch onto a line and follow it. It can be a banister or a strip of carpet. It can be a line that you map out for yourself. I've got one of these for going to the toilet at night. I mapped it out when we first moved to into the room we are in and I just retrace my mapped-out line all the way to the toilet bowl and back (this can be a problem if you stay somewhere else). I mapped it out with conscious and voluntary intention but I can use it from point A to B whether I am disconnected or not (the only problem is then getting from C or D or E to B).

Perceived lines too often cut off at a wall or something is left in the way. One way to make permanent lines for people with this problem is to draw linking or connecting lines between rooms that people can latch onto if they get 'stuck'. Brightly coloured electrical insulation tape can be stuck onto carpet in a line from room to room. The lines can branch off but should be wholly connected.

The only potential problem with using this technique is that having problems of control can interfere with its benefits. So, for example, someone who has no such linking or connection problems might find themselves compelled to follow *only* the lines. It is a matter of weighing up the benefits and losses.

Expressed intention as a trigger

Another way I have found to make links and connections is to express intention which then commands to be followed through. This sometimes works and from childhood right up to now I often announce publicly 'I'm going to the toilet' or 'I'm getting some food' or 'I'm going to bed' just for the purpose of using the compulsion to follow through with what was announced as a way of making sure I make the physical connections to get there. Often it works and because it worked, it didn't matter how many ignorant people tried to train me out of announcing such things. Sometimes it doesn't work and the person who heard me will say something like 'I thought you were going to the toilet' or 'I thought you were going to bed' which will command me to be 'true to my words' and make the connections. Sometimes I end up having to say, 'I'm trying but I can't get there' and sometimes I can't make the connections to ask for help in that way. Sometimes I get the command but the sort of answer comes back 'how?' and I lecture my body on the physical mechanics (either out loud or in my head) and that sometimes gets me started. Sometimes I end up stuck until physical need is so extreme that it triggers a 'have to' and that usually works.

Tuning in

Another way of getting all the links together to complete an intended action is to tune in to someone else's. This is what some people call echopraxia. It isn't about mimicry. Mimicry, as most people use the term, is conscious and voluntary. Tuning into to another person's movements and moving as them is automatic and involuntary, sort of like stepping onto an escalator. I used this for most of my life to eat, go to the toilet, wash, brush my teeth and go to bed. One of the problems is that you get forever told off for copying people and following them into the bathroom. The other problem is being able to get off the escalator. If you tune in because you can't get to the toilet and someone else seems likely to go there or even says they're going but doesn't, you end up stuck wherever they went.

One of the most important things that people with this trouble need, is understanding. They may not need to be drilled out of using useful strategies by ignorant people who tell them 'don't follow me into the toilet', 'just because I'm eating, doesn't mean you have to' and 'have a mind of your own'. It also doesn't help when people don't understand the role of some kinds of rituals in aiding functioning and deliberately sabotage them rather than try to understand them and develop new rituals for new situations.

Transferring

When information doesn't transfer as it should to new situations, you can find yourself helpless, in danger, exploited and told off.

'Rules'

For me, sense of danger sometimes doesn't transfer much, memories of helplessness don't transfer, memories of having been exploited don't transfer, but memories of being told off in the form of 'rules' does seem to transfer, sort of. I say here, sort of, because it is not as though I fear being told off (having the 'rule' stated again) in a new situation that is similar to an old one, but that the original telling off ('rule') can have a sort of mental replay.

For me, this is like a tune being triggered in your mind, only it isn't the tune, it's the original telling off (the 'rule'). More specifically, it is my mental echoing of the original telling off, like 'sound memory' used in a serial-memory way (I've called this 'audiographic' memory to draw the parallel with photographic memory) and this was how I was able to repeat long strings of things I had heard. When it is replayed, it doesn't feel like a personal memory in the same way that something personally significant might be recalled; it is more like me telling me off (stating the 'rule') as the person who originally did the telling off (stated the 'rule').

This can be a good mechanical way to get around not transferring information properly from one situation to the next. There is no point telling people 'silly girl' or 'you'll get hurt'. Things like that don't tell you what to do or what not to do. Things like 'don't ask people how old they are' or 'no playing on the stairs' are good because the cues of seeing signs of age and the urge to comment on it can fire the replay of the rule, 'don't ask people how old they are'. Being on the stairs and starting to mess about can trigger the replay of 'no playing on the stairs'. These work like 'have tos' and they usually work for me in stopping me from doing a lot of things that might have caused me some trouble. It wasn't that I'd learned about these things, it was that I'd stored rules about these things and I paid attention not so much to the content of these stored rules, but to the 'not' command within them.

Behaviour modification isn't usually about teaching rules, it is about making people take account of consequences. This teaching of consequences usually didn't work so well for me because part of my information processing problems involved the transfer of lessons learnt to new situations. This was why, in spite of constantly being sworn at and physically abused for my unintentional but compulsively addictive and manic repetitive door-bell ringing, I never seemed to get the message. If I'd simply been firmly ordered, 'no ringing', the cue of approaching the doorbell might have triggered the rule, 'no ringing' and I might have knocked instead.

The same was true at school. Particular students led me into doing certain things and when I was caught I was told off for not having common sense or not knowing any better. If, instead, I'd been told, 'don't do what so and so tells you to', then next time so and so told me to do something, the stored rule might have been triggered and I'd have had to follow my 'have to' (which was the 'have to not follow what so and so asked me to do').

Sometimes I speak these stored rules out loud. One of the problems with this is that I often do this in the voice of the person who made the rule. If someone else hears these, they often don't realise the original context or the importance of having the rule.

I might say 'get your coat' on the way out the door because leaving the house had triggered a rule someone made that had stayed in my head. It might do no harm to take my coat, rain or shine, and a lot better than having no coat on a cold day because I didn't remember. Someone else, seeing it is sunny might say, 'no, you don't need your coat'. I'll insist that I do because I know that I often can't use judgement and that the rule has only ever helped me and never hurt me and that to get sloppy about 'have tos' is to jeopardise the huge degree to which 'have tos' assist me in being 'high functioning'.

I have seen so many professionals training people out of useful 'have tos' that are causing no harm, just because they don't look 'sensical' or 'normal'. Some of these 'have tos' have led to me putting other people's dishes away, picking up laundry in other people's houses, turning lights off in other people's houses ('no wasting electricity').

Of course, there are some rules that don't work when applied all the time. One of these has been 'no wasting water'. One of the things these got triggered by, was any sound of running water, including the flushing of the toilet. This meant that the toilet didn't get flushed often. Also, if there were spare glasses of water laying about, they got used by watering plants (whether they needed it or not) or in assisting the washing out of a dirty sink. I also had a rule 'don't waste paper' which, before it got controlled, led to using the minimal amount of paper, including in the toilet. An 'autistic' definition of 'most minimal' can be what is called 'logic before practicality' so 'have tos' can have all sorts of unforeseen consequences. Rules have to be used with people like me very carefully but they can be used with a lot of success too if thought goes into them.

Categorising

One of the things that categorising usually does for people is helps them to locate things. As a child, I learned the skills of categorising, but learning the skill doesn't make it happen automatically when you need it. The result was that I just kept categorising the same things over and over again and still couldn't recognise that one thing belonged in the same category as another or another or another.

I could have been looking for flour and because the bag of flour I was looking at wasn't exactly the same as the one I had in my mind, I may not have recognised it as flour even if it would do exactly the same job.

The problem with not being able to use functional categorising skills when they are needed is that things often have to be almost exact replicas of the thing I have already had experience of for me to recognise it (and this connects with 'what to do about it'). This makes me look, sometimes, like a brilliant locater of things because I can often pinpoint *particular* things instantly, but it is only because nothing but the near exact copy of what I am looking for jumps out as 'similar'. Everything else can be as irrelevant as the shelf that the objects are on.

The problem here isn't a psychological one, it is the way that I store information. Too often, I don't form and access a general *idea* of something (such as flour), I don't form any idea. Mostly, I store the *experience* rather than the idea and those experiences get used *as* ideas.

This means that if I have stored 'conifer trees' by smell, then unless it has the smell that I originally stored, it doesn't matter if it looks like a conifer tree. If I stored 'Paul' by his hair or beard, it doesn't matter if it is the same Paul after cutting his hair or shaving his beard, it doesn't feel like it. If I knew the entrance to someone's house by the sound of the doorbell and they changed their doorbell, I may well fear I am at the wrong house. If I stored jelly by its wobbliness, it doesn't matter if a harder jelly is made from the same things, it isn't jelly, even if I might comply with the expectation to act like it is.

This form of storage relates again to the role of decoding and long-term memory. The storing of 'templates' for the recognition and categorisation of new information is about forming an *idea* of what an experience is like, not the experience itself. When people store and retrieve the original experience and use it to categorise new experiences, this is what I call 'serial memory' and it is not the same thing as storing an idea. The use of serial memory in this way limits what you tune in to and how you tune in to it and it also affects how you relate to change. It may, however, be all you have and so even with its set-backs it may be better than nothing.

Reading the labels

There are some ways to get people to rely on comprehension (ideas) rather than sense impressions to find what they are looking for. 'Home-brand' products may be good for this if the person can read because they all have the same label and can be in the same packets but there can be sugar in one packet and flour in another. What this may do is get people actually to *look for* things as opposed to relying upon certain things *jumping out* at them.

When things 'jump out' at a person, this is a trigger that occurs when a match is made with a pre-formed mental imprint of what a particular thing looks like. Its a bit like an automatic 'bingo' siren going off. That is not the same as actively looking for something and sometimes what 'jumps out' isn't even what the person may have gone out to get but just happened to be an irresistible match that 'felt right'. Being triggered is more like exposing yourself to a situation where certain things can 'find you'.

Here's an example. If the first experience-based imprint of a tin of baked beans is one with a green label and black writing, then it is only that sort of tin of beans that will jump out, in terms of attention and processing, as a tin of baked beans. Having people rely on reading labels instead of waiting to be triggered, may lead them to find what they need or want in a wider variety of possible forms and make it less likely that they get out things purely on the basis of triggered recognition (which can feel like compulsion and be confused with real need or want). Of course, even 'home-brand' products can become categorised according to word length or shape and so the reliance upon actually reading the labels may easily become redundant.

I can sound written words out phonetically but I know other people with 'autism' who know all printed words solely by their pattern and shape and yet can read reasonably fluently this way. I used to rely on this system quite a lot and this was how I could scan piles of books very quickly and found that my mind had eventually processed the information. I am fortunate, though, that I can use both systems. Reading the labels is also very limited if you think about having a triggerable pre-formed mental imprint of what a particular person looks like. People don't wear labels.

Teaching body language

Even though people don't wear labels telling what they think or feel, some people with 'autism' can be formally taught to read facial expressions and body language in a mechanical, though generally limited, way. Even if you can't recognise trouble about to happen in human form because your categorisation skills don't work efficiently, you can learn to read each person.

'Autistic' people can be taught to recognise simple and individual signs of sexual harassment, for example. They can be taught to recognise simple and individual signs of anger or boredom or annoyance or fatigue. Many do, however, learn these signs in a fragmented way. So, for example, I learned that if people's mouths hung down, they were frowning and that this meant they were angry. One day, at the railway station, I felt very anxious that almost all of the people were frowning and angry. Fortunately, I expressed this anxiety and the person with me had the sense to ask how I knew this. I explained how I could read these expressions and she calmly pointed out that to recognise a frown, you looked at people's foreheads too to see if they were crumpled up. I took a look around at everybody's foreheads and almost none of them were crumpled. I asked what to make of their hanging-down mouths and was told that this was probably because they were bored with waiting.

Taking account of more than one sign at once can be very hard for some 'autistic' people but, despite some of the misunderstandings, learning none of the components of composite signs at all can leave you much more frightened, overwhelmed and helpless than at least having learned some mechanically.

To augment reliance on fragmented signs, it may be a good rule to 'check with one person you can trust' (someone who won't make a joke out of what you say and who will not take advantage of your 'naivete') whether you have got the signs right or not.

One last word about signs. It is very important that if 'autistic' people are taught signs by which to tell when they can trust or feel safe, that they *also* be taught to read signs by which they can tell when they should not trust or cannot feel safe. Without teaching both it should be realised that people who can't be trusted and are not safe will try to pass themselves off as though they are.

Rules

If you have trouble recognising that you are in trouble when confronted in a way which is similar to a previous time, or if you keep leaving the supermarket because you didn't see a bag of flour among a whole shelf full of bags, then you can get around these problems of categorisation by using rules.

Rules can't help you categorise but they can help you respond in routine ways to particular experiences. If someone hurts you and then someone else does and someone else does and someone else also does, all in the same way, then you have to acknowledge that you are probably not stupid but you may have a problem with categorisation.

You also need some strategy to protect yourself. This strategy can be a rule. Some examples of such rules might be, 'all new "friends" have to be met and approved by Paul' (or whoever is a person you can trust). Another rule might be, 'When meeting people Paul must always be with me' (or whoever's judgement you can trust).

If you can't find something or someone because the packet has changed, the label is different, the smell has changed or the coat is missing, you can develop a rule to 'ask someone for help to find what you are looking for'. Even some 'autistic' people without speech, or inhibited in their use of speech, can carry helpful cards they can use to ask set questions.

As a child, I was often sent to the small local shops with a shopping list and the shop assistants would often just gather up what was on my list. This isn't so easy with many large modern stores now but even in the modern stores there are assistants hanging about the aisles who are sometimes very helpful in actually getting things on your list for you. Again, cards requesting the help you need can be really useful. If you can't follow instructions, verbal or signed, you can still have a card that asks 'please take me to this' and you can then point to the item on your list.

Definitions

Stored definitions can't help you categorise but they can help you know what to do with something. If you are hearing your name being shouted but this isn't exactly the same person calling you as the first time you stored the experience of 'being called', you may not respond to it as being called at all.

If it were night-time the first time but it's daytime now or if you were painting a picture the first time you stored the experience of being called but you were jumping on the bed this time, the same thing can happen. One way of learning to respond to these things when categorising doesn't work for you, is to use definitions. An example of a stored definition might be, 'hearing your name shouted equals being called'. Now this might help you know you are called and might even trigger the serial memory response of responding to being called (if there is one) and that might even be followed through ('played out') in action. The linking of hearing your name shouted with the definition 'hearing your name shouted equals being called' might not result in responding to that calling. For this, you might need to link it with a rule such as, 'when you are called, you must respond'. In fact, many definitions can be part of the rule, cutting down on processing time. An example might be, 'when you hear your name being shouted you must respond (by going to where the shouting is coming from)'. You might also have to include safety features to this rule (I must respond to my name being shouted by going to where the shouting is coming from *unless* the voice belongs to so and so). This way you don't answer to your name if you are being called by someone who is not a safe person for you to be near.

Other uses of definition might be, 'a round green thing with a short thin stick protruding from the top equals an apple' and you might have another definition which is 'apples are for eating'. Of course, these definitions might mean that only green apples will be eaten, those without sticks sticking out from the top will not be eaten, a green ball with a piece of stick stuck to it might get eaten or every green apple that is seen might get a bite taken out of it.

Definitions, in spite of their possible setbacks, can be better than having nothing. If you are constantly confronting plates of food and staring at them without connecting that these are in the same category as every other meal that made you full when you were hungry, then a definition such as 'plates with things on them are meals to be eaten' may lead to more independence than having no definitions at all. The job is to keep non-food stuffs off your plates and to refine and expand the repertoire of definitions to decrease the likelihood of non-functional or dangerous errors.

In my view, poor functioning has room for improvement and is better than not functioning at all. Too many of the techniques used to try to teach people how to respond to things give them no definitions to work by and assume that functions, such as categorisation, are going to come into play by themselves. For some people this will never happen and you are better off developing strategies which *can* be used to compensate.

Matching

When I was a child and particularly because I processed what I saw piece by piece and not as a coherent whole, I knew people in other ways. As an infant, I knew my mother by her tone and pace and smell. If someone else smelled of cigarettes or beer, had sharp movements and spoke with a similar tone, I responded to them as though they were her.

I knew many people by the pace and style of their movements, their vocal tone and the sounds they made as they moved. I knew people by their 'edges' so that I could read the 'feel' of people (some were brittle, some were hard-edged, some were sharp-edged, some were fluffy, some were scratchy). Edges had nothing to do with any particular behaviour or mood nor even to do with personality. Edges influence personality but personality doesn't influence edges. It can be overlaid over it but someone who senses edges may be confused but won't be fooled into taking personality in place of edges (though they may fluctuate between reliance on the two very different systems – that of 'be' which is about sensing edges and that of 'appear' which is about mind and involves interpretation). I have met some people with seemingly lovely personalities in whom I sensed distinctly sharp edges and in whose company I could never relax no matter how kind or understanding they might be. I have met people who were nasty or callous where I still felt secure in their company because I felt stable in the presence of their hard edgedness. I have been with people who have been firm and highly organised and logical who still brought out lemons on me because I couldn't help but sense their distinctly fluffy edges. I have been with people who have behaved responsibly and had many people depend upon them but in whom I sensed such brittle edges that I could never find instinctually the feeling to rely upon them. I have been with people who have counselling skills and are calm and gentle in their behaviour but in whom I couldn't help but sense scratchiness. Later, I knew people by certain components of their dress or their hair or their body shape or size.

As a small child at the big supermarket, I kept latching on to strangers because they wore the same colour or fabric as my mother on that day. I was always horrified when 'my mother' didn't make sense because the wrong type of hair would be attached to the clothes or she'd be moving in a way that wasn't hers. I have gone to the wrong houses because they had an important identifying component but gradually everything else didn't fit. There was a shampoo that was in the bathroom that smelled like strawberries and no amount of times tasting it could seem to have me learn it wasn't what it smelled like (unfortunately, I didn't communicate this and it was the regular shampoo for a long time). Dominoes looked like chocolate biscuits. A milk saucepan had the same curve and depth as a bowl. The white toilet paper and a white towel hung on rings on the same wall by the toilet. The white bath, the white basin and the white toilet bowl all had the same curvature and place where the water went down.

Analysing the source of mismatches

Matching that relies on sensory-impression rather than idea of a person, place or thing, may have its limitations but it's better than nothing. Too many people spend their time trying to teach through reward and punishment, which things are for what or what responses are appropriate. If these people put their efforts into analysing upon what sensory-bases people are making mismatches, they can rearrange the environment to make many mismatches less likely without the emotional confusion of a system of rewards and punishments that can make a person feel persecuted or patronised.

For example, if someone is peeing in the bathtub or the basin, putting in their mouth anything that looks like a biscuit, drinking shampoo that smells of food or sweets and using the towel as toilet paper, you can pretty much assess that these mismatches are the result of using sensory-experience rather than 'idea' to recognise and respond to the use of these things. There may be little point using reward and punishment systems with someone who is having these difficulties because if they cannot use sensory-information in a composite (non-fragmented) way, they may find it very hard to have much idea what your rewards and punishments are relating to. It is more humane and sensible to put the toilet in a room where there are no similar objects.

It is the carer's job to analyse the basis upon which the mismatching is occurring. Is it that the objects are all made from a similar material (ie: porcelain)? Is it that they are all curved in a bowl-like shape? Is it that they are all the same colour? Is it that water runs down into a hole in all these things? Is it that they all have the same temperature or texture when in contact with the body?

If the towel is getting used in place of the toilet paper, is it because they both hang on rings? If so, hang the towel on a hook instead. Is it that they are the same colour? If so, never use the same coloured towel as toilet paper in the same room. Is it that they are both flexible as fabrics can be or that both are soft? If so, put the towel well out of reach or stepping distance of the toilet.

If the dominoes and the scrabble tiles are ending up in someone's mouth, is it because they are shaped or textured like something edible? If so, make cardboard ones. If it is because of their colour, dye them or colour them.

If the shampoo is getting tasted, have a smell of it. Does it smell like anything edible? If so, get one that has no fragrance. If the bottle has pictures of food on it or words like egg-creme or green-apple on it, get a shampoo that doesn't indicate food. If it is in a bottle that is like a bottle that something edible is kept in or has a similar cap or is coloured like some kind of sauce or topping or juice, get a shampoo that isn't.

This system of analysing what is causing mismatches can be applied to all sorts of places, people and things.

Definitions

By expanding upon repertoires of definitions by which people recognise things, mismatches can also be minimised. If, for example, there is a mismatch happening between the dominoes and biscuits, introduce a component they don't share as a definition. Biscuits can be broken easily, dominoes can't. Make sure it is something you want to see again, though. If you use 'biscuits can be crumbled' (or biscuits are crumbly things) and 'dominoes can't be crumbled' then you have to expect that this new definition might be used to identify these things. That's fine for the dominoes, but will the person be able to eat the crumbs after crumbling the biscuit and can you cope with the mess?

The bath can be distinguished from the toilet by its elongation or the absence of a flush level. There may be no point just saying this or showing it, especially if visual or sound processing is slow. Learning through your body can be of help and a person can learn this new distinguishing sensory experience by running their hand around the inner perimeter or looking for the flush lever *before* they relieve themselves. You might have to keep a pretty clean toilet if this is going to be your strategy and you have to be prepared for the eccentricity of people flushing before they actually use the toilet. Having a different coloured toilet might help some people make fewer mismatches as long as attention is drawn to colour as a distinguishing feature. The best idea is to distance potential mismatches from each other, preferably in different rooms. That is not always possible.

Rules

By making rules to check out information or check before doing things, some mismatches can also be avoided. Teaching rules such as 'check with Paul before eating things' (or whoever is the most trustable person), for example, can mean that the some of the mismatches are stopped before they happen.

Locating

Long-term memory helps people to locate things. Serial memory can also be used to locate things but it works differently and it is less flexible and has its limitations. Like so many other strategies, it is still better than nothing.

I often can't make any use of verbal directions or instructions even if they involve pointing. I have trouble making use of these things because I don't have the sort of recall required. To be able to make sense of verbal directions, you have to be able to use *general* 'ideas' you already have about stores and streets and transport and people and machines etc. These general 'ideas' are stored in long-term memory and are used like templates by which to make flexible use of new information, including directions and instructions. For some people who don't have this, or in whom it is poorly developed or limited in its development, serial memory can be a compensation that is better than nothing.

Serial memory works to make use of some directions or instructions by being able to access a serial memory of the last time you were in a certain place or time. Usual verbal or visual directions and instructions make no direct link to any stored memory of a specific place or time so, to someone who relies on serial memory, they don't give you any 'map' to follow. The good news is, you can make those maps and you can ask for them.

Body mapping

I have learned to make use of directions and instructions by mapping them through my body. I do this by acting out on a small scale all the steps involved as the person speaks or shows me where to go or what to do. If they say or indicate 'turn this way', I physically turn that way as they give the direction. If they say, 'go up the stairs', I step as though going up stairs.

If they say 'walk for a few yards' then I walk on the spot. When they leave me, I replay what I have mapped out, except that I don't do it all on the spot. This doesn't always get me to where I'm going but it usually gets me in the rough direction and at least, when I need directions again, there are fewer instructions needed to complete my journey.

With instructions, if I am told to pick something up and take it to the desk, I mime what I am told as I am told it. When I set the instructions in motion I have to locate some of the actual things I have to use.

The thing that most sabotages the ability to use these strategies, is that nobody helps you learn them and if you do evolve them for yourself, too many people are more worried about the appearance of eccentricity than they are about functioning. I too often been told to 'stop fidgeting' and listen or watch when I've been trying to map out what I'm being told or shown, but most people show or tell me things at a pace that is way too fast to map out accurately or adequately. On top of this, when I've done my best and been unsuccessful (because I was stopped from using my strategy to my best ability), I've been told I 'should have paid attention'.

Creating new serials

Another way that you can learn from instructions or directions is to get someone actually to escort you to where you are *intending* to going or to what you are *trying* to find. I have highlighted these words because too often people think they can establish patterns in people where there is no intention or attempt on the part of the person being taught. Compliance is compliance and it doesn't help to map out much at all.

In the supermarket, I don't ask 'where is the peanut butter', I say 'show me where the peanut butter is' (non-verbal people can use a card to do the same). This way, I am more likely actually to be taken to the peanut butter. Not only is this more likely to get me the peanut butter this time, but I will be able to replay the serial memory of being taken from A to B to find the peanut butter again if I need it and can't find it. When the shop assistants take off to actually get my product for me, I often follow them. I may still have no memory of what aisle number the peanut butter is in but I can always go back to the spot I was in when the shop assistant first took me to the peanut butter and go along the same path till I get to it. This can be time consuming but it can work fine until the peanut butter gets moved.

I have used this system to go places as a child. I thought of it as 'the snail system' because I watched snails follow their own tracks to return from places (this became quite an obsession and I collected them in shoeboxes and followed their tracks around my room the next day).

When I was older I used this system to drive to and from home and university and the shops. If I needed to go somewhere new, I often followed other people there and developed new serial-memory maps. Like the peanut butter, the only problem was road detours which almost always got me lost. I relied on the only system I had and turned around like the snail and went back to where I got lost and tried again. Of course this can have you going around in an endless repetition because redoing the whole thing doesn't take the detour away. This happened to me once because of roadworks and I went around and around about four times before throwing a bad wobbly in the car. After I'd screamed and hit and cried for a while, I decided to pick a totally different path and just see where it ended up. It eventually hit another road that triggered another serial and even though I went in the opposite direction to where I intended I didn't feel lost. When I got to the end, I turned around and went in the other, equally known direction. Sometimes having a rule such as 'find a phone box and call someone when you are lost' can be a help. Even non-verbal people can carry a card instructing someone that they are is lost and who to call.

One of the biggest obstacles to people using this strategy is that non-autistic people try to stop them using such systems because they see them as 'inflexibility'. If this is someone's only way of functioning, my view is you are better off working with the compensatory strategy and developing an independent and higher functioning individual than strangulating these strategies in the pursuit of making someone appear to have efficient or reliable non-autistic systems that they don't have.

Reversing

The information stored in long-term memory can usually be used in a flexible way. It is not a *linear* system. It does not run in a *single direction*. Because of this, people who can rely on long-term memory information can deal with information much more flexibly in terms of direction. For example, if someone finds they have driven towards the shopping centre from a direction they don't usually come from, that person can usually still assess what moves they will need to make to turn into the shopping centre. For someone who relies on serial memory, this is a very difficult thing to do. Serial memory doesn't run backwards and these adjustments don't come easily.

I have found myself in the vicinity of somewhere I wish to go but been coming from a direction I don't usually come from. As a passenger, this is not such a problem. If your intention is known, the driver can just take you to where you want to go. If you are the driver, though, it is much harder. There are two things that have happened to me in this situation. One is that I make the turn as though I were actually coming from my usual direction. This feels right but doesn't get you into the supermarket, it makes you turn away from it. The other thing that happens is that in order to get into the supermarket, you have to come from the direction that you usually do. If this was the opposite direction from which you are travelling, you do this by turning the car around. I have done this too soon, before passing the supermarket and it just took me back to where I came from in the first place. I finally managed by driving past the supermarket and then turning around to approach the supermarket from my usual direction. This worked because the turn off that was mapped out according to serial memory happened automatically. From this example, it should be easy to see that serial memory can be used to do something as high functioning as driving, but it has its limitations in that it isn't always as efficient as being able to rely on long-term memory information. Still, it should be easy to see that in the absence of anything else, it can lead to independence even if that has to be managed independence.

Trouble reversing and the reliance upon serial memory to compensate is very important for non-autistic people to understand. Too often, people are stopped from doing things in particular directions or in a linear way, only to find that they can then not seem to do a particular activity at all. So many more people who are considered 'low functioning' could lead useful and more independent lives if their compensatory strategies were understood, fostered, developed and refined. If non-autistic people did this, they might be more worthy of the trust and co-operation of some 'autistic' people and more comprehensible to them.

Sense of Self and Other

When everything is strung together and linear, it is hard to separate things out from the times and places in which they occurred. Because of this, it is very hard to build any composite pictures independent of serial memory. This greatly affects the ability to perceive of yourself or anyone else as an 'identity'. Being like this, you accumulate experiences with people and facts about them, but these things don't translate into telling you what the person is like.

Serial memory and relationships

I can tell you personally about experiences had with someone. I can tell you facts about them based on these experiences such as 'Paul mows the lawn when the grass gets long' but I can't tell you whether Paul is a person who likes mowing the lawn. I can even tell you that 'Paul has smiled whilst mowing the grass'. I cannot tell you if that meant he was happy.

I am in my own serial memories too. I can tell you, 'Donna types books on the computer' but I can't tell you that 'I like typing books on the computer'. I can tell you 'Donna sings songs in her mind when she wakes up'. I can't tell you, 'I enjoy singing songs in my mind'.

I have serial memories that hold both Paul and I in them and can say 'Paul reads Donna stories at night'. I can't say 'Paul and I are interested in hearing stories'. I have been able to accumulate enormous strings of facts about people based on serial memories and can relay them all to sound like I have been intensely interested in someone or something but it could just as easily have been a relay of every experience ever had with a toothpick as every experience ever had with a person. It is impersonal, factual and detached; part of regurgitated category.

Relationships are usually based on people feeling that personal rapport is building and that personal connection is happening. Too often, 'autistic' people who store and recall information differently don't build up rapport, they build up an accumulation of information. Most people's egos can't sustain feeling deeply for someone who can only accumulate experiential information about being with them. They feel left out or hurt or robbed of something. Yet non-autistic people engage in a relationship with televisions, computers, even cars. There is absolutely no reason why 'autistic' people cannot have meaningful relationships with non-autistic people as long as non-autistic people don't expect them to process information as though they were not 'autistic'.

Sensory-experience based relationships

Aside from building up detached serial memories of my experiences with and of Paul, I have also developed sense-memories of him. Like some foods, fabrics and sounds, I have developed a taste for Paul and a familiarity with him as a collection of sensory-experiences.

Paul's hair is a texture that I find sensorily pleasurable and it has a smell to it which I like. His nose has a texture that is like velvet, which I like too. He is the source of scalp massages which I find very pleasurable and calming and relaxing. He is a fun climbing frame and the source of gravity experiences such as holding me by the feet, which I like. He is the bringer of food that my taste enjoys. He is the source of pressure when my muscles need it. All of these are sensory experiences and I *do* feel very personally about them. They are the entire source of my joy and pain and all feeling of 'humaness'.

I also get these from the sound and the smell and the effect on my body in space as a wild wind pushes me about. I get these from food and its textures and tastes and colours and the different ways of handling it as it is eaten. I get these from haberdashery shops that trigger sense memories of the sounds of buttons and buckles clinking together and the textures of fabrics and the exquisite order of rolls of material, categorised for colour, pattern, quality and texture. I get these from plants and leaves and twigs and their smells and colours and shapes and the different ways they pull apart in your hands. I get these from hearing someone repeat a particular familiar pattern of words in exactly the same way as this person has said them ten times before. This is like hearing a familiar song that I know that I could almost sing along with in a way I can never predict or keep up with the flow of most blah blah. I get these from seeing someone clean up a mess in exactly the same order as they have done several times before. This is like viewing a work of art I am familiar with. Paul is the source of so many of these things and so many more than the wind alone, for example, holds for me. These things make Paul a rewarding experience for me.

Many non-autistic people train 'autistic' people out of experiencing people as sensory experiences. Then, sometimes, they find these people feel nothing at all. Rather than training people out of sensorily enjoying the company of people (or anything else), 'autistic' people could be trained to restrict indulgence in sensory experiences to certain environments or times. Many 'autistic' people understand rules and use them themselves for so many things. This is much better than teaching them that there is to be no pleasure in life for them. Teaching people out of being able to sensorily experience company with people and objects and the elements may amount to teaching them there is no pleasure in life for them as these people may not store and retrieve information like non-autistic people do. So much of the deep depression and rebellion seen in some 'autistic' people may be because they are being systematically suffocated out of being able to feel for things in the only ways available to them.

Non-autistic people are often using each other as sensory experiences, even though they disguise this as all sorts of other things. 'Autistic' people who enjoy overtly sensory experiences as their way of building 'relation-ships' with people, things and places are doing no worse than what so many non-autistic people are already doing covertly. Perhaps this treads on some people's toes and may even be why non-autistic people seem so appalled to see their own covert behaviours so overtly flaunted by 'autistic' people. If non-autistic people have a problem with this, it may be that they should be working on their own hang-ups before considering themselves qualified to come down heavy on 'autistic' people for 'being different'.

CHAPTER 10

'Hyper-Connection'

So far, I have talked about problems of connection that are mostly to do with *delayed* processing. Sometimes, there can be an equal number of problems, though of a different type, when people process information too quickly. This second problem of connection, I will call 'hyper-connection'.

Some people with 'hyper-connection' have been labelled as having Attention Deficit Disorder or Asperger Syndrome. Some are merely considered to be odd or lazy or uncaring or uninterested. I don't care what label is on the pickle jar, I just want to talk about what I have found to be in it.

Just as the rate of information comes in without sufficient filtering for some people with 'autism', this can happen for people with 'hyper-connection' too. The difference between someone with delayed or inefficient processing, accessing and monitoring and someone with what I refer to as 'hyper-connection' is that in both cases too much is coming in but in one case, the person is unable to keep up and in the other case the person keeps up but still spends a lot of their energy making connections that have no relevance or significance.

So, for example, someone with 'hyper-connection' may be driving, see the car behind them and think about how many cars of that type are on the road at this time, where each of them might be heading, what kinds of jobs each of them do, how old each of the cars is, how the letters in their number plates vary, ALL WITHIN A FEW SECONDS. Another example might be that upon hearing a knock at the door, someone may have run through every conceivable possibility of who was there, what they wanted, where they'd been all day, what they'd done or had for lunch, the range of reasons they could be there and hundreds of different logically possible scenarios about what they will want, say or do when they come in, ALL WITHIN A FEW SECONDS. These things may not sound so bad at first and are almost the image of 'genius' but they can have extreme disadvantages.

One thing that is important to point out is that 'hyper-connection' is *not* conventional daydreaming. Conventional daydreaming is something that is governed by personal significance. People may daydream with conscious intention or unconsciously but the daydream is usually about something they wish they were doing or liked doing or somewhere they'd rather be or who they'd rather be with or a remembering of a non-serial event that was personally significant to them. Conventional daydreaming is also not reliant upon cues or triggers.

'Hyper-connection' is *not* about personal significance. 'Hyper-connection' *is* about cues which trigger *serial memory*. Serial memory is not where events are stored because of personal significance. Serial memory is where events are stored as information, irrelevant of their personal significance.

If someone offers me a toothpick right now and it triggers a serial memory of me taking toothpicks out of the cupboard one week ago and putting them onto a particular shelf next to the herbs and spices, to the extreme left and then putting away the dishes, this has nothing at all to do with whether toothpicks are personally significant to me or whether I enjoyed getting the toothpicks out or whether that had been a particularly good day for me. Conventional daydreaming, on the other hand, is governed by personal significance and relates to how you feel about your present and whether it interests you or whether you care about what is going on at a particular time or if it bores you. 'Hyper-connection' happens whether you are interested in what is happening around you or not and has nothing to do with caring or motivation. It has been a great source of mental and emotional cruelty for people with 'hyper-connection' to be unjustly treated as though they are unmotivated, uninterested or uncaring. It would be a good thing if such ignorance could stop by illustrating how two things which may look similar (daydreaming and 'hyper-connection') are in fact not similar at all. I would like to take the reader on a journey through some of the losses that happen to people because of 'hyper-connection'.

Imagine the effect of this type of processing on the ability to keep track of conversation. In the short break between two halves of a sentence, there may have been triggered a huge number of tracks, leading to tracks leading to tracks.

For example, at the time the speaker said, 'on your way home...' an image in the listener's mind may have been triggered of the home she once lived in, which may take her careering down a serial memory path of what was in the loungeroom at that time and who put the ornaments on the shelf and where each of them came from and when they were bought and what someone said at that time they were first put there and what was on the television in the room at the time and how long that programme had been running. In the meantime, the speaker may have continued with 'I want you to take these eggs...' at which point the word 'eggs' might trigger a serial memory of an article about battery hens that the listener read on the train last week as she drank a bottle of mineral water which came from French mountains which is where her friend, Peter, comes from who lived there in that house in the postcard that he sent on which he wrote about his cat that looked like the one that... By this time the speaker may have said five more words, none of which have been processed. By the time the listener gets out of their serial memory and back to trying to make sense of what she is being told, she didn't hear that the eggs had to be dropped off at an aunty's house. She then gets given the eggs, whereupon she stands there wondering what to do about them. She either asks what to do about them and gets told off for not listening or assumes they were given to her and eats them or gives them to the first person who seems they could use them.

Serial memories can be triggered by smells, by a certain colour or pattern, by a sequence of words, by a particular physical action, by touch...by just about anything. Seeing the black and white stripe on a toy plane can trigger the memory of eating humbugs in a classroom decades before and might run into who was in the class on that day and what was being taught and the noise that the school-book made when snapped closed and the exact path the teacher travelled across the room at a particular point and, and, and...

'Hyper-connection' can also affect the ability of these people to express their ideas or feelings in writing or speaking. Paul (who was 'Ian' in two of my books), for example, might write part of a sentence just fine but will get to a word which will trigger a serial memory and off he goes down a track that ends up completely unrelated to the word that triggered him in the first place. If he doesn't go back and read what he wrote, he may have an assumption about what he had been writing that is not the same as what he really meant to write. Even if he rereads what he wrote, the original feeling or significance has been lost because of the track he has just been down. If this happens fifty times in the course of writing a one page letter, it becomes very unrewarding to write, not to mention difficult. Even if he forces himself through the activity, by the end, he has likely written very little of what he originally meant to write.

The same is true for Paul with speaking. He is triggered so often onto long serial memory tangents that by the time he gets back to attending to what he meant to say (if he does at all), he has lost not just his original track, but most if not all of the connection he had with feelings and significance relating to what he was saying.

Any processing of one's own emotions or body messages whilst these explosions of connection are taking place, is also affected. Mostly, they don't figure. Nor is there much processing of what is *personally* thought about what has happened to or around you. Whilst someone's brain is running through the entire range of theoretical possibilities or half a dozen serial memories, what was *personally* significant to them may either be embedded in a mountain load of theoretical possibilities or not be there at all.

Paul would go to work and be triggered all day in between trying to do his job. He generally had only theoretical ideas of what he might have thought or felt about anything he'd done all day and had often not been to the toilet all day nor eaten. He might have used the excuse of having been too 'busy' but even when he stood doing 'nothing' he was most often lost in triggered 'hyper-connections' and his body messages and personal thoughts or feelings generally neither got processed nor attended to.

Not being able to perceive or process your own body messages or emotions consistently can put these people at a serious social and personal disadvantage. They often won't know what they feel about things even though they seem almost exceptionally capable of attention and have seemingly high, even exceptional, intelligence. This means they are often measured against non-autistic people and blamed very harshly for 'not listening', 'not conversing', 'not being affected', 'not showing expected emotional responses', 'not remembering what is significant to someone' and for 'being boring' by going off onto long unrelated tangents.

In place of all the feelings which don't get processed, they may learn all the facial expressions they are meant to have, even learn that people like people who smile and so walk around with a smile stuck permanently on their faces regardless of what they think or feel (if anything).

In place of not being able to remember what is significant to people, they may put a lot of energy into pleasing people and buying acceptance. To disguise their inability to know what they think or to talk about what they think or feel, they may mirror whatever everybody else seems to think, be interested in, like or talk about. In place of not being able to stay on track whilst listening, they may pretend to be hard of hearing or pretend they understood what had been said when they didn't.

They may learn to impress and clown about or avoid people altogether in order to hide the problems they are having and avoid being blamed for them. They may establish themselves in a child-like or 'client' role to cater to the useless attempts of ignorant non-autistic people who think they are 'helping' them or 'correcting' them but whose 'help' and 'correction' does nothing at all to help them process information in a way they can experience personally and emotionally with a feeling of belonging.

Strategies

Some of the strategies that can be used to help these people include:

- cutting down on unnecessary information when speaking or expecting speech or writing or reading or activities which may act as cues or triggers for 'hyper-connections'. (Examples of unnecessary information may be movement, intonation, body language, facial expression, background noise, smells, objects in the room, touch etc whilst verbally explaining something. There are many other examples like this, specific to cutting out information that is not essential to what you wish to teach or share.)

- maintaining a 'normal' pace when speaking or demonstrating (provided there is no receptive language problem) in order to decrease the space in which the mind can fly off onto triggered tangents.

- provide breaks regularly (such as at 10, 15, 20, 30 or 45 minute intervals, depending on the situation and person) to avoid fatigue that will lead to the increased likelihood of triggered distractions.

- provide a healthy and non-toxic diet and environment and nutritional supplements where these will decrease the risks of fatigue and lessen the effects of chronic stress. (Small healthy non-toxic, meals that have no refined sugars may need to be taken every two to four hours to meet these needs in some people.)

- make sure these people get into good regular sleeping routines to counter some of the effects of chronic stress and decrease the tendency towards fatigue.

Checking

Checking is a laborious mechanical way of helping people with these problems to find some non-theoretical, personal feedback about what they think, meant to say, felt, want to do, like, are interested in and what they do/are not. It may also be invaluable to people who have great difficulty in accessing their thoughts or feelings for themselves.

Because these people often have virtually no idea of these things, they may develop theoretical ideas of what they can (possibly), could (potentially), should (morally) or are expected to (ie: fashion), think, feel, be interested in, like, want to do or write or say.

As theoretical ideas of these things may be all they have, and because these things may have been rewarded by people (for selfish or unselfish reasons) these people may fiercely defend these things as 'real self expression'. For example, they may take 'can say', 'could think', 'should want' or 'am expected to do', to be things like 'intended to say', 'really thought', 'actually wanted' or 'enjoy doing'.

Sometimes, in spite of how these people may defend these things, they are either in danger doing them or look miserable, even bullied, as they do them (in spite of the smile they may have permanently stuck on their face). Because of these things, even if these people may never have known any better, it may be important or just humane to help them find out what they really wanted, thought, felt, meant to say, do, etc. The only way I know of to do this is 'checking'.

Checking is a way of impersonally listing potential wants, likes, intentions, thoughts, interests and so on in order to prompt *natural* responses in body language and facial expression to these prompts. Of course, someone with these problems may have stored theoretical ideas of what emotional expression a person is meant to express in response to each item but even this can eventually be identified and ignored. Sometimes, however, these triggered 'plastic' unfelt expressions so dominate *natural* connected body language or facial expression that one may be limited to reading things like muscle or eye response.

The two parties involved in checking must be committed to not pre-empting the responses to these prompts. It is important that the person assisting the one checking does not give away any indication of what they personally want to hear or the person checking may easily just mirror this as their 'own' response. It is also important that the person checking realises that checking is not a weapon used against them but is there to assist them in getting to what they truly want, think, meant to say, etc. In

other words, checking should be entered into voluntarily and not compliantly.

If it is entered into compliantly, the annoyance at forced compliance
will only block the flow of natural feelings coming through and defeat
all chance of the technique being successful. Because of this, the person
checking has to be personally ready to use this technique and follow
through with what has been established as 'real wants'.

It may be that the compulsive grip of commitment to stored wants will
be confused with feelings in the checking process and that defensiveness
may be so high that no real feelings will get through at all. It may be that
even when real feelings do connect with expression they may not be (or
psychologically acknowledged or admitted to be) felt and the person
checking must understand this and sometimes be committed to following
through with what the assistant perceives as a 'real want'. Videotaping
could help here.

The person assisting has to be capable of telling natural expression
from stored expression as well as have an established rapport and trust
with the person who is checking and be truly committed to arriving at
the truth rather than what they wish to be the truth.

Checking can be done verbally or through demonstration. The person
checking can present the information for checking or the person assisting
can present the information. Checking prompts should be simple and
impersonal. Here are some examples:

CHECKER: (*pointing, signed or spoken*) 'This is the one I want'.

ASSISTANT: *watches for response.*

CHECKER: *moves to the next potentially or assumed wanted item indicating,*
           signing or saying 'This is the one I want'.

ASSISTANT: *watches for response.*

This goes on until either a natural response is seen or the potential or
assumed wants are exhausted. If at any point there is a clearly stored
response based on an assumed or expected want, this should be ignored
if possible. Only once a natural want is found should the assistant disclose
their observation of the person's real want.

Sometimes, to avoid rebellion where the person fiercely defends clearly
stored wants, it is important to go through as many potential wants as
possible. It may also be important that if the person really feels their stored
want is a natural and felt one that you check it for 'not want'. To do this,
you have the person check what they believe is their want by indicating,

signing or saying, 'this is NOT what I want'. If the person is defensive, there may be no response to this. If, however, the person is truly committed to the personal usefulness of checking and is not defensive, then a clearly natural 'not want' response will reassure the assistant that they were right.

This model can be used for 'likes', 'is interested in', 'wants to go', 'wants to do', 'thinks', 'meant to say', etc. If the checker is not able, or is too defensive, to do the prompt themselves, it may be necessary or helpful for the assistant to indicate, sign or say the prompt. Pictures can help in choosing places to go or activities or who someone wants to see. Lists of words or sentences can be used to check about what one intended to say or write. The relative intensity of a 'like' can be assessed by referring to an assumed or established 'like' and rating it on a scale of one to five or one to ten.

The system of checking is one that can be much better than nothing and can give people a feeling of connectedness and control over their leaf-in-the-wind or tear-away lives. It is also one that can establish a feeling that someone really cares who the person *really* is beyond appearance and *will* have the time and patience and commitment to find out. In caution, though, checking is a technique that, used badly or by the wrong people, can be abused and lead to exploitation. It is something that should be taken on voluntarily by the person requiring it and should be monitored very carefully to be sure that it *is* beneficial to the person with 'autism'.

CHAPTER 11

Problems of Tolerance

Problems of tolerance, in my experience come into two basic categories:

- ○ sensory hypersensitivity
- ○ emotional hypersensitivity (and/or exposure anxiety).

Sensory and emotional hypersensitivity can occur in many other conditions which have nothing at all to do with 'autism' but are very often confused with it. Like compulsion, obsession and acute anxiety, sensory and emotional hypersensitivity can be due to chronic stress and chronic stress can come from any source.

Ongoing psychological or social problems can cause extreme chronic stress, as can psychiatric problems and emotional disturbance. Ongoing physical stress such as that caused by allergies or metabolic problems can also cause chronic stress. It is only when sensory and emotional hypersensitivity occur together with problems of connection, that the source of the chronic stress can be assumed to be caused by information overload. It is this last case that I will be focusing on here.

Sensory Hypersensitivity

In my own experience, sensory hypersensitivity has happened both independently of information overload and as a direct result of it. In the first case, it was caused by allergic reaction, toxicity and metabolic problems. In the second case, the pain of sensory hypersensitivity seems to be an instinctual warning device that is meant to trigger avoidance behaviour when a state of information overload is imminent.

By triggering adrenalin rushes in a state of information overload, touch and bright light and sound can become so intensely sharp that it becomes natural to avoid them.

The problem in someone like me is that the efficient processing of the significance of this sensory pain doesn't always happen. Nor does the efficient accessing of the connections necessary to protect myself or escape a sensorily painful environment. What that means is that although my brain may instinctually trigger the adrenalin release that is meant to make me sense impending danger (overload) and avoid it, I often don't do enough with those messages. In response to its messages not being responded to, and information overload persisting, my brain instinctually ups the intensity of its 'hint', resulting in sensory hypersensitivity. When this happens, rather than becoming avoidant, I sometimes become captivated by the sensory intensity I experience – as though the whole world suddenly gets a fairground atmosphere. For me, the adrenalin rush triggers a compulsive rush towards the intense sensory stimuli, seeming to be trying to top each sensory high. This is like addiction and is difficult to fight. The result, however, is that this can reach a painful peak of intensity where the instinct is finally to have an extreme aversion (even terror response) towards the same stimuli that held me captive a few minutes before. The compulsion to self-abuse seems to serve a similar function by resulting in an instinctual closing off.

Sensory hypersensitivities in any form can make it difficult to concentrate, to trust, at attend to things other than the source of the hypersensitivity, to join in or to relax. If the discomfort or distraction is extreme enough, they can detract from the ability to learn.

The initial answer for these people is to remove these sensations where that removal will not seriously interfere with the development of interaction, communication or education and to assist these people in shifting focus.

People who are in a constant state of stress and discomfort also develop strategies to help calm themselves. For some people, this might be rocking or humming or tapping themselves. For others, this might be carrying something around with them. These things should not, however, be treated as distractions as long as they actually help the person to feel more able to be involved and part of things. Security strategies and security objects are not the same as compulsive or obsessional ones.

If someone's self-calming tapping or rocking or humming is interfering with their freedom to interact, communicate or attend to their learning, I do not feel that the answer is in removing these things. Instead, I would suggest that other people could compensate for these actions.

Having an assistant tap or rock the person in a reliable, consistent, calm, non-invasive, impersonal and rhythmic way, may be enough for some people to be able to let you do this important calming work for them and free them to interact and communicate and learn more broadly. For some people the constant provision of a constant background rhythm, such as a metronome, might be of help. Any assistant helping in this way, however, must be attentive to the fine line between calming and hypnotic. There is a point in helping someone to lower their stress level but there is no real point helping someone to lower their stress level to the point of self-hypnosis if that means they will just tune out to everything around them.

For me, sensory hypersensitivity is a fluctuating condition and rests in the hands of information overload (though I should note that, though fluctuating, sensory hypersensitivities can be chronic problems due to the chronic problem of overload). Information overload is due to problems of connection. It is about a hyper-saturation of information. It has nothing directly to do with stress level, nor personality or resilience, even though it does affect a person's stress level and can shape the expression of their personality.

For me, sensory hypersensitivity results when I have taken in more information than I can keep up with (become 'hyper-saturated'). So, for example, if my ability to keep up with the processing of people's blah-blah is failing as I fall further and further behind, more and more unprocessed information keeps accumulating. If I run away from more information coming in, or close my eyes and ears, I might not reach overload. If, however, in spite of falling behind in my ability to keep up, I continue (as trained) to try to understand and at least look as if I'm listening, my hearing sensitivity may become painfully acute.

When hearing becomes acute, sounds that are normally inaudible can be as audible as usual sounds. Because too much information is already coming in for the brain to keep up with its connections, the perception of these additional sounds can make them intensely unbearable. Sometimes, it is not that certain pitches are causing the problem, it is that 'good training' by non-autistic people has led to behaviours that stop someone from properly managing an information processing problem in a way that will avoid 'hyper-saturation' and ensuing sensory hypersensitivity.

The same thing can happen with touch. When I have been taking in a lot of visual or sound information, my sense of touch can be overly sensitive, sharp as a pin and to be touched can be 'shocking' as though being jolted. The problem, however, is not with touch, the problem is that I remained too long attending to information I could not process efficiently at the pace it was coming in.

Before having special lenses to correct the overload of visual information the same was true of my vision which would make many types of bright light physically very uncomfortable and distressing. One of the most unfortunate things about this is that whenever I developed strategies by which to cut down on information overload and avoid 'hyper-saturation', I was ridiculed for these and taught out of these 'quirks'.

In each of these cases, what lead up to the heightening of these senses was the progressive increase in inefficient processing of incoming information. So, for example, my senses would become so painfully hypersensitive when the meaning and significance of what I was seeing or hearing had *already* began to fall out.

You can teach people with in a state of 'hyper-saturation' to 'act normal' and this might have learning benefits for them, within limitations. On the other hand, I think it makes more sense and is more humane to help them to manage both the cause and the symptoms of 'hyper-saturation' and to aide them in reading the signs of it approaching so they can better manage it for themselves.

One way that non-autistic people can help is by reducing information overload, as mentioned these things earlier. Suggestions for this include having non-autistic people slow down their own pace.

- If people speak more calmly, with less intonation, more slowly, concisely and economically, and cut down on any unnecessary background noises, there is less unnecessary information to process and more time to process it in. That translates into being able to keep up and avoid 'hyper-saturation' for longer.

- Similarly, people can be more conservative with unnecessary movements or facial expression, move slowly and cut down on unnecessary light (which causes light refraction; 'shine' that can cause the visual effect of shooting out sudden streams of light), particularly where there is natural light. This cuts down on the bombardment of visual information and may give some people with 'autism' more time to process things.

- Touch, also, should not be used except where it is part of information you are trying to get across. Touch should be slow and as predictable and purposeful as possible and only used where necessary. This will stop people using up so much processing capacity in being on guard.

- ○ Finally, cutting down on the need to extract information or translate it from one form to another are two other ways that non-autistic people can increase someone's information processing capacity. The more concrete and able to be visualised the language, the quicker it can be processed and the longer 'hyper-saturation' can be kept at bay.

Unfortunately, all of these things are what is generally *not* being done with people with 'autism'. I have seen people in a serious state of hyper-saturation where non-autistic people are patting and rubbing and praising and trying to make themselves interesting by using more animated movements, facial expression and intonation.

Instead of demonstrating information in the contexts in which it happens, it is embedded in songs or stories where people who are having trouble keeping up, have little processing time for the luxury of extracting embedded information or connecting it to an experience that is not immediately experienceable.

In my view, what would be far more 'interesting' to people with 'autism' is if people working with them could cut out unnecessary, bombarding, self-satisfying behaviours so that people with 'hyper-saturation' could keep up for long enough and process, access and monitor efficiently enough, *to* be interested in something.

The other thing that non-autistic people can do to help people with 'autism' keep up and avoid 'hyper-saturation' leading to hypersensitivity, is to give information in short bursts and leave the person with these problems *completely* unstimulated for at least five to fifteen minutes before starting up again.

When I was a small child, my threshold for processing blah-blah was only a few seconds. When I was about ten or so, my threshold for processing blah-blah was about five to ten minutes. When I was a teenager and up to my twenties, this threshold was about fifteen minutes to half an hour. Now it is about twenty to forty-five minutes. In a more accommodating environment I'd say that these thresholds could have been much higher than they were.

In my view, people who are in an extreme state of 'hyper-saturation' should ideally only be stimulated with new information for around five to fifteen minutes AT MOST before a (*real*) break. Also, it is important to be aware that some people with information overload can look as if they are keeping up much longer than they actually are and some switch to autopilot and give stored responses to cover for having stopped being able to process anything else coming in.

If someone with 'autism' suffers from hyper-saturation I would say that stimulation with new information should not go on for more than forty-five minutes without a break (based on one-to-one interaction). This should certainly be for a shorter amount of time if interaction is on more than a one-to-one basis.

'Hyper-saturation' results in sensory overload in me for several reasons. First, 'hyper-saturation' can result in poor filtration of incoming information, resulting in an excess of sensory information. Second, inefficient processing results in a lot of anxiety, confusion and frustration and this raises the stress level dramatically, causing a sharpening of the senses. Third, overburdened processing means that the brain is also slow in making internal connections, such as what to do about, and how to make sense of, the discomforts of sensory hypersensitivities and this can result in not taking actions to close stimuli out (so can training at the hands of ignorant people). Fourth, as the brain is already battling to keep up with processing a backlog of information, sensory hypersensitivities don't become easily dispersed or adjusted to quickly enough as they otherwise might, such as through expressing the problems you are having so that someone can help by turning lights off, turning radios and TVs off, shutting up and not touching you. Fifth, the sensory hypersensitivity itself puts an even higher burden on processing problems by giving the brain even more to process so that it has a tendency to 'top itself'.

In a nutshell

In a nutshell, some things which can be used to reduce some anxiety and stress for people with information overload-related sensory hypersensitivity are the following:

- Fatigue makes people more susceptible to the effects of any kind of stress. Fatigue can be minimised through a healthy non-toxic diet and environment, regular exercise, a good sleep routine and nutritional supplements such as B-complex vitamins that help handle stress and vitamin C which combats fatigue.

- REAL breaks of between five minutes to an hour in between participation can help people to sustain personal stress or information overload caused by participation. Breaks should be a peaceful and relaxing time with no non-calming and non-welcomed stimulation.

- A lessening or absence of *unnecessary* stimulation.

- Providing a gentle, quiet, steady calming physical or sound rhythm where this is found to help.

- Allowing people familiar *self-chosen* objects of attachment where these do not seriously impede interaction or communication and where these are observed to give these people security or orient them during experiences of extreme stress or discomfort.

- No unnecessary touching unless it is clearly sought by, welcomed and comforting, calming or relaxing to the person receiving it.

- At least twenty minutes after the stress or discomfort has clearly died down and the person can process receptive communication, ask these people (in sign or written or spoken word), if possible, if there is anything that you can realistically do to help them to better cope with you in the future (you could present some options).

Available therapies

I really don't know if hearing therapy or auditory training works for everyone but it may work for some. However, it is worth considering that it is the nature of hearing to adjust and readjust naturally to all different sorts of environments. This means that even if a few weeks of playing noise at the problem frequencies does result in change, a change in usual environment could alter the readjustment leaving the effects short term only.

Second, these 'treatments' generally attempt to alter pitch, without addressing cases where sensory hypersensitivity is due to information overload. In these cases, what is needed is not to treat the symptom of a difficulty with pitch, but to treat the cause by reducing the rate and pace and intensity of sound sources so that they can be processed more efficiently, anxiety kept low and hypersensitivity to pitch less likely to result.

Third, these treatments do not address the situation where a hearing sensitivity problem is merely a secondary result of a primary problem.

The condition called Scotopic Sensitivity Syndrome (SSS) is a perceptual problem to do with how the brain processes what the eyes see (*not an eyesight problem*). For me, this condition primarily affects the ability to CONSISTENTLY interpret what I see. It is *not a visual problem but a perceptual one.*

The main known cause of SSS is to do with a problem in filtering different wave lengths of light. The main result is that overloaded visual perception is generally fragmented and there is trouble making sense of visual context. These problems are heightened by bright or harsh light and by an excess of unexpected, fast or varied movement around the person.

Seventy per cent of information processing is done through the eyes and they take in information at a faster rate than any other senses – the problems in other senses are caused, in people with the syndrome, by these senses compensating.

Secondary problems, caused by having to use other senses to compensate for these processing difficulties, involve a similar inconsistency in getting meaning from what is heard or even in making sense of the meaning and purpose of touch.

In the case of hearing, this means that although the person listens they may have difficulty in *consistently* processing what they hear as more than just a cacophony of sound. These problems are heightened by sound or voices coming from more than one source at once, excessive variation in a speaker's voice, high pitch in voice or sound, and by constantly changing sound (such as some music) or people speaking too fast to process.

The heightened stress from this sort of sensory and information overload can result in hearing and/or visual hypersensitivity. In cases where the underlying problem is Scotopic Sensitivity Syndrome it may be that any success seen with hearing therapy or auditory training may possibly be attributed to a placebo effect by virtue of having instilled trust through the long awaited recognition of the 'autistic' person's altered perceptual reality and the raising of hope through renewed belief in recovery. In some cases, dealing with sensory hypersensitivity in other ways may be cheaper, more effective and more long lasting.

Ways of finding out if a person with autism *may* have Scotopic Sensitivity Syndrome include the following:

- A related family history of dyslexia, learning difficulties, hyperactivity or light sensitivity.
- A family history of migraine.

○ A tendency to sit in the dark, lie under the bed, sit in the cupboard etc (to cut down on the ongoing stress of light and colour).

○ A tendency to look predominantly at feet whilst walking up the street or in shops (to avoid visual bombardment).

○ Does the following *compulsively or continually*:

   • rubs or pushes eyes (to relieve strain, self-stimulate and avoid usual bombardment by seeing colours rather than what is around them. This also gets rid of visual 'white noise' and after-images.)

   • blinks or switches lights on and off continuously or looks at things in short quick glances (to break up and slow down visual input)

   • squints (to cut down light and narrow surrounding 'context')

   • turns one eye inwards or defocuses and appears to look through things (to put things out of focus, cut down on bouncing light and shadow and take the sharp edges off of what is seen)

   • views scenes through cracks or tubes rather than directly (to cut down on surrounding 'context')

   • seems often to have noticeably more difficulty staying aware/concentrating or keeping control of behaviour when under fluorescent lights

   • seems to lose sense of the purpose or meaning of what is seen, either totally or intermittently

   • echopraxia – the generally unintentional 'parroting' of what is seen

   • has extreme reactions to certain colours or shine (light refraction)

   • appears to see the part and lose the whole

   • sees things in greater detail than most people

   • has parallel problems to any of the above with what is heard.

Sensory hypersensitivity and biochemistry problems

Sensory hypersensitivity can also depend on other stressors such as allergies, vitamin/mineral deficiencies and imbalances, hypoglycemia and the amount of new information or emotions being tackled at a given time. Even some of these metabolic and chemical problems can be due to chronic heightened stress caused by sensory-perceptual problems. In this sense, the two can become a vicious circle.

Vitamin B, magnesium and zinc deficiencies can relate to pitch and brightness sensitivity, although whether these vitamins and minerals are consumed in coping with these sensitivities or whether they make a person more vulnerable or susceptible to these sensitivities is a question that research may one day be able to answer.

Zinc deficiency shows itself as white spots on the finger nails. Vitamin B6 deficiency shows itself in distinct vertical 'grooves' running the length of the fingernails. B2 deficiency shows itself in an 'abnormally' red tongue. Calcium deficiency can be seen in brittle fingernails (splitting layers and soft flexible 'paper' nails). Vitamin A and D deficiencies show themselves in hair and eyelash loss (see how easily they come out). Vitamin C deficiency can be seen in bleeding gums and easy bruising. Any of these could be hints that sensory hypersensitivities have underlying metabolic problems which should be addressed.

It is possible that there are some 'autistic' people for whom hearing sensitivity is the major cause rather than a major symptom. It may be that for such people the temporary relief from one of the symptoms gives them some time and space to adjust their attitude and focus on working on combating the restrictions of their 'autism' rather than being eaten up by them.

Sensory hypersensitivities and management strategies

If someone finds some tactile, auditory or visual sensations overwhelming and you appear to force that person to put up with these things (or block their escape from or aversion to these things), this can undermine social trust and want and interest. On the other hand a person needs to be pushed towards development. The answer is to address both with as much empathy and understanding as possible.

Auditory problems

The symptoms of auditory hypersensitivity can be addressed with cup-type headphones which cut down volume enough to STAND listening.

Slowing down auditory input and cutting down distraction can help a person to process and comprehend that input now it is at a bearable pace. Ear plugs, headphones or cotton wool can be sources of self-control over associated stress levels and also show the person you understand and respect their sensory difficulties. This may go far in developing trust of others and the environment and empowering the person in a way that encourages them to believe they are not just passive objects in their wider environment.

Speaking in whisper, in a room without other noise sources, or quietly through a tube, can cut down on excessive noise sources and unnecessary sources of distraction from what is being said. This can encourage interest in words and develop listening skills in a way which will not sensorily overload.

Speaking slowly on a one-to-one basis in a relatively even voice, or relatively middle pitch, may allow for better processing of what is said and less distraction caused by extremes in pitch or intonation. Quiet voices have less reverberation and are easier to tune in to for some people with a processing problem or hypersensitive hearing. Few words, low or whispered, even, rhythmic voices are easier to process in a shorter length of time.

Loud voices can send someone into being a statue because of overload and shutdown due to perhaps a combination of noise sensitivity and emotional reaction.

A person with 'autism' can be encouraged to control this with cotton wool, earplugs, or headphones and carrying a card explaining how people should speak to minimise difficulty could also be useful and an easy way for the person with 'autism' to take control of their difficulties and manage in spite of them. If a person has hypersensitive hearing they will still hear in spite of ear plugs or other measures, just now at a more normal level.

Tactile problems

Regarding tactile sensations, if it is fabrics or textures that seem intolerable, find out which ones. If someone insists on a coat or jumper where it seems socially inappropriate, the person may have good sensory reasons for this that go beyond mere habit.

Visual problems

For some people with visual-hypersensitivity or visual-perceptual problems, coloured light bulbs of various colours may be tried throughout the house and a diary kept of their effects. Find out what lighting seems to be best or worst for concentration and involvement. Some parents have tried out different coloured light bulbs and found dramatic changes in concentration, application, comprehension and expression. If these are too dark for everyone else in the house, low wattage (25–40 watts) pastel shades of an effective colour can be used in main rooms in place of any 'white light'. If there are rooms with fluorescent lighting, lamps can be used in those rooms instead. Lamps that reflect light upwards rather than downwards can create less visual distortion. This is no replacement for Irlen Lenses but may be better than nothing.

Sunglasses can help some people cope with hypersensitivity when they go out and can help some people to cope with bright lights and sunlight (including indoors). Whilst sunglasses, unlike Irlen Filters, do *not* correct visual-perceptual problems, they can, at least, reduce some visual hypersensitivity to light and may be better than nothing for those people who are unable to be fitted for Irlen lenses.

Emotional Hypersensitivity (and/or Exposure Anxiety)

'Emotional hypersensitivity' is a vague term that can mean many things. It is important to point out what I will and will not be dealing with here.

'Emotional hypersensitivity' can mean having intensely strong emotional responses to the sources of obsessions, compulsions or acute anxiety. I will be dealing with this in the next chapter as a problem of control.

'Emotional hypersensitivity' can mean being intensely emotionally affected by finding too much significance in things, such as what happens to some people with mental health problems like 'paranoia' (to do with persecution) or 'megalomania' (to do with grandiose ideas). I won't be discussing these problems.

'Emotional hypersensitivity' can mean having a flood of affect in one of two extremes, such as in the case of what is called 'manic depression'. Even though many more 'able autistic' people and people with Asperger Syndrome have sometimes been misdiagnosed with this label, I won't be dealing with this here either.

'Emotional hypersensitivity' can mean being avoidant of letting affect come in or being avoidant of sharing emotions that you feel. It can also mean that if one pushes oneself beyond one's level of emotional tolerance, the exposure and self-expression anxiety that this causes may result in systems dissociation (where these systems switch to autopilot and operate only on a subconscious level beyond voluntary, conscious, control) or may result in an accessing shutdown so that no matter how much one may want to interact or communicate, one may be cut off from accessing one's own knowledge and connections. It is *these* aspects I will be looking at in this chapter.

These types of 'emotional hypersensitivity' can be roughly put into these categories:

- 'Emotional hypersensitivity' due to what I call 'self–other' or systems integration problem. I will refer to this as 'emotion-preservation response'.

- 'Emotional hypersensitivity' as one form of sensory hypersensitivity to do with body messages, due to information overload. I will refer to this, again, as 'hyper-saturation', since it is similar, although of a different kind, to the sensory hyper-saturation explored earlier.

'Emotion-preservation response'

'Emotion-preservation response' is what is used by some people who have difficulty holding onto an emotional experience for any amount of time. This problem is related to being mono where an emotion is rarely processed and held onto before more incoming stimuli leaves it tuned out again.

'Emotion-preservation response' is basically about closing out anything that would distract from the emotion being experienced. This might be experienced by outsiders as someone avoiding sharing their emotions with other people or avoiding talking about what they are feeling. Some people might consider it a sort of 'emotional selfishness'. In fact, because any attempts to share it would rob the person of the capacity to experience their own emotion, any actual selfishness is in the hands of the person who wishes to be shared with who would put their neediness for sharing above the need of a person to experience their own emotions.

For some people, any shift in focus away from their emotions, including the acknowledgement of someone else or the cognitive or verbal naming of the emotion being felt, is enough to cut them off from the experience. Many people in the environment of these people take this personally when it shouldn't be taken so personally. For people with this problem it is not a matter of not trusting someone with the emotions they are feeling. They may very much trust the person in the room with them as they are having their feelings. The other person in the room may even have been the source of those feelings. For people with this problem, it wouldn't matter how much they trusted and were close to someone; by attending to *external* information (the other person), they would lose track of the experience of *internal* information (what they are feeling).

'SELF–OTHER' PROBLEMS

Some people with problems of 'emotional hypersensitivity' have them because they cannot simultaneously process incoming information (from outside of them) and what is happening inside of them. This is a form of being what I call 'mono' and these people work on single tracks more than most people. This problem is part of what I call a 'self–other' problem.

'Self–other problems' can have all sorts of effects. They can make it difficult or impossible to keep track of your own thoughts whilst listening to someone else articulate theirs.

They can make it difficult or impossible to be aware of your own physical existence, whilst attending visually to someone else's.

They can make it difficult or impossible to be aware of being touched whilst you are doing touching.

'Self-other' problems can mean that one can talk on one's own track or on someone else's track but can't talk in an interactive way that requires combining or taking simultaneous account of the two (such as comparing or contrasting views or working together with someone else to come up with a synthesis of ideas).

Self–other problems can also make the concept of 'social' difficult or impossible to grasp and things like loneliness or boredom very hard to make sense of or act upon. Worst of all, 'self–other' problems can make emotional experiences within social interpersonal contexts very rare and also make it difficult or impossible to perceive and experience emotions whilst simultaneously attending to external information.

These things can have a devastating effect one one's sense of self and feelings of imprisonment in the necessity of emotional isolation as well as being a considerable obstacle to the development of tolerance of affect which comes from the consistent and socially comprehensible conscious experience of having emotions.

STRATEGIES FOR HELPING PEOPLE WITH SELF–OTHER PROBLEMS
RELATING TO EMOTIONAL HYPERSENSITIVITY

- Not expecting or assuming they do not have the problems that they do.

- Welcoming or inviting self-initiated open communication about how they experience these things.

- Welcoming or inviting open communication about how people without these problems can give these people the social space to experience their emotions.

- Recognising that in people who do not consistently experience their emotions, when they do connect, they often come out bigly. This means that even happiness or being 'moved' by something may make someone cry and shake and this shouldn't necessarily be seen as a negative thing, nor one requiring intervention.

- Decreasing bombardment of external 'other' information when it is clear that someone is experiencing non-destructive emotions (many ignorant people stick an arm around these people when they are feeling 'moved' by something and this drastic bombardment of external 'other' cuts them off completely from their feelings – after which they, ironically, are expected to appear grateful for being 'comforted').

- Not staring or asking if the person is all right until they have had a chance to experience their emotions, unless they appear agitated or in danger. If such a person is crying it may be because they are moved by something and the last thing they may need is to be watched or have to reassure you they are all right just because their emotions are too big to be expressed in a more casual and controllable way.

- Don't enquire about the emotion the person has had *until it has clearly passed* unless the person appears agitated or in danger.

- Without emotional expectation or need, you can make a genuine and unselfish open offer that the person can come and be in your company when they feel emotions *provided the person is not experiencing their emotions at the time.* You could also reassure the person you will not bombard them in any way if they take up the offer.

- Accept that if *you* need to share emotions with someone at the time they are sharing them, you may have to find someone else who doesn't have these problems with whom to do this. Accept, also, that needing this from someone else doesn't mean there aren't a whole range of other rewarding things you still *can* share with this person.

○ Accept that people with these problems can be sometimes be useful, innovative and creative when working 'alone' (with or without assistance) even if they are incapable of 'team work'.

Also, it may help these people for others to realise that, just because they may be unable to make comparisons or contrasts between their own views and those of others, this is not the same as their being without views of their own, or comprehending those of others. They may simply not be able to do both within the same context. (This may have important implications for education, especially at post-elementary level where the ability to work as 'a team' and the ability to compare, contrast or synthesize information may often be assumed. Educational design could easily be more flexible so that students without these capabilities can still work productively on comparable topics using mechanics that do work for these people.)

'Hyper-saturation'

Emotional hypersensitivity due to 'hyper-saturation' is like sensory-hypersensitivity; they are both about information overload. As emotions are felt physically these, along with general body messages to do with physical pleasure or discomfort, are one form of sensory feedback.

The brain has to process sensory information. People who have delayed processing have a problem in keeping up with sensory information, including emotions. The more of it there is, the greater is the problem in keeping up with it and the more likely the result will be discomfort and overload.

Information causes affect when it is at least partially processed for meaning or significance. In someone with a problem of connection, such as an information processing delay, there may be plenty of sensory pleasure or discomfort that looks like emotion but there may be very little experience of emotion triggered by personal significance *within the context in which a stimulus, that would otherwise register as personally significant, occurs.*

Where meaning and significance connect so rarely in the context that provokes them, the emotions that these cause may be felt extremely, yet out of context. This may mean that, when they are felt, they may be both intensely foreign and difficult if not impossible to comprehend or diffuse.

The effect that emotion can have on a system which cannot make meaningful sense of it can be much more extreme than emotion would be for most people who generally experience it meaningfully in the context in which it is provoked.

Emotions are experienced physically. Without comprehension to help diffuse or make sense of the emotions, the effect on the body may be so extreme that it may feel that it is too much for the body to sustain. These extreme reactions can mean that even being emotionally 'moved' in a minor degree may result in severe tremors, palpitations and hyperventilation.

The physical experiences register in the brain as a form of sensory information. In such extremes and with little experience by which to make sense of (and diffuse) what is being experienced, these physical (sensory) sensations cannot be reasoned away psychologically as harmless because there is usually no idea of what provoked them or even what they are there for. Because of this these extreme physical sensations due to affect may be made sense of according to the only information that the brain has about intense, out of control, physical sensations; DANGER.

The intense, unintentional, out of control physical sensations caused by things that have no traceable meaningful cause may be wrongly perceived by the brain as an attack on the body, as though it were a kind of invisible physical onslaught that needs to be defended against as a matter of survival. This can trigger even worse flow-on effects.

In someone who has extreme problems of connection, such a danger signal, especially with little information or previous experience by which to make sense of and diffuse it, may result in an adrenalin rush that puts them into a hyper-alert or hyper-reactive state. This can result in such a sudden and extreme processing demand that the flood of incoming information causes 'hyper-saturation': information overload.

In the situation where expressing oneself in front of another person (or even thinking about doing so) results in this emotional hypersensitivity, if a person persists in pushing themselves (or being pushed) beyond the limits of their emotional tolerance, any of three involuntary things may happen.

(1) Systems may become dissociated. That is, consciously and voluntarily accessible systems may switch to 'autopilot' which is a subconscious level of processing, accessing or monitoring beyond conscious awareness or voluntary control. A dissociative switch to autopilot in a 'mono' person can happen on any channel and affect one's connection with movement, accessing

of stored verbal responses or stored responses to 'social' touch or other social cues.

(2) Systems shutdown may occur. This can affect communication or movement so that the person becomes involuntarily frozen out of expression. It can also affect thought and feeling so that one becomes cut off from one's own recollection of knowledge that one has, or the ability to connect with thoughts and feelings that may even have been intensely present before the shutdown. This is what I call a 'mental stutter' and may be similar to what some students experience as 'examination anxiety'.

(3) Acute anxiety of overload, triggered by anxiety that is related to emotional hypersensitivity, may be enough to result in painful sensory hypersensitivity on the way to systems shutdowns.

The journey from sensory hypersensitivity to systems shutdowns may be a fast one, in which case the sensory discomfort may be short lasting or not experienced at all or the journey may be a slow one and the sensory discomfort may be prolonged.

The information overload may be diffused before it leads to systems shutdowns or it may not. If it is diffused before it reaches this point, a person may experience severe sensory heightening (colours becoming too intense, light becoming too bright, certain pitches becoming intolerable, certain patterns becoming obtrusively distinct, touch may feel 'prickly' or 'ticklish' or provoke 'shock') yet continue to process and be able to access information.

If information overload is not diffused in time, systems shutdowns may, for example, mean that there will be a temporary inability to process touch, sound or visual information for meaning. (Systems shutdowns may also, as mentioned, result in an inability to access connection to movement or speech efficiently.)

The social consequences of emotional hypersensitivity
Having any of these problems can seriously interfere with consistent interaction, communication and learning.

If your mind learns from these experiences of emotional hypersensitivity that being affected feels dangerous and causes the pain and discomfort of sensory overload, all your motivation may be directed towards avoiding anything that will cause personal affect.

If, your mind has also learned that being affected causes the chaos, confusion and turmoil of sharp perceptual shifts in the ability to make sense of what you see, hear and feel or even your connection to your own body, these are very big survival-based motivations to avoid furiously anything that even begins to cause affect.

Now if all these things happen before you even know what this affect is called or why it is there, there is nothing to tell you that all your urges to avoid affect are misguided. Even if you do learn what emotions are called and why they are there and what use they are and that they aren't dangerous, this may all only be comprehensible many years after you have established a pattern of avoiding the things and that avoidance has become an integral part of your identity.

The job of developing a comprehension and trust of affect can be a very slow one that takes more courage, endurance, motivation, intelligence, commitment and resilience than most people with this problem may have. Nevertheless, here are the steps I used to manage it.

IMPROVING INFORMATION PROCESSING AS A KEY TO REDUCING
EMOTIONAL HYPERSENSITIVITY DUE TO HYPER-SATURATION

The main cause of this type of emotional hypersensitivity is delayed and inefficient information processing in the first place. Where inefficient information processing does not allow much meaning and significance to sink in in the context in which the stimuli happens, this can lead to a whole load of affect happening once the backlog of delayed information processing has cleared and the context has passed.

In terms of the accumulation of information, this may result in the accumulation of a huge stock of factual information that is not consciously and voluntarily accessible but which may be able to be 'triggered' unintentionally by directly related external cues.

This information can happen on all levels and result in impromtu triggers of brilliant examples of delayed echopraxic and/or echolalic replications. These can be of conversations heard, commercials or programmes seen, the voices or accents, characterisations, even whole concertos regurgitated but not processed with meaning at the time they went in, nor sometimes even as they are coming out. The person's personal relationship to these brilliant displays of 'talent' may be one of detachment, apparent indifference, even alienation, or be followed by distress at being the subject of what is sometimes experienced more as a possession than an expression.

The effect on the affect associated with this information may be that it is experienced without any conscious awareness of the experiences or events it is linked to. Unlike the storage of factual information, affect, when not processed in any interconnected way with that information, may simply build up just like a full bladder. At bursting point it may be attended to, in one great meaningless (uncomfortable, overpowering, and frightening) purge of unnamed affect.

By improving the efficiency of information processing in general, more things connect more quickly within the context they happen in and more things are likely to be processed for significance. This makes experiences of emotion happen more consistently and when they happen more consistently, the mind can begin to form some ideas of what these things are, some of the differences between different feelings and some of the sorts of things that can cause them. This means that the mind gets used to handling and making meaning of the feedback (the physical effect of the emotion and what that means and why it is significant). There are many ways that inefficient information processing can be made more efficient, such as by decreasing stress and fatigue. There are also many nutritional and environmental ways this can be done which have already been mentioned.

Other ways of improving general information processing are to cut out unnecessary information as much as possible, to slow down the rate and duration and number of simultaneous sources of incoming information and to give REAL breaks to allow people the processing time they need without pushing them constantly into information overload.

With people who have problems of emotional hypersensitivity relating to information processing problems, it is *very* important that these people, even as young children be taught in a calm, even detached, theoretical way, what the physical experience of emotions feels like, what these feelings are called and why they are there and that they are not, themselves, dangerous. My younger brother said to me that my problem was that I hadn't learned, like him, that fear is an illusion. I think it might have helped me a lot if I could have been taught to understand that my brain was 'playing a trick' on me and that emotions wouldn't hurt me. I don't know how anyone could get that through to someone who couldn't consistently process blah-blah or actions or touch, but it has, at least, helped me a lot as an adult, once my visual and auditory receptive language skills were developed enough to process information for meaning for some sustained time.

If someone has such an aversion to being taught such things through direct interaction, advertisement-length, video learning with the use of a home-movie camera, may be a way around this.

BUILDING UP TOLERANCE

Improving information processing so that personal significance triggers emotions more consistently, is one way of building up a tolerance. For me, I had to do this more mechanically than that. As an adult I did this by 'daring'. 'Daring' is about testing your limits in order to stretch them at your own pace and within your own control. Other people can't get you used to emotions by making you do things. All they get is emotional-detachment and compliance. Forcing people when they aren't ready cuts them off from their feelings so they don't get used to having them, even if they learn to do a lot of other functional things in the absence of emotion.

Trouble with emotions may co-exist with 'normal', even pleasurable sensory responses to some kinds of sensory stimulation (such as textures or sounds or patterns). This is not the same as the sort of affect that comes from something being personally (not just literally) meaningful or significant. Many people confuse the two and either can't reconcile one with the other and find the person disturbed, or figure the person doesn't have trouble with emotions at all.

Daring to feel or even explore affect cannot, in my experience, begin with sharing that affect. When someone has not even been able to stand sharing affect willingly with themselves, they will not be able to sustain this daring with someone else. That's like having a pair of shoes you've never tried on, giving them to someone else to wear and then trying them on for yourself. By this time, they are stretched and altered and not one's own at all. One is then trying on the other person's shoes.

This doesn't mean that someone else cannot help someone with emotional hypersensitivity by reassuring them that affect is emotions and that they are natural and can't hurt them. It just means that if you haven't learned to know, be familiar with, and accept something in yourself, it can be too invasive, bombarding and threatening to be expected to share with someone else what you have not yet experienced meaningfully as your own.

Especially with people who deal with emotional hypersensitivity or exposure anxiety, the best way to do such 'counselling' is in an indirectly-confrontational way. If the person with autism seems to like stories, 'write' (or make up) and read a story (or series of stories) about a boy/girl/

man/woman who had some very big feelings which made him/her feel very very out of control and scared (and describe these states and their internal feelings and external displays) and write about how he/she couldn't talk about these things because he/she didn't know what these feelings were or were called or what people did to make them less scary or annoying. You can use familiar characters that the person identifies with or likes. Whether it is Mickey Mouse, Thomas the Tank Engine or anyone else who is going through these things, it won't make too much difference. Some people may be able to sustain this sort of assistance through letters (particularly typing as this is to handwriting as formal detached speech is to informal subjective speech) though not face-to-face, and the giving of such a letter should, too, be indirectly confrontational. The point is to convey the understanding, capacity for trust and hope, and the knowledge and advice without overloading the person by being too personally direct.

If the person with autism doesn't like stories, you can 'talk to yourself' in a similar way, referring (out loud to yourself) to 'an unknown friend' who has these problems and merely allowing the person with autism to listen in, however peripherally this may be (and many will be unable to allow you, or even his/her self to notice he/she is actively or consciously listening).

Praise and acknowledgement, too, can be given in the same way – by writing it into a story about someone the person identifies with or even eventually writing it into a story about the person themselves (though perhaps still going through the motions of reading it as a book rather than telling it direct). Again, telling these things out loud to yourself as objectively as possible, referring to the person not (directly) using 'you' but indirectly and formally by name without seeking eye contact (the more formally, generally the easier to bear listening). Praise may also be able to be given by letter, especially typed letters, but remember that the giving too may have to be indirectly confrontational – a 'leaving' more than a giving.

Remember, as praise provokes feelings beyond one's own control, this forces conscious awareness to a level the person may not be able to bear emotionally. The response to these feelings in a person with extreme emotional hypersensitivity and exposure anxiety may be an extreme misfire, resulting in an unwanted and unintentional strong aversion or defensive response (even spitting, swearing, violence or further with-drawal) so praise has to be handled with care. Surely, even the person 'allergic' to praise may strongly crave the self-feedback and confirmation they cannot endure. The job of a carer or professional here is to redesign the ways you give praise, knowledge or understanding so these can be tolerated and then very gradually work from the indirectly confrontational to the directly confrontational over time as the person naturally breaks beyond the restrictive boundaries imposed by the unintentional and instinctual responses caused by emotional hypersensitivity and exposure anxiety.

When people reach the point where they are becoming acquainted with affect, support and encouragement can *very* gradually build to one way sharing. There is no point in imposing your emotions upon someone who has spent all their life closing them out. They will have no personal experience by which to make much sense of the meaning of your feelings, let alone their significance. When such a person gets to the point of being able to share their feelings, this will be part of their courtship with their own emotions.

When people get to this point, the only way to get people to 'dare' may be with calm, firm, non-bombarding, non-provoking, non-threatening, sometimes even detached and impersonal encouragement. For many people with these problems, however, having another person involved may be just more information causing overload. The only way around this may be to help or encourage in an 'indirectly'-confrontational way.

What this means is that if someone is overloaded because you look at them as you reassure them, look at the wall and give a general and impersonal reassurance about the topic rather than to the person. What being indirectly confrontational means is that, if the reassurance of directly and personally touching the person is too much and causes aversion, gradually getting physically nearer over time in a way that is not personal nor directly confrontational may be easier to tolerate. Allowing the side of a foot to touch the person whilst not showing intent may be all that that person can endure without aversion, but it is a start.

If they cannot stand being spoken to because it causes them affect, speaking out loud to yourself about the topic, rather than to the person, whilst not looking directly at them, may be indirect enough for them to stand. Again, it's a start.

If someone is so emotionally hypersensitive that they cannot stand the affect caused by the self-exposure of demonstrating an interest, then demonstrating things as if to the air may be indirectly confrontational enough for the person to dare sneaking a few glances. Over time, the person may build up a tolerance to this dared self-exposure and be able to watch something you do openly and directly.

What is important is to realise that the fear of affect that can develop from this type of emotional hypersensitivity can be so extreme that to demonstrate interest, appreciation or awareness may trigger an acute anxiety warning that affect may follow.

If even self-realisation there has been an interest, appreciation or awareness, triggers affect, this may run so deep as to freeze not just expression, but thought. Where this is the case, 'indirect interaction' and 'indirect communication' may be the best, even only, way to gradually build up these people's tolerance without forcing them into robotic or puppet-like compliance.

Exposure anxiety is something all people have at some level if pushed far enough. In some people, it takes a lot for this instinctual reponse to fire. In others it is triggered much too easily, making conscious awareness experienced as painful regardless of the emotion attached to it. The conditions of agoraphobia, exam anxiety, fear of public speaking, 'intense shyness' and compulsive hypersensitivity found in 'autism' is this state at its worst and for some, the only answer may be to indulge almost constantly in attempts to hypnotise oneself out of conscious awareness.

Exposure anxiety is not intentional and nor are its often reactive, avoidant or defensive and distancing results. It is an uncomfortable state for everyone, especially the person with this condition. It can make life itself feel like an infliction, a place of pins.

The result of exposure anxiety is an intense rawness that is easily mistaken for 'pain' and because the expression and interaction of others are often the cause of its provocation, intentionally or unintentionally, the result is the same; they cause the pain. It becomes easy to reject them as the mistrustful enemy who, regardless of good intentions, refuse to acknowledge this power they have and show no mercy in the apparent power they have to inflict discomfort. Some people with autism get past this 'war' and focus on the exposure anxiety itself as the enemy that robs them of a shared, freely expressed life with others, and some can make the transition from warring with the world of people to warring with their 'autism'. The role of the carer or professional is to use an indirectly-confrontational approach to gradually break down the basis of 'war' with the world of people and to assist them in making the transition to recognising that others didn't cause the problem and, as intensely uncomfortable as the sensation is, to work on a co-operative and creative programme to gradually and progressively build tolerance.

Some other forms of indirect interaction that can at least get people like this willingly attending to information, include impersonal and controllable sources of affect. Video learning is one such source. Video learning can be attended to without forcing acknowledgement of what is being learned in the way that interpersonal face-to-face learning does. Computer learning is similar and computers are one way in which interaction can be filtered *through* something else and, thereby, experienced as less impacting, less direct. Communicating through objects was something I wrote about earlier to help process information more easily and efficiently. It can also be beneficial with these people because it has a less direct impact.

All of these things can be good ways to teach the *topic* of emotions, what they are, how they feel, what they are called and why they are a good thing. I could attend to the cat being made to dance and what he was being made out to feel even if I couldn't have stood watching someone dancing and telling me what they are feeling.

MIRRORS

Relating via mirror reflections can also make interaction feel less direct for people who had developed some tolerance already. Reflection can seem like another world.

Mirrors may be a way in which people can experience each other without forcing acknowledgement of that interest. I remember watching the people at the bank this way in a way I could never have done at the time by looking directly with such intent and interest. This may also help lessen some of the intense emotional needs of parents to become personally familiar with who their emotionally evasive child is. Sometimes, these people are able to express far more on their own than when they are in company simply because the risk of affect is so much less when social interaction does not provoke acknowledgement, awareness or reflection upon what you are expressing.

CHAPTER 12

Problems of Control

Pink Street Light 'called'
and it tickled me.
It had my body in ecstasy.
It wound its way through my body and soul.
It blinded my mind,
I had no thoughts at all.
It triggered a switch
inside of my head
and nothing else mattered
but Pink Street Light, instead.

For some people, compulsions, obsessions or acute anxiety are psychological or physiologically-based states that are unconnected to cognitive problems of making connections. I won't be discussing the problems of these people.

In other people, compulsions or obsessions may actually not be outstanding responses at all, but merely stand out by contrast with all the other actions and activities that are not repeated again and again. These sort of compulsions or obsessions may come about because connection at a deep level is a rare experience.

When these people make such a connection, it may sometimes be repeated and repeated as the only sense or source of *controllable* affect, in a world that seems devoid of it. It may even happen that, just as non-autistic people use information they already have to make sense of new information, further connections for people with compulsions or obsessions of this sort may be filtered through these first 'significant' connections and they may then filter out anything that can't be made sense of in relation to these things. This is what I will be discussing in this chapter.

Obsession or compulsion may arise because of problems of connection and the effect these have on processing for significance.

If you have problems of connection, sometimes very little may be sufficiently processed for meaning for it to be possible to process it further for significance. When so little is experienced as significant, then it is that SIGNIFICANCE that may be the basis of obsession or compulsion in some people. In other words, it may be a case of what slipped through the net.

It may be that these people merely appear obsessional or compulsive because so little does get processed for meaning and then, more deeply, for significance, that all of their affect comes to be poured out on the few things which *did* hold significance for them. In this case, the problem is not that they are obsessional or compulsive but that they have an information processing problem so that, whilst processing is efficient enough to allow limited and sporadic experiences of significance, it is not efficient enough to allow constant processing for significance.

Where emotionally-hypersensitive responses to those things that *are* significant are causing a problem in teaching or interaction, I don't think the solution lies in taking away the only things which feel significant to these people. Instead, it may be possible to USE THESE THINGS AS BRIDGES for attending to and making connections regarding new information that does not get through with significance.

This technique is what I, and some other people with 'autism' call 'bridging' or 'building bridges'. Bridging is about taking an 'interest' and expanding it. If someone loves the ocean, you can get posters, books, cards and pictures related to it and things from the ocean. You can make a brief home video-documentary slowly and concisely talking about the ocean and what sort of creatures live in it and how the water tastes and so forth. The same sort of thing could be done about rain, animals, puddles, flowers, nature, going to the toilet, having a bath, getting dressed, getting breakfast…just about anything. It is important, in my view, to speak slowly and clearly and simply, without intonation (which can distract a mono person from the meaning of words themselves). Keep gestures and facial expression simple and undistracting. Use no unnecessary or unrelated background noises and keep the scene uncluttered and orderly.

Any and all collections can be expanded on. If this is done in front of the person or too many changes are made too soon, this could feel invasive and even cause them to reject their collections (which could otherwise be great sources of bridging to other skills). Silently and privately leaving things you have observed someone to like may be a way of expanding on their tendency to collect things in a way which may feel less invasive or personally exposing.

If the person seems to like fish, pictures of fish and toy fish and scale-like fabrics and patterns can be collected. Eventually, these could be made into a collage or used for a project. You could see if you can borrow picture story books with categories of fish or trees or whatever the category is (age is not relevant here). There are poster charts with all the types of trees and fish and other things. Stamps with these things can be collected and swapped as can swap cards with fish or trees or whatever on them. If the person goes to a mainstream school this may give them 'interests' to share and a basis for, albeit limited, conversation.

Trees can gradually expand later into forests. Fish can expand into oceans and rivers. Both can expand into geography (I studied atlases for the distribution of such things across the world). There are nursery rhymes and songs and poems and stories about fish and trees. Borrow some tapes from the library if possible. When and if the person uses song as speech, it can be responded to at first as song but after some time it can be used to expand into speech (about fish or trees or whatever).

An interest in noses or ears can be built upon by making clay or fabric replicas, collecting plastic ones from button shops or novelty shops, by making a project about types of noses, races of people, the role of noses, types of handkerchiefs, noses on masks and so on).

An interest in combs can be worth encouraging because it can be something others could be involved in. Combs can be swapped as a basis for learning to swap other things. Combs can also be used to make noises (as fingers or teeth are run along them) and this can be expanded into zithers or other related home-made musical instruments. Collections can be expanded upon, ordered for size, colour, pattern etc. These are skills which can transfer to other interests. They begin narrow but can expand. Combs can lead to fences or ladders.

You have to understand the basis for the 'interest' and build on it. This could help show the person is understood and accepted and that if they can't meet you, then you are willing and interested to meet them.

One of the benefits of tolerance of so called 'bizarre' behaviour is the expansion of repertoires – sometimes in very constructive ways. My interest in fabrics was expanded into collection and then crafts and sewing and I later became a machinist. My thing for tidying and ordering was channelled into housework tasks (like sorting the pantry shelves and the laundry, for example) and I later became a cleaner and worked in a storeroom. My narrow repetitive interest for rhythms and patterns have become music and art.

If the person's interests are sound-oriented, where the pitch is constant or monotonous, consider introducing wooden or metallic percussion instruments, many of which can be made from household objects.

If a person likes textures, you could get books of wallpaper samples, carpet samples, vinyl samples, tile samples, fabric samples and so on. If they took to these, later you could give them a model of a house they could experiment with (this is another thing my mother did…and I spent time changing the wallpaper and carpet in the toy house. Now I do this with my own house. These are SKILLS, skills built upon so called 'bizarre' obsessions and interests).

Shoeboxes or icecream buckets can be collected to house various collections. The person may grow up to work in a warehouse or store room. I was able to work in a storeroom because of my obsessions about order.

If someone seems to find ladders significant, incorporate them into as many activities as possible. You can use them to lead up to a bed bunk to go to sleep or even design a bed that is surrounded with ladders. You can make ladders on a plate of food using carrot or celery sticks or asparagus, out of mashed potatoes and peas or out of grated carrot or grated cheese. You can paint or draw ladders that lead to charts that need to be paid attention to and even step by step charts can be drawn up as ladders. You can make cardboard ladders and tape them down to make tracks between rooms where things like teeth-brushing (or other avoidables) get done. You can make string ladders and lay them out on the ground from the house door to the car door to get people where they have to be with less force.

If there is a compulsion to spin, spin everything you want attention to be paid to. If spinning things makes them user-friendly, you can spin the jumper that's got to be worn, the shoes that have got to be put on, even the chewy old chop on your plate that has to be eaten or the toothbrush that's got to brush your teeth.

If someone has a compulsion to tear paper, collect all your recycled paper and put them to work. A bucket full of shredded paper can be then soaked in water and put into a brick-making mould, turned out, dried and then burned in place of logs. The shredded and soaked paper can also be finely mulched and scooped up with a screen before being turned out, pressed and dried as recycled paper and cardboard. Shredded paper can also be used for animal bedding and put into garden compost to help aerate the soil.

A compulsion to press buttons can be gradually turned into using a cash register, operating an elevator or using a keyboard – all of which can lead to employment. A compulsion to line things up, categorise and order things, can gradually be turned into housework, filing or library skills. A compulsion to roll things down stairs can be gradually turned into bowling.

The more you use compulsions or obsessions as bridges, the more you diffuse extreme emotional attachment to one particular ladder or spinning one particular type of thing. It may be more advantageous to meet and share with these 'autistic' people on territory that does make sense to them, than to take away the only things that do hold significance for them in favour of compliance. Some carers and professionals really need to ask themselves whether they might not be able to have a little more tolerance of eccentricity than they already have, not just regarding the 'autistic' people in their care, but in themselves as well.

The other alternative to using obsession or compulsion as motivational forces is to address, as already previously discussed, the underlying cause of these problems of control: information overload. In particular, where compulsions are instinctual, involuntary, attempts to correct information-processing or accessing-related problems, then addressing information overload may be the most effective way of decreasing these compulsive behaviours.

CHAPTER 13

Communication

My other books have brought me into contact with a wide range of people with 'autism' of varying 'levels of functioning' from all around the world, and I have come to see that this group share more in common, in terms of the mechanisms of adaptations to their 'autism', than in terms of the FORMS those adaptations take. So much of what is assumed and misassumed about 'autism' is based on those forms: on what 'appears' rather than what 'is'. 'Autism' can affect all systems of functioning; recognition and comprehension on every sensory level including proprioperception, relationship between body parts, sense of self, sense of other, cognitive visualisation, sequencing, categorisation, synthesis, analysis and retrieval skills relating to information on all levels (sensory, emotional, mental, proprioperception, social-interactive) and the integration of those systems.

All individuals with 'autism', if not countered at every turn, may be capable of finding (consciously or subconsciously) their own adaptations to their condition. That is, they will find their own way of managing the relationship or non-relationship between their various systems and how they operate in interaction with 'the world'.

This means that, for example, someone whose systems are not sufficiently integrated, may ignore all emotional signals, but be able to accumulate and process factual information in an unemotive, purely logical way.

It may mean that auditory processing is 'switched off' whilst visual or tactile processing is 'switched on'. It may mean that auditory comprehension is 'switched on' but the processing of all 'body messages' (such as need to use the toilet, hunger, cold etc.) are put 'on hold'. It may mean that someone who is with difficulty holding awareness of two things at the same time, such as internal and external, may switch awareness to one or the other but be unable to make sense of both at the same time, or interact at a functional level when required by the environment to use both internal and external awareness at the one time.

These different combinations of 'systems forfeiting' are almost infinitely variable but help minimise 'overload' (and its behavioural consequences). They may be almost unimaginable to people without 'autism' in whom systems of functioning have a reasonable degree of working integration. This inability, on the part of some people to imagine (and thereby plan out how to work successfully with) this manageable ('autistic') state of disarray, can lead to (among many other things) two unfortunate circumstances.

(1) The use of inappropriate (sometimes self-justifying) testing techniques that are sometimes based on misinformed premises and faulty assumptions.

(2) Misinformed assumptions (and proclamations) of how things work or don't work that can sometimes undermine the credibility of claims of capability on the part of some people with 'autism'.

People with 'autism' are generally pushed and pulled in all directions by people who don't have 'autism', whose systems of functioning are reasonably integrated and who, therefore, make sense of interaction, environment, sensory stimuli, emotions, body messages, and make mental connections and so on, in the 'usual', non-autistic way. When people without 'autism' assume that people with the condition are merely 'slow' or 'broken' versions of themselves, they may not only insult, but in addition confuse and frustrate the person with 'autism' with behaviour that naturally stems from such arrogant and ignorant assumptions.

The person with 'autism', in my view, may learn that the ways of people who don't have their condition do not work for them. What is more, I feel some learn pretty quickly that when they attempt to manage or sort out (and, inevitably, react to and be frustrated by) their own systems' chaos, people without 'autism' will generally treat their attempts as a 'problem' and will interfere like dentists working with garden tools. One result of this may be that, often being highly sensing, people with 'autism' generally learn to 'smell out' the dentists who come along with garden tools and arrogant assumptions. An inability to read body language or intonation or even auditory comprehension is not necessary to 'sensing' when a 'brick wall' is approaching you. Many animals have this sensing and it doesn't require mental telepathy nor complex conscious processing.

Prompting

Though prompting may look like control, there is a definite distinction in practice when it comes to getting a valid or sensical response.

Though I can speak exceptionally well on many logical, intellectual, concrete topics (that may require categorisation, systematisation but not visualisation), when it comes to social language or personal-emotional expression. I can sometimes have great difficultly. The production of nonsense when there was previously sense is something I have experienced under frustration. Here is a recent example.

After making a whole string of provoking statements, I was asked what it was that I wanted. I had been wanting something for many weeks but was unable to organise how to have this want fulfilled (which, unless having observed someone else get the same thing, requires a complex process of expressing it 'in the real world' out loud and getting someone to help me plan the steps to follow it through and then having them prompt the action to follow the steps).

At the prompt of 'what is it that you want?', my first answer was 'I don't know' (though I did know but couldn't connect and access). My mind ran amok with stored evasive responses. I had wanted to say 'a pottery wheel'. The stored picture that jumped into my head came, first, from a category of 'things we couldn't have'. Instead of saying 'pottery wheel', I blurted 'cat'. When that response was checked, I again wished to say 'pottery wheel' but the stored picture that jumped into my head (which I compulsively named) came from a category of 'things we already had in our house' and I said 'ironing board'. There was no way that I wanted an ironing board nor a cat (which we couldn't yet take care of). I had been preparing a pottery shed for the past weeks and was thinking of a pottery wheel but was totally unable to organise fulfilling or even expressing the want without being prompted or triggered to do so.

My husband is a person with 'autism'. His prompting was not a matter of control, nor did he give me a selection of 'his' tracks to follow (though sometimes that is required when I cannot come up with a selection of 'potential responses' by which to get closer to expressing the one I meant).

Self–Other Problems

One of the problems that can arise from a lack of systems integration is an inability to hold awareness of two tracks at the same time, which I call being 'mono'.

On a simple level, this sort of 'mono' can mean that one can process a sentence about 'what John did' as long as John remains the central or only subject. When one of the things that John did was to meet the dog who did X, Y and Z, cognitively, either the part about the dog doesn't get processed or the part about the dog gets processed and the part about John may get aborted as useless information. 'Mono' happens on every information level.

Another expression of 'mono', on a more complex level, is the inability to monitor consecutively a sense of 'self' and sense of 'other' (internal–external) at the same time. I call this the 'self–other system'.

Whilst there are many versions of this 'difficulty', what it means, essentially, is that there is 'awareness' of either only 'self' without a sense of 'other' or the other way around; a conscious sense of 'other' with no conscious sense of 'self' (or a fluctuation between the two or, in some cases, a shutdown or forfeiting of the entire system with no awareness of either).

Techniques and therapies used with people with 'autism', unfortunately, may take no account of the adaptations the person with 'autism' may have worked out regarding sense of 'self' and 'other' (internal–external). Here are some examples or one or more possible types that a person may have:

(1) One version of a self–other problem may be to be *consciously aware of and voluntarily responsive to external 'other'* (the other person, one's own hands, objects around oneself) *but be only unconsciously aware and only automatically responsive regarding what one is expressing* ('self'). In this version, what one 'wants' to express may be difficult, if not impossible, to retrieve voluntarily upon request (as required, for example, in a test situation), though it may (like dreams) be prompted or triggered by someone outside of oneself. This would be comparable to something like post-hypnotic suggestion being able to trigger the recall of subconsciously-processed information that the conscious mind may be unaware of having.

(2) The opposite case is where one may be *consciously aware and voluntarily responsive regarding (internal) 'self'* but *have no conscious awareness of (external) 'other'* (including one's own hands or body). In this case, the initial prompting of touch might sometimes be able to bring someone's body-connectedness 'on-line' enough for them sometimes to connect with their body to communicate

this awareness. Getting someone to connect with their hand to express something through typing, whilst still maintaining connection with 'self', may, however, require less 'mechanics' and be more manageable than getting them to connect with the larger range of mechanics involved in verbal speech (which involve the co-ordinated and constantly varying connections and modulation in the use of one's mouth, tongue, lungs and voice box). One is a one-ring circus, the other a four-ring circus.

In the case where someone has only conscious awareness and voluntary responsiveness regarding 'self' and no awareness or responsiveness to 'other', what they express may be more likely to be more idiosyncratic and less accommodating (or not accommodating at all) of someone else's attempts to guide monologue into dialogue.

(3) Not all people with 'autism' have developed the technique of simultaneously maintaining conscious/voluntary and subconscious/automatic to get around self–other difficulties. Such a person, in practice, may have *only subconscious awareness and automatic responsiveness of 'self'*.

In a relaxed flexible situation, such a person may be able to express fluently but be unable to know whether he or she is making sense. Pushing such a person to become consciously aware of their actions (i.e. through praising, touching or making them pay attention to what they are doing) may freeze up expression as it shifts from a subconscious to a conscious level. This is particularly relevant to testing techniques and forms of directly-confrontational interaction which may wrongly assume this form of expression to be consciously controllable, and use testing techniques or a too-direct approach that may effectively extinguish the ability to communicate.

(4) In the opposite case, a person may have *conscious awareness only of (internal) 'self' and no awareness, subconscious or otherwise, of 'other'*. Such a person may be as intelligent as anyone regardless of a mountain of labels but be unable, no matter how much physical guidance or prompting they have, to connect with a means of expression to demonstrate any expressively-trapped awareness of 'self'. In such a case, someone assisting the person with 'autism' might only be able to be ultra-attentive to the barest (if

any) impulse from the person and have to guess the rest, stopping at intervals to attempt to detect any counter impulse.

(5) Where someone is *subconsciously aware and automatically responsive to (external) 'other' but has no connection with 'self'*, this person may be very vulnerable to the manipulation of others. Such a person might be like a puppet.

(6) Where someone is *consciously aware and voluntarily responsive of 'other' but has no connection to 'self'*, this person may be robotically compliant and equally vulnerable to the manipulation of others.

Where someone's adaptation to self–other 'difficulties' is to fluctuate between several of the above combinations, there is bound to be a dramatic shift in the nature (and quantity) of expression. As different situations cause information overload of different sorts and to different degrees (including the provocation of even 'good' emotions, for example) then someone who shifted between one of these adaptations and the next might be found to be distinctly different in different sorts of company, in different environments and when confronted with different types of processing and communication demands.

These fluctuations are also very difficult to cater for in terms of test designs (based on a non-autistic, integrated, non-mono, perceptual, cognitive, emotional, linguistic and social reality). Crude testing based on assumptions of a hidden lesser-developed, non-autistic, reality within 'autistic' people produce, in my view, no more valid results than some of the archaic and culturally-biased intelligence tests of once upon a time. Those seeking to test people with 'autism' might begin by daring to imagine that these people may not be lesser-developed versions of non-autistic people but, rather, people who HAVE developed, sometimes substantially, along a very different track from non-autistic people. Looking at how 'autistic' people measure up to non-autistic people according to a non-autistic developmental path tells the researcher nothing about how far the same person may have developed a whole range of adaptations, compensations and strategies along an 'autistic' track.

Measuring non-autistic people by this type of development would often find them failing miserably and appearing to be thoroughly 'subnormal' by 'autistic' standards.

Having a 'dysfunctional' or 'abnormal' brain organisation does not dictate the level of one's intelligence. Nor does it even dictate the level of one's functioning, as functioning is subject to a wide selection of adaptations and shifts. That people without 'autism', with integrated systems, need to learn consciously how to read and write or play music, do mathematics, design, paint and so on, does not mean that people with autism, with poorly integrated systems, cannot learn subconsciously and have this subconscious learning triggered under the right conditions – conditions requiring fewer connections and less direct interaction (such as writing).

That the person with autism may be able to absorb subliminally, process unconsciously and use senses peripherally does not mean that they will therefore use what they 'know', for one can have much subconscious knowledge without consciously knowing one has it.

Some people with 'autism', who have been assisted in their communication via verbal or physical prompts or the learned expectations of others, have sometimes expressed things that others have found distasteful or disturbing. At this point, fingers sometimes get pointed and one of the first places these fingers point is towards the person assisting the person with 'autism' to communicate. Rather than saying that the person with 'autism' misled, lied or fantasised, it is generally assumed, instead, that the person with 'autism' was manipulated in their communication or even incapable of it in the first place. One of the reasons that the finger is least likely to point at the person with 'autism' is because the same stereotypes which often portray them as incapable of communication, also portray them as incapable of imagination, deceit, the capacity to reflect expectations back at someone, or even (in some cases where mental illness co-exists with 'autism') delusion.

Assisting 'autistic' people in expression may produce fact or fantasy. Though many people with 'autism' may not be consciously capable of fantasy, lies, or reflecting someone's expectations back at them, the subconscious mind may still be capable of these things and communication is not always the expression of a conscious mind. Some facts or fantasies may tread on the toes of other people's morality, ego, power and theories. Despite the stereotypes, some people with autism can fantasise, mislead, evade or even lie but it is also the case that most of the people with 'autism' I have encountered deal in facts which are generally more concrete, observable, tangible and reliable to work with cognitively than something as evasive and difficult to monitor as fantasy or lies.

In communicating, particularly if it is on a subconscious level, people with 'autism' may be more likely to be more graphic and detached in what they express than someone without 'autism'. Just because someone else finds something distasteful, disturbing or even false, doesn't mean that the person who expressed such a thing should be denied assistance in their communication if this assistance is the key to their ability to communicate.

Non-Verbal?

People seem to make a big deal about the distinction between verbal and so call 'non-verbal' people with autism.

I've heard so called 'non-verbal' people speak in audible autie-speak that's generally incomprehensible to non-autistic others. I've heard others speak out loud but only to themselves and heard others speak in such a quiet whisper or mumble that they are generally inaudible or incomprehensible. A 'non-verbal' friend said the phrase 'I like it' (whilst releasing cut grass in the wind) at such an exaggerated slowed down pace that the sounds would have been generally unrecognisable as words or a phrase except to someone else who had done the same in playing with words. I heard another 'non-verbal' person speak at such a sped up pace that their words were an incomprehensible jumble. I have heard 'non-verbal' people speaking only when alone in their own room. I have known of 'non-verbal' people who have written about speaking in thought without using their mouths to make that think-speak audible to others and have heard others singing phrases to themselves without socially directing these phrases to make it directly known these are responses. There are so called 'non-verbal' people who speak in some environments but never in others.

So what is this term 'non-verbal'? All these so called 'non-verbal' people speak so differently and when they are all labelled 'non-verbal' it tells nothing of what is going on for any particular person, what systems are on-line and what systems are off-line and why.

If someone has functional speech but no personally expressive verbal speech, or speaks only to themselves or to their reflection or when alone or only in certain environments, might this not say something of that person's feelings about sharing themself with others, or about the relative impact of information overload in different environments and might that not say something about the sort of real help needed?

If someone speaks so quickly or quietly or with such poor pronunciation or goes on and on or is repetitive or seemingly nonsensical and unaware of what they are saying, might this potentially not have as much to say about emotional hypersensitivity as about difficulty with simultaneously accessing and monitoring the production and feedback of one's speech? In such cases, what is the role (or the point) of traditional speech therapy?

I have been around so called 'verbal' people with autism and I've heard people talk in a functional way but not a personal one. I've heard people talk in monologue in front of others without juggling social dialogue. I've heard people talk using stored language that involves no self-exposure and no provocation of emotion. I've heard people talk to themselves without apparent relevance as to who their talking is for. If the others are called 'non-verbal' then what are these people – 'seemingly verbal'?

I have had letters from speech therapists asking for advice in working with people with autism. Some of the things which may be needed might include teaching people to take action to identify, indicate and reduce information overload in their environment, including emotion-related overload, in order to improve their processing, accessing and monitoring, or their own speech-related mechanics. What might be needed may be to restore trust in the ability to comprehend the emotions provoked in social interaction and to establish trust in them and trust in the right and means to control their intensity. What might be needed may be the reduction of nutrition related problems that slow down information processing and unnecessarily compound information overload, resulting in limited or inflexible use of language and limited invitation to others to further contribute to information overload through verbal interaction.

Speech therapists are often dedicated people and it may be that some of them can combine dedication with the daring and imagination to tackle things in a way that few autism professionals are yet trained to do, for the simple reason that many may not yet have been able to see beyond non-autistic theories and the artificial categorisation these theories created.

CHAPTER 14

Sleepwalkers–Sleeptalkers and 'Savant Skills'

Tell me of language,
I who cannot see your words
nor hold developed thought
with conscious awareness.

Tell me of language,
I who cannot experience the creation,
only the product.

Words on the wind, words on the wind
Like falling birds they fall
From a sky that does not exist
With a thud that is not even heard.

For some people, ongoing conscious awareness is a luxury that overload cannot afford. Yet subconscious processing, accessing and monitoring may still continue, sometimes well outside of the context in which the information or initial motivation to respond would otherwise have occurred.

A person can react tomorrow to the unprocessed emotions of today's events or those of the whole week. A person can have prompted or triggered recall of entire passages of writing in a book that was read without awareness last year. They can have prompted or triggered recollection of a formula or statement heard in a class, seen on TV, or seen in an advertisement and yet be unable to recall its context, significance or implications at the time.

When someone else would (usually incidentally) prompt an automatic and subconscious response from me, I was often surprised to find myself blurting out understanding and knowledge and quotations that I didn't even know I'd acquired. Sometimes it would be a visual memory of a page I'd read or an audio memory of a series of phrases I'd heard which would automatically get blurted when triggered.

Not everyone can cater for someone who functions predominantly in a triggerable state of subconscious 'autopilot'. Conscious awareness and conscious capacity to voluntarily access what one knows, thinks or feels, is often assumed by those to whom such things come as easily as breathing.

In response to someone who expects conscious voluntary accessing, rather than triggered responsiveness, a person who relies on triggered responsiveness might express nothing, or might express something that appears entirely off track, purely because some situational trigger caused a response. Triggered subconscious responses don't go by the same rules as conscious conversation but that doesn't mean they are any less valid as a form of self-expression.

Triggering

When people are communicating on a subconscious and automatic basis, if they are responded to, not with prompts but with comments, exclamation or praise, it may jolt them into a shift to conscious awareness and result in the loss of their links to subconscious automatic expression. Equally, comments, exclamations or triggers can, unintentionally, serve as triggers for an entirely different and unrelated track of subconscious, automatic expression.

In a triggerable state, a comment may not be a comment, but a situational reminder of a key element in a triggerable serial memory that comes out verbally or through typing. An exclamation may not be an exclamation, but be a pitch-related trigger that happened to provoke the expressed recollection of a door bell someone once had. Praise may not be praise but a trigger of an emotion that is linked in serial memory to events that have nothing to do with the other person's intended track. All are still expression, even if they are not conversation and it is expression, not necessarily conversation, that is important.

Just because expression is subconscious and triggered does not mean that what is communicated is not real or factual or the result of the autistic person's understanding or feelings. The only valid question may be whether the self-expression was intentional. All I know of myself is through experiencing my unintentional self-expression. Subconscious automatic expression is my walking frame. Would it be right to take this from me because I lacked conscious intention or used subconscious triggered response in place of conscious social communication?

Arguments about intentionality have their place with regards to the unintentional mirrored expression of others, or the mindless meeting of their expectations or assumptions. I accept and celebrate my automatic and involuntary self-expression, as long as it isn't the mirrored expression of others or the mindless meeting of their expectations or assumptions, and yet it has taken me most of my life to weed out one from its entanglement with the other. It is for non-autistic people to tell the difference between these two things, and to acknowledge that both may co-exist.

Sides

Before I was three, all that I knew as my sense of self was a sensual side that thought nothing because I was so robbed of conscious processing that, as far as I knew, there was nothing to question nor think about. This was the side of me that consciously perceived without interpretation or significance.

It was this side of me that, robbed of meaning and significance, could hardly feel the emotion that comes with realisation and yet I was showered with out of context, unprocessed emotion that belonged to information that was processed beyond my conscious awareness, and beyond my ability to access voluntarily the unknown knowing that was within me.

It was this side of me that felt part of the things around me, not with them, but *as* them. In sensing them, yet sensing them without the selfhood of interpretation, significance and realisation, I became 'one' with the things I sensed. I sensed pattern and form, colour and texture, variation and contrast, category and similarity. I sensed the pace and style of movements and tones of voice and knew fluffy-edged people from sharp or hard-edged ones, brittle or scratchy ones.

Another side to me was a logical side, a hidden side. This was the part of me that had stored and recorded everything peripherally – personally detached, objective and purposeful. This part of me asserted itself like a sleepwalker–sleeptalker, like the person who responds in an accident with strength they didn't know they had, except my sleepwalker–sleeptalker came more and more often and stayed for longer.

Another side to me was an involuntarily reactive side. This was a side that would lash out involuntarily, slapping, biting, scratching and punch-ing at what confined my soul – the flesh that enclosed me that had been perceived by my brain as external, foreign and part of a world that, in a state of overload, needed to be distanced, but wouldn't leave. This side of me clapped when a system of functioning needed switching to tackle information elsewhere. It held my breath in an instinctive attempt to keep everything 'out there' and maintain control in a state of instinctual alarm where it perceived there to be no self-control. It drove my body to weave from side to side in an instinctive attempt to correct some inner balance and flow that was out of sync.

The inability to get consistent meaning through any of my senses in an environment that demanded that I did, meant I developed another side; a side with an acute ability to respond, not to meaning, but to patterns.

It was through rote learning, stored rules and stored definitions, through mirroring the words and actions of those around me and storing theoretical knowledge about what 'a person' is meant to 'like', 'want', 'think', 'believe' and 'be interested in' and how 'a person' is meant to respond, that this side evolved a mechanically constructed patchwork façade in place of an expressed and social identity.

It didn't matter that personhood was meant to be more than a bundle of stored regurgitable information, mimicry and mindless compliance. For a long time, as far as I knew, this may as well have been my personhood. I had virtually no socially-shared nor consciously, intentionally expressed, personhood beyond this performance of a non-autistic 'normality' with which I had neither comprehension, connection, nor identification.

This disconnected constructed façade was accepted by the world around me when my true and connected self was not. Each spoonful of its acceptance was a shovel full of dirt on the coffin in which my real self was being buried alive, and without hope of ever living, expressed, in the world, beyond the sensual being that I was; one with little ability to process information in the context it happened in, one with little ability to access consciously and voluntarily the capacity to express myself fluently and comprehensibly as myself, one with little ability to monitor my own actions and expression in order to be assumed a responsible, rational and equal being as myself.

That logical part of me kept the video going, recording that battle, but I wasn't allowed into the projection room. That part of me was beyond the iron curtain of my conscious awareness and intangible, yet more and more it left its tracks. By the time I was eleven, I knew that linking with that part of me would be the key to being able to live functionally as myself and not just spend the rest of my life as a patchwork façade made from foreign fabric labelled 'acting normal'.

Typed Words

When I was ten, I could hear sentences just fine, even repeat them back as I'd heard them, but I could only process a few disjointed words in each sentence. Words were cues for my monologues and not part of dialogue.

I could not read consistently with meaning. No images happened in my mind. I could read the sentences, but my conscious mind generally did nothing with them beyond being cued onto other tracks by the occasional processed word here and there and finding myself stuck on those few words I'd never seen before. Around this time, I began, not to read, but to digest dictionaries, street directories and telephone books. It was as though something within me, in spite of a lack of conscious interest, had a huge appetite for information, category, order and structure.

When I was ten, a typewriter was left in my room. I smelled it, licked it and tapped at the buttons. I felt its texture and the sound it made when touched, its shiny surfaces and its rough ones. I explored its mechanisms and its systems, fragment by fragment. I typed onto the roller, strings of letters and then patterns of letters. The roller became indented and covered with overlays of letters. I worked out how to put paper into it and typed strings of letters and then patterns of letters. I typed words onto the page, strings of words that had good visual patterns, words that had felt good in my mouth, words that had sounded good to my ears.

By the time I was eleven, I had typed lists of words running down the page and the words jumped back at me with imagery and feel to them in a way written words that had come from other people, never had. These had come from my own context from somewhere within me, beyond my conscious mind. The typed lists had pattern to them. The words written had a relationship between them. There was an inherent humour in some of the lists as the words shifted from one to the next. There was hurt and anger and beauty in those lists. There was an understanding of categories: things in nature, animals, feelings, describing words, advertised products.

By the time I was twelve, those lists had begun to look like poems. By thirteen, those poems were waterfalls falling out of my fingers.

The first I ever knew of the thoughts or feelings that came out of those poems was in reading them off the page. My feelings were 'fear' because I didn't know where these were coming from. I hadn't experienced the thoughts and wasn't aware of the feelings. I couldn't conceive of the personhood on these pages as having come from me even though it was the first reading ever to be consistently comprehensible and cause me affect and empathy.

I felt 'shame', because now surely my mother was right, and I was truly possessed, like a shell into which some other soul had jumped like a opportunistic spiritual leech that would cash in on my trappedness and the void that was my expressive self beyond the 'acting normal' façade that others chose to think was 'me'.

I felt 'in company', as though sharing with an invisible comrade who had trusted me with these rich things, this rare experience of 'other' in a state of wholeness, so rare in a lifetime of the fragmentation, meaningless-ness and insignificance I had found in the company of others.

I felt 'chosen', maybe even honoured, that I *was* worthy of the trust of this invisible yet comprehensible other who, like no-one else, could reach me. It would be more than another decade before I'd realise that this spirit that had communicated back to me through writing had been my own expressively-crippled soul.

Music

Growing up, I had always had a memory for long strings of patterns; patterns of movements and patterns of sounds. TV advertisements and jingles were unintentionally mentally recorded and triggered by other people who said a words or used a pitch or moved a body part that made a match with a key fragment of some stored string. Even the sounds of objects could set these off. Sometimes they fired mentally in an involun-tary replay that I had not consciously nor voluntarily accessed. Sometimes they blurted out in words or actions.

From the time I was small, something else had happened. As I had mental replays of music, my fingers would dance to them. As pitch climbed, my fingers danced one way in larger or smaller jumps. As pitch lowered, my fingers danced in the other direction.

By the time I was thirteen, my head was not just filled with mental replays of heard jingles and tunes, but with unintentional compositions, first simple, then progressively more complex. I, however, did not feel like their composer, for they composed themselves of a volition I was unaware of, according to feelings I was disconnected from and expressing with a depth that I knew myself incapable of. As far as I experienced these things, I was in the position of someone observing a dream happening, only the dream was mine and my mind was both outside of it and in it, conscious and subconscious.

When I was fourteen, my mother rented a piano. It was not for me and I was not forced to play it, even though I was not stopped from exploring it any more than I was stopped from exploring anything else in the house. There was not a corner or cupboard or drawer or box nor the contents of any of these things that I hadn't acquainted myself with and the piano was just one more.

I had sneaked peeks at the piano and hit one note here and another note there. I was left in the room with it and I played the range of its notes. Just like my fingers had danced one direction as pitch rose and danced in the other direction as pitch fell, the piano did this too. I had hands and it was gloves. I put my hands on its keys. A composition created itself in my head. My fingers danced along the keys. The sound coming back was coherent and whole and beautiful.

I had been heard by someone else in the house. I was made joltingly aware of what had come out of me; aware at a time before even I had had much time to know how I thought or felt about what had come out. I decided that expression through music was too threatening and didn't play again for five years.

When I was nineteen I got my own piano. Classical music poured out of me; music that spoke the force and variation of wind and rain, sunshine through clouds, stars, the contrast and magic of dusk and dawn and flying.

Some of this musical capacity may well have been influenced by early daily exposure to classical music (ballet suites) and though no conscious processing or thought was happening about these musical experiences, they had a definite effect on me emotionally (along with the non-classical music my parents had such as Bill Haley and The Comets, Little Richard, and Elvis). Some created definite feelings of aloneness, some made me wild and manic, some made me cheerful, some felt 'beautiful'. Regardless though, without having conscious awareness, others were not invited to meet me in music in any directly confrontational or personal way, for to have done so was to jolt the exposure anxiety that came with knocking on the door of conscious awareness. Nevertheless, even on a preconscious level, and perhaps particularly because it was unprocessed, I must have mapped out music patterns and structures at a very high level (I was also around many statues and have found the same 'savant' skill in sculpting and carving).

Tunes poured out reminiscent of sit-coms and jingles, blues and jazz. What was poetry now poured forth as lyrics; the words angry and sad, alone and celebrational; songs about stray cats, if I had a wish, beyond the when beyond the where, about blue eyes looking nowhere, shoes going to Berlin, next time around, don't know who's me and nobody nowhere. The lyrics spoke my life and the music spoke my emotions. And I shared none of them with anyone.

When I was twenty-two I let someone else hear them. Though I still lived as a façade that spoke and moved according to stored patterns of movements and postures, stored intonation and phrases that had sprung from other people's expression and not mine, in music, poetry and lyrics, I was free to experience the thoughts and feelings that I still couldn't consciously and voluntarily access.

Art

As a child, I had drawn the same picture over and over again. It was a ballerina on a stage dressed in a tutu. I drew that picture from the age of four to the age of ten and the picture never changed.

It was very clear to me that that was what I wanted to be because my mother had said so. I had heard her more times than I could count telling people, 'Donna wants to be a ballerina'. I'd be brought out and made to do the arabesque I'd been positioned into so many times and the splits I'd been put into daily as a child. I'd smile the plastic stored smile I'd been postured into in front of the mirror and hold my ballet fingers in exactly the positions they'd been put into. I'd pull my bum under and my shoulders back and my chin up to where they'd so often been put and I'd perform my well trained party tricks on cue so that my mother's ego could swell and I'd be told, yet again, how lucky I am.

That was me, dressed in a tutu and sent out to play. Retards don't wear tutus I suppose or maybe they just look more attractive when they do. Little girls who get taken to the ballet are lucky and it doesn't matter if they don't know what they are there to see, nor what, if anything, they feel about it. And there were the pictures, drawn again and again. The girl in the tutu on the stage and the word, ballet; a solitary word I could write before any other, at the age of four.

By the age of ten, I'd stopped doing ballet. Something had begun to develop in me that put up a barrier to my mindless compliance. Whatever that something was, it didn't want to go to ballet lessons, it didn't want to be a ballerina and it didn't draw ballerinas.

Given that my repetitive picture had been the limit of my artwork up until then, no-one expected much of me in the way of art. When I was ten, however, I drew something different. I drew cows. I drew Freisian cows and Jersey cows and Guernsey cows. All the cows faced in the same direction; always facing to the left. That was the only cow I could draw;

a cow facing left and cows were the only thing I'd been motivated and free enough to draw. Soon after cows, I began to draw cats and then birds and then dogs. Then came something quite different again.

By the time I was twelve, I'd begun to draw things that I didn't set out to draw. They just came out. I drew sparkles. I drew boxes. I drew shapes. I drew patterns made up of lines and dots and squiggles that made waves and cliffs and clouds. I drew as people blah blahed at me, hardly looking at what was coming out until it had got there. Then I saw the expression of that same invisible someone.

A new full set of oil paints and paper had been left in my room. A painting came out of me; it was a picture of me as a child. It was not the kind that a child might paint, it was like what an adult might have painted who worked as an artist. In the picture, I was standing there just as I had been in a photo I'd seen. The plastic smile, however, that had been in the photo was gone. The child in the painting merely stood and there was no smile. I felt haunted by this picture and awed and fearful of the ability that had come through my body but which I did not know myself to possess and had never seen before. After a few days, I took out the paints and smeared them all over the picture until the whole thing had been blotted out.

Another painting came out; a white background with a stark black dividing line down the centre. On one side of the painting was a shadow of a human being. On the other side was the same shadow but running off behind it were seven reflections, each in a different colour of the rainbow. The picture upset me. I knew it was saying something but didn't know what. I put it where it couldn't make me look at it.

Haunted by the picture, I kept visiting it. I spent a long time staring at it as though waiting for it to speak and help me understand the feelings I felt about it. After a few months, I gradually understood what the picture was about. One side of the painting was about what was seen by others. The other side was about what was behind the façade that was seen by others. That invisible stranger inside of me was bringing to my conscious awareness an understanding of how I lived, who I was and who I was not and showing me the dividing lines between the effects of my 'autism' and who I was, regardless of the constraints of my condition. I eventually took black paint and blotted this picture out too.

In those pictures I saw humour and depth, turmoil and sadness. I saw aloneness and frustration and desire to escape. Again, I became scared because these things were outside of me and could be seen by others and because I felt a kind of perversity and shame that such complex and highly developed and expressive works were coming out of me when I had never built up these abilities nor even knew I'd had them.

I stopped allowing the drawing to happen. I moved from where the paints had been and never took any action to get any more for more than a decade.

After writing my first book, I bought some paints and paper and paintings emerged; paintings of landscapes that captured feelings of freedom and happiness, solitude, belonging and individuality, paintings with cats in them which captured a sense of tomorrow, fear of sharing, hidden dangers, exploration and loyalty. This time I wasn't afraid of what was coming out of me. Even though I couldn't experience its creations and only its product, I had come to trust that nothing that would hurt me was going to come out of me even if being party to my unknown knowing was going to make me feel and result in understanding, growth and the change that entails.

The art of others, by contrast, seemed almost always to speak only of alienation. From topic to technique, to colour to approach, with only a tiny minority of exceptions (maybe one per gallery) I could sense no freedom in the expression of these people, no breaking out, no setting free of soul, only of mind and of learning. In their works, I saw, almost exclusively, the work of conscious minds that seemed painlessly to take account of the other who would view such works and to whom the works themselves seemed directed. My works had the feel of being distinctly expressed from self to self, as coming from preconsciousness and not consciousness, and the expression of which had no direct relationship, nor even conception of the relevance of the viewing of any other. By contrast, the art works of almost all others spoke of the system of interpretation, the loss of sensing, the dominance of mind and ego and a grounding firmly in the non-autistic world and its perceptions. Viewing it, like so much other expression from non-autistic people, only confirmed my own alienness and I had no desire to look upon the works of gentle gluttons to whom such reaching out, such expression, such directness before and for others came so easily, so inconceivably easily with all the alienation that entailed. The works of the few which were exceptions seemed buried like a scattering of jewels in a vast expanse of mud.

Writing

The letter strings of a ten-year-old became the lists of an eleven-year-old, became the poems of a twelve-year-old and the lyrics of a twenty-year-old.

When I was nineteen, I returned to education. I had left school when I was fifteen, barely passing some subjects, failing or unassessable in others. At nineteen, I enrolled at a further education college and with a lot of remedial English and remedial mathematics I was able to do the work required of me and to pass.

I sat in those classes consciously processing only a few words in each sentence, consciously unable to squeeze meaning out of the words in the books we had to read and unable to use a calculator or use punctuation. I passed that course by writing on prescribed topics, automatically in cued response to questions I didn't understand, but some part of me did. The student who had barely been able to pass subjects in the third year of secondary school, had jumped three years and was passing with average to above average marks in the equivalent of a sixth and final year.

From there, I went to university where I was required to read books I still couldn't understand and listen to lecturers blah blah without knowing what I thought or felt about what they'd said. I went to classes where I was asked to respond. I had nothing to say because I thought nothing. Someone else would be asked something. Out of my mouth would blurt the answer without my even thinking or knowing that I had it. I couldn't access my thinking, but it could be cued. I took home stacks of books week after week and scanned the pages, as though some part of me was gorging itself on the words.

I could now read with fragmented conscious comprehension by labouring through word after word as it was strung into a sentence that was then strung to another. Yet I could scan within minutes an entire book and had come to trust that it was from here that the knowledge that was being triggered had come from. An essay question would be in writing before me. I'd begin to type and the essay would form itself.

I was twenty-five when I landed in London and bought a typewriter. The words began to pour out of me, telling the story of my life. The typed words and sentences, like tormenting ghosts, triggered the memories as they hit the page and I relived my life with affect and personal significance in a way I had never experienced so wholly. Because my mechanics were broken, it had to come from me, get outside of me and come back to me for me to be able to experience it with consistent meaning, personal significance and feeling. As it did, I was handed the ownership over my own life because I didn't just know theoretically who I was and who I had been, but I was able to feel too.

What This Did for Me

Self-dialogue is the building block to a true motivation to share and any true interest in others. Most people have that self-dialogue from the time they are born, maybe earlier. They are aware of having thoughts, feelings, body sensations, body connectedness. They are aware of their power to use their own conscious mind, to access thought and feeling and the means to express it. They are aware of the ownership of their own expression, not just because it came from their own understanding and feelings, but because they are able to monitor it and guide it with intention and will.

Robbed of any consistent conscious experience of these things, I had no building blocks. Sharing was a role I was taught to perform. Curiosity and interest and social affect were things I was meant to act like I had if I was worth something.

The subconscious self-dialogue within me fought with me and gradually guided me towards giving it a voice through my fingers. I did that with a pencil, with a paintbrush, with the keys of a piano and with a typewriter. It became my truest friend and gave me the greatest gift a friend could give; selfhood, a mind of my own. Without that, all I had to share with others was the patchwork façade of stored repertoires they'd programmed into me. Without that, the only interest and curiosity I had was based on stored theoretical knowledge of 'what a person should be interested in' or 'what a person should be curious about'.

My subconscious mind did not abandon me, nor did it permanently take over the space in my shoes. Through the products of its visits, it parented me where no parent could ever have reached me with meaning and significance and affect. It assisted me in becoming the person I am today.

You cannot see my invisible walking frame. You probably don't even know that the words you now hear were mostly written without conscious thought, nor awareness of what I had to say. You probably wouldn't know that as this writing emerged through my fingers onto the screen, the words that had come from within me had scared me and touched me and that even after writing three autobiographies, I hadn't even been aware of some of the feelings and realisations expressed here until they came up on my computer screen. You probably wouldn't know that without these pages, my words would be like wading through mud and I mightn't even be able to tell you how I'm feeling beyond the stored response of 'fine'.

What This Did for My Communication with Others

It would be nice to be able to say that achieving this level of automatic communication did as much for my communication with others as it did for my awareness of self.

My automatic, subconscious expression did not instantly take the place of stored responses based on theoretical knowledge of what I should think, feel, believe, be interested in, want, like, say or do.

On a conscious level, I continued to have to rely on stored responses that had no connection with self-expression, merely in order to function. A piano or painting could speak my feelings but couldn't express my thoughts in words in a way that could help me verbally dialogue with others. A typewriter or computer was not always available to me, nor even pen and paper.

People continued to ask me if I wanted a cup of tea and I continued to say, 'black, no milk, no sugar' even though I didn't want the damn thing and was surprised when it showed up. I continued to go along with people's invitations without any thought of whether I wanted to or if I was safe, merely because their expectations and wants had provided my only context for behaviour without any ability to access my own feelings or know how to act upon them.

I continued to find my life out of control but I gradually found that if I could get away from all direct influences and sit down with paper, I could write out what the problem was and a sequential plan for solving it would come together. I hung these on my walls and doors:

- how to tell when you have a want or a not want
- what to do when you want people to go
- what to take with you when you leave the house
- things I need if I am to stand being somewhere
- how to tell safe people from unsafe people
- what to do about unsafe people or places
- how to ask for things I need.

I learned to control my environment according to these plans. I learned to write notes to take with me so I could raise issues I needed to understand. I learned to take notes to ask people for help if I was in a crisis. I learned to draw diagrams and scales so that other people could see how I thought and what I understood and what I didn't. I invited them to add to my diagrams and scales, to bridge the gap between how the world of non-autistic perception and relationships were and how I conceived of them. I learned to teach people to 'show me' via objects and to get them to role play what my responses to things were like and what the alternatives ways of understanding and responding might be.

I gradually learned to control most of the automatic responses that came from stored theoretical knowledge, to hold them at bay long enough to reflect upon my feelings and have some idea of whether these responses were true to my feelings and thoughts even if they didn't spring from them. I learned to guide these responses so that even if they weren't true self-expression, they came progressively closer to things I at least thought or felt, even if I didn't think or feel them at that moment.

I progressively developed an ability to speak as myself. It wasn't fluent or developed or complex or impressive like the triggered speaking that came from stored theoretical responses. Nor was it with the depth of expression that I was capable of on subconscious automatic, such as that that came through typing. But, for the first time, I wasn't merely remoulding someone else's expression, I was using my own and mostly it was comprehensible even if it was limited.

That has developed to the point of being able to engage verbally in simple conversation on familiar self-generated topics. I use mime-signing to monitor my words so I stay on track, don't repeat myself and can see that I am comprehensible in a way that sound alone can never reassure me. I use a lot of words that I've constructed for myself in the absence of access to the words others might use or in the absence of non-autistic words to describe experiences and perceptions these people have never had to discuss or name. I am still ashamed of my expression as myself because the ease with which it is judged as stupid or mad has left a big imprint upon me and I also hear every day, if only via the TV, that other people do not express themselves as I do when speaking consciously and verbally as myself.

When I need to explain something at a level of complexity for which spoken words evade me, I still run off to the computer and let my fingers talk. The fax machine speaks for me much of the time and so do my books. My radio interviews are read in read-speak from my typewritten responses to questions submitted in advance. My print interviews involve handing journalists my typewritten responses and then taking them out somewhere for a non-blah blah, spend-time-with-me, orientation so that I am more than a bunch of printed words to them. My TV interviews mostly involve my reading what I had written in response to pre-sent questions, then speaking my read-speak at the interviewer. My public talks involve my read-speaking what I have to say to people.

For me, subconscious automatic self-communication, whether through art, music, typing, creative movement or sculpture, is a means of self-feed-back that is essential in building enough of a sense of self that one knows who one is fighting for, and why it's worth it.

Self-communication is the building block of expressive interaction with others. If the only way that can be achieved is through subconscious automatic response, then it is a start. The rest is about building bridges.

Subconscious, automatic expression can come from the delayed proc-essing of information for not just literal meaning, but also personal significance. Rote learning can also happen on a subconscious level. Both are triggerable by other people outside of oneself even if they are unable to be self-accessed. The first, however, is true self-expression. The second, albeit sometimes functional, is not. The two are liable to be confused with each other and purport to be each other. Both are liable to exploitation for the sake of people other than the person with 'autism'. Both can be valuable bridges that can be expanded to bridge the gap between disability and ability.

Gradually, over time, the conscious self may be able to take steps along those bridges towards self-initiated, spontaneous interaction and commu-nication with others.

'Savant Skills'

'Savant skills' are highly developed skills that seem to 'come out of nowhere' without formal teaching or practice. They are sometimes called 'gifts'.

People who may be unable to read a note of music may be able to play Beethoven. People who may be unable to tell you the number of days between Friday and Monday may be able to tell you the day of a specific date at any time in the past or future. People who may be unable to draw a simple picture of a cat on request may be able to draw a masterpiece from their mind.

Many forms of intelligence testing take no account of an 'autistic's' processing reality and that intelligence can exist even where there are seemingly clear signs that it does not. It is often claimed that 'autistic' people cannot teach themselves to read without step by step confirmed instruction by a non-autistic person. Yet critics who make this assumption would sometimes put up no opposition to accepting the automatic mathematical, musical, impressionable or artistic 'savant' skills of 'autistic' people.

My first book, *Nobody Nowhere*, was not thought about and then written. I could not have grasped those thoughts and connections mentally nor articulated those thoughts verbally – my brain doesn't work that way. But when I put my fingers on the keys they produced the written version of the video in my head that I merely set to play. My typing spoke for me without effort and I saw my thoughts appear only after they hit the paper – enough that I was shocked by the awareness I was not aware I had. The action was automatic and awareness and intention would have blocked the whole mechanics as it had in life. The same is true of my music composition and playing. If I think about it as I do it, it doesn't come out and playing often stops in mid-air in a mental stutter in which I sometimes involuntarily disconnect from the 'memory' of the ability to play. The same is true for me of art. I have also acquired several foreign languages largely through memorising lists in dictionaries and reading foreign labels and advertisements. I also had many seemingly 'clairvoyant' experiences which may also have been related to so-called 'savant skills'.

So many forms of ability testing used on people with 'autism' assume conscious awareness of what one knows. However, one does not always know what one knows, but one finds out when these things get triggered or cued and just 'pop out'. Rather than realising that 'savant-type' skills are like a video or audio being triggered, people testing intelligence or ability generally seem to assume, instead, that a person is somehow poised with waiting self and the conscious flexibility of expression required by their testing techniques.

Ask many people with 'savant skills' how they do what they do and most might say they don't know or they didn't try and it just happened or came out. For me, it is like I'm not always in on the secret of what a more inner-me knows or is aware of.

Maybe that's how it's meant to be. Maybe conscious minds are too clumsy and too backward to be let in on what the subconscious mind does with ease, so far beyond conscious and voluntary capabilities. The important thing is that people with these skills aren't sold short and that the non-autistic world realise that 'savant skills' are not limited to the places where stereotyped impressions expect them to be. In my view, they can and do extend beyond art, music, mathematics and 'calendar memories'. In my experience, they can extend into mimicry, speed-reading, automatic writing, the acquisition of foreign languages and, in some cases, to the intermittent presence of so-called 'clairvoyance'. Taking into account these wider areas in which 'savant skills' may be found, a larger percentage of so-called 'savants' may be present among the 'autistic' population than is presently realised.

In 'my world'

Not only was my first book, *Nobody Nowhere*, typed out of me in just four weeks, but poetry began composing itself out of me in minutes since I was about ten or eleven years old, shortly followed by classical music and songs, each produced in between ten and thirty minutes, sketches and paintings produced in the same amount of time and, recently, sculpture much the same. All of these have been of what socially is considered a very high standard that would normally require many years of training. Yet none of these involved any conscious learning of the skills involved nor any applied conscious trying in producing these works. It felt, quite simply, that they had a life of their own; they produced themselves. My only active role was in not stopping them from coming out.

Someone once asked me who had taught me to play and compose music. I pointed upwards and said 'God'. Like so many words, without discussion, the word 'God' developed its own special meaning for me; a 'my world' definition. For me God took two forms, the internal map and the external map. The internal map was the real and unadulterated non-ego self, the part of self that absorbed information peripherally and without judgment or evaluation, which met this information without mind or conscious thought and somewhere in unknown knowing danced with this information until the miracle of triggered expression which bore that dance for the conscious mind to perceive through the senses. The external map is the destiny, the specially set-aside potholes of life when these miracles are triggered. For me, 'God' made music happen, made painting happen, made poetry happen, made sculpture happen and made personal writing happen. The 'I' of the conscious mind didn't take a hand in these things, they had created themselves and merely came out. They required no teaching. They had come from 'God'.

For me, a 'my world' is the entire shadow realm of unknown knowing. It is the place of preconscious thought and waking dream states. It is an existential twilight zone and it is the source of expressed or as yet untapped 'savant' skills. A 'my world' is the place where the self lives when it finds the world too impacting or too overloading, and one cannot go into a 'my world' by conscious choice. Instead, getting into a 'my world' involves giving in to its hypnotic call, no longer fighting for consciousness or processing or resilience in the face of overload or hypersensitivity. One

merely gives in to it in a way similar to how one gives in to sleep and
often there is no active part in that giving in. Like sleep, sometimes one
is taken before one has any awareness of the taking. Problems of
connection, tolerance and control make people with autism more susceptible than most to being swallowed up by the hypnotic pull of a 'my world'.

What people think of as 'the world' is basically the natural world
around us all; what we can see and hear and touch and smell and taste or
just sense. The external place of 'the world', however, is also the social
and communication system shared by those who live consistently and
self-expressively in that world, not just in its metarepresentations within
one's head. Though sensory and perceptual problems meant I perceived
and sensed the natural external world differently from those who didn't
have these problems, I was often still sensorily a part of that external world.
It was the fact that I was devoid of any consistent interpretation of those
sensory experiences which meant that I had great difficulty in being a
consistent part of the social and communication structures and ways of
people in that external 'the world'.

When 'the world' ways make consistent meaning and sense and one
can consistently manage involvement and express oneself in the social and
communication structures of 'the world' then one's soul takes a grip on
one's place in that world, a grip that causes one to put up a fight when a
'my world' state of conscious attempts to draw its curtains over awareness.
If problems of connection, tolerance and/or control have so interfered
with that consistent meaningful experience of and involvement in 'the
world' ways, then there is basically nothing to grip. On the edge of the
cliff between the solid ground of 'the world' ways and the freefall into
the void of a 'my world', there are only crumbling edges that give way
easily, so easily, under one's feet.

Many people imagine there is active thought in a 'my world'. There
may be passive thought processes but, for me, there is none of the active
thought that involves what could be conceived of as an 'I'.

Fantasy and imagination are conscious self-indulgences and for me, a
'my world' may be a place of symbolism but it is not a place of imagination.
Imagination involves some conscious awareness of thought. Imagination
is imagination. It is of the mind. A 'my world' is not imagination. A 'my
world', if nothing else, is a place devoid of the presence of mind. A 'my
world' exists at a deeper, less tangible place, where there is no 'I'.

A 'my world' can be like a spiralling staircase. It has different levels.
One may be more easily called back from some levels than others. One

may more easily use the conscious mind to call oneself back from some levels than from others.

A 'my world' can be a sensory world, devoid of interpretation, where no reasons are given or sought and reasoning and wonder are non concepts, as intangible as floating clouds. For me, a 'my world' can be a place of preconscious metarepresentations of every relationship that might otherwise exist in the external world that people call 'the real world'. In a 'my world', beyond the curtain of consciousness, there can be a sense of being in the company of oneself and oneself can take the form of every person ever encountered peripherally in the external world. Here, in such a 'my world', one basically becomes a God, able to make the entire external world and all its inhabitants, and all they might offer, redundant. This is the ultimate power against the crime of daily, even hourly, felt alienation that autism, and the responses of others to it, can cause.

A 'my world' can be a storage shed for preconscious 'laws' that form with each re-entry. Emotional hypersensitivity triggering the shutdown that makes entry into a 'my world' as easy as going down a waterslide can create a sense that emotion (even happiness or excitement) equals impact, which may mistakenly be assumed to be 'hurt' and a preconscious law can form that 'emotions are against the law'. Sharing, causing emotions or information overload can cause the formation of a 'my world' law, 'sharing is against the law'. Finding that closeness can call one out of the womb-like void of a mindless 'my world' can result in a loss of control that can form the law 'closeness is a crime'. In the shadows of a 'my world' the list of preconscious sensed 'laws' may be endless and because they are not consciously accessible, they are not easily reasoned with or resolved. As experience challenges these 'laws' it can create an internal war; a 'my world' versus 'the world' war. For those who identify a 'my world' with their sense of self and special place, this war can challenge identity to an intolerable level – even splitting it in two.

Not all the people with autism I've met have a 'my world'. Many more able people with autism either describe or seem to have left theirs behind and developed conscious abilities. Some people with Asperger Syndrome seem never to have had a 'my world'.

A tiny handful of those more able people with autism I've been in touch with still have a 'my world' which they allow (by not fighting its grip) to take them from time to time. An even more tiny handful, often called 'savants', seem to reach out into 'the world' from a 'my world' and basically function almost exclusively on automatic pilot. It is my view that a large number of so-called 'lower functioning' people with autism live firmly in the grips of a 'my world', cut off from conscious connection but still sometimes capable of untapped triggerable preconscious expression.

From my experience, making consistent meaning and having consistent true self-expression in the social and communication system of 'the world' involves the forfeit of a 'my world' just as waking forfeits sleep. Some people, however, cannot maintain a grip on 'the world' and can only visit. Living in the hands of a brain-affecting food and chemical intolerance, I have been one of those. Having dealt fiercely with these intolerances, I am finally beginning to be able to stay on the other side of the fence. Time will tell what price I pay for that in terms of automatic preconscious skills. If, like other savants, I pay that price, there will be no turning back. The social and communication systems of 'the world' are full of mind and of ego and of the arrogance and ignorance born of these. But it can also be a place of tangible and interactive social experience on some level and there can be a warmth in that which, once known and held with any non-elusive consistency, has its own addictive call. I can only hope that if it costs me all place in what I knew as 'my world', that I will say, 'it's worth it'.

CHAPTER 15

Personality

'Autism' can have a huge impact upon sensory, perceptual, cognitive (thinking), emotional, language and social development. Because all of these forms of development shape identity and personality, it should not be any surprise that 'autism' can also have a huge impact upon the formation of identity and personality.

As problems of connection, tolerance and control can all severely restrict the ability to process incoming information consistently in the context in which it comes in, much information may be perceived consciously without meaning or significance, yet still be stored and worked through on a subconscious, though impersonal, purely logical basis (that may be all that is left when processing occurs out of the context of affect that should have resulted at the time). This can affect the consistency of any identity, personality or selfhood one associates with one's comprehension of, and feelings of, personal and relative significance about experiences.

In the absence of consistent processing within the context in which information occurs, there may develop a sort of division between the conscious mind that is aware of sensations, though without meaning or personal or relative significance, and a subconscious logical mind that is aware of the literal meaning of experiences and may even be able to assess them impersonally for relative significance, according to stored (personally detached) moral values. In this sense, one may be divided into having a conscious and sensual side and a subconscious logical side.

If this sensual side is less functionally able to meet the demands of the environment and survive, the subconscious side may break through to connect with action or expression (comparable to sleepwalking or sleeptalking). Over time, if the sensual side's inefficient processing continues to get in the way of functional development and the environmental demands continue to increase with age, this 'breaking through' may establish a pattern and what might otherwise remain an unexpressed, subconscious logic-driven part of self, might come to govern waking life as though it were a conscious mind.

The sensual-self, on the other hand, being denied its experience of waking-time, may exert pressure (i.e. via emotions such as depression, anxiety or frustration) enough to jeopardise the smooth functioning of the logical mind which has taken over, resulting in it getting into a struggle of continually gaining and losing its place as the expressed self. Though not the same as the Jekyll and Hyde split most people might associate with dual personality, this might, nevertheless, be considered a case of dual personality.

As problems of connection, tolerance and control can all severely restrict the ability to connect consistently and with awareness with one's own thoughts, feelings and body sensations, this can also affect the consistency of any identity, personality or selfhood one associates with one's own thoughts, feelings and body sensations. In the absence of consistent connections of this sort, one may establish little or no consistent sense of self, nor be aware of having a real self to 'defend' even if one may still exist on a subconscious level.

In place of a real self, people in this situation may sometimes take on (or merge with) the pre-established identities of others (complete with copied movements, phrases, intonation, facial expressions, and even cop-ied patterns of 'emotional' expression, copied patterns of 'beliefs' and 'thought' and 'morality'). Over time, though these stored repertoires may always remain purely cued and triggered and never spring from self-initi-ated self-expression, some people may come to identify with these as their own and even fiercely defend them as such.

Even with awareness of one's thoughts, feelings and body sensations, problems of connection, tolerance and control can also severely restrict the ability to connect consistently and with intention with the means of expressing one's own thoughts, feelings and body sensations. This, too, can severely affect the development of identity and personality. Some of these people may remain so-called 'low functioning' because of these problems of connection. Others may develop one or more 'external' facades or apparent personalities with their real self still internal and basically unexpressed but an evolved or constructed external self (or selves) that is able to function according to stored rules and repertoires.

Some people who develop in this way may come to give up on their real self and live as wholly as possible through this stored (or series of stored) 'alter ego'. Others may find themselves in an ongoing battle between accepting this as a path to 'higher functioning' and feeling suffocated by the abandonment of hope for true self-expression that this 'bargain' can entail. These people may constantly swing between being apparently 'able' and 'not so able', 'high functioning' and 'not so high functioning'.

In each of these cases, problems of monitoring can mean that monitoring is not 'on-line' or functional in someone, these mechanisms can go unchecked and unchallenged by the self within, who may put up no battle (even if, when monitoring is back 'on-line' such a battle may start up again).

As problems processing, accessing and monitoring can all happen in the same person at various times, it is possible that one person may, at different times, find themselves in more than one of these predicaments.

'Characters'

When I wrote my books, I mentioned characters or 'alter egos' and the mention of these made sense to some people, created confusion in others and may have scared some others. Yet, my mention of these things, however, has not been the only one. Many 'able' people with 'autism' have written about or been described by others as having 'two sides' or having some inner enemy that distorts their freedom to express themselves as themselves or express themselves at all, or seems sometimes to take on the behaviour or voices of those around them (including TV characters or even cartoons).

For me, I developed not as one person, but as three. Yet of these three, I identified myself, Donna, with only one; my sensual self. This sensual self, however, had little consistent or controllable connection with intentional expression and very inefficient processing of information in the context in which it occurred. Because of these things, I came to think of myself as someone who could not connect with my body and the world beyond it and as someone who made some meaningful 'sense' in a world which didn't

I came to identify myself as the person whose realm was within what I called 'My World' rather than in the world around me. I was connected to my sensory-perception and could perceive the world around me (albeit without meaning or significance) but I learned that I had little developed ability to respond, with intention, to that world nor could I comprehend, with meaning, its response to me.

I developed another persona that I came to identify as separate to what I knew as myself. In order to make sense of its invasive take-overs, I identified it with the name Willie. I had been unable to conceive of where it existed in space but did know that it existed separately to me in some way. The earliest trace I had been able to make of my awareness of its existence was associated with sleeping underneath my bed and believing (or fearing) that the two iridescent green dots (they were part of a night light plugged into the socket under the bed) I could see must have been its eyes.

Willie was basically the embodiment of my logical mind and the separateness of this character my have been because of the information processing delay I had in making sense of incoming information. This meant that a part of my brain still continued to accumulate information which was processed on a subconscious level, though usually not on a conscious one. Because of this, this information was processed by another part of my mind, beyond my direct awareness and access, so I did not identify myself with that part. I became aware of this other part when its logic began to assert itself through my body and I found myself on the receiving end of repercussions for behaviour I had been unaware of.

As this subconscious mind asserted itself through connections with the body I had been unable to connect with, it began to establish for itself something of an identity. Over time, it came to defend any threat to that identity as a matter of survival, including any internal pressure from me, as the sensual self, to connect with the means of expression.

As my conscious-living subconscious mind, Willie was also able to monitor and accumulate logically that which came in through my senses when I consciously could not keep track. Unlike me, this part of me was also able to process what it had accumulated (albeit purely logically and with personal detachment) beyond conscious awareness. Though I could not access this information, its expression could be triggered by people in the environment that my body lived in. Willie may have been a natural 'fight' response that was put to work as a compensation.

I also evolved a highly refined ability to mimic and to store mimicry which could also be triggered. I also did not personally identify with it but found this mirrored and echoed expression to be better than having none at all. Nevertheless, in spite of sometimes wishing it was intentional self-expression, I distinguished between this mimicry-based expression and myself as well as distinguishing it from the logical reasoning of Willie, by naming it after one of the first people I had ever been aware of it having involuntarily mimicked in actions. I named it Carol. Carol may have been a natural 'flight' response that was put to work as a compensation.

Some people might call this process, 'splitting' and might have considered the first 'split' to have made me a case of so called 'Dual Personality' (DP) and the next 'split' to have been part of being a so called 'Multiple Personality' (MP). Furthermore, as the role of what I called Carol came to be to mimic anyone I had dealings with, some people may have seen this as an indiscriminate merging with others and called it 'Borderline Personality Disorder' (BPD). Whether I like these labels or not, words have to be used to describe things. Though the conventional and popular descriptions of these conditions does not apply so well when applied in cases of 'autism', these labels are currently all there is.

'Borderline Personality Disorder' ('BPD')

Many people with 'autism' have difficulty thinking for themselves. For some of these people, this results in inactivity. Others, however, may compulsively mirror other people and compulsively store the information they can gather from others as though this fills the gaps left by the absence of their own thinking. Some more apparently 'able' people who are like this occasionally have been labelled as having 'Borderline Personality Disorder' (BPD).

People with BPD generally have little definition to their own personality. This is something which could easily happen to a person with 'autism' who has a social communication problem, as it is through social interaction that one expresses who one is and establishes a conscious sense of identity and conscious awareness of one's own personality. Lacking definition or boundaries to one's personality also means one isn't quite firm in knowing who one is or what one thinks or feels so such a person may sometimes indiscriminately follow everybody.

Borderline Personality Disorder is considered by some people to be part of the spectrum of 'autistic' disorders and many of the very able 'autistic' people who have written to me describe the problems of BPD.

Some people with 'autism' have few personality problems. Some people with 'autism' have 'autism' and also what seems like BPD. BPD involves the compulsive mirroring of others. It can be part of appearing so called 'high functioning'. It may be no coincidence that what looks like BPD exists in people with 'autism'. BPD may be an elaborate and complex older version of immediate echolalia and echopraxia (immediately echoed speech and mirrored movements of others).

People with what seems like BPD can sometimes make other people feel claustrophobic – as though the person who is trying to please all the time, prompt all the time, mirror all the time, is trying to take away or drain the selfhood of the person they are mirroring.

People with BPD may talk in a seemingly argumentative or circular way. This may be because, basically, they have no *personal* commitment to anything they say but have merely accumulated chunks of argumentation or discussion that others around them have used. This may happen because they are lacking the boundaries of definition to their own personalities which would otherwise direct their focus of interest. I had contact with two able 'autistic' women, one who had what seemed like 'BPD' and the other who did not. The second found the first to be eager to please but sensed that she had no 'self' of her own.

'Multiple Personality' ('MP')

Over the years a number of people with 'autism' have written to me about their own 'alter egos', 'personas', 'faces' or 'characters' (around one third of those who wrote had these things or wrote of BPD-related problems of mirroring and merging with others and some wrote of having both MP-related and BPD-related problems).

Though a percentage of these 'autistic' people have been abused by others, *most* of these people have not. Though some 'autistic' people with MP-related problems had problems with self-abuse, this was generally not a reflection of abuse received from others.

This is distinctly different from MP in the general population where it is considered extremely rare and where those who acknowledge its controversial existence often tend to attribute it to severe childhood abuse, usually of a sexual nature. This was certainly *not* the case for the majority of those 'autistic' people who wrote to me with MP-related problems. This would have major implications for the appropriateness of the therapy they receive.

Some people with an MP-like condition knew (or had given) names to their 'characters'. Some were aware of particular roles they played in their overall functioning or their basic 'nature'. Others just knew, sometimes from the reports of those around them, that they had 'characters' and that they 'took over'.

As a larger number of these people with MP-like conditions had been self-abusive (without ever having been abused by others) I considered whether it could be the case that some cases of so called MP in a person with 'autism' could be the result of fear of unintentional, yet uncontrollable, self-abuse caused by the 'autism'; as though they were, unintentionally, their own abusers. I know that I was at times far more afraid of the sudden involuntary, compulsive self-abuse (common to many so-called 'less able' people with 'autism') than I was of abuse by anyone external to me (although, being unintentionally self-abused also made my body – which was perpetrating this against me – feel external to me).

I also considered whether the presence of self-abuse in such a number of these people might sometimes have been related to the expression-related frustration of a self cheated out of expressive connection by a 'character' or whether self-abuse was just one consequence of information overload which had led to a character taking over because of processing problems and their effects on the consistency of functional ability.

I considered whether dissociation, or 'splitting', could happen in some people with 'autism' purely because their condition has such a degree of perceptual and sensory problems as to lead to self-abuse, because of unavoidable and uncontrollable information overload. Most recently, I have considered the role of self-abuse as a sort of purging behaviour for the unintentional and uncontrollable self-distancing from closeness, emotion, involvement, sharing; from life. In myself, it came as a terrifying, almost unbearable, shock when finally I had enough processing to make the conscious realisation that one of the many sources of my own self-abuse was the compulsive necessity to do this in order to forgive myself for the unintentional and unwanted social-murder of my selfhood.

The more my autism-related problems compelled me to reject connection with those I loved, liked or could have loved or liked, the more I hated, murderously hated, myself for what I could not control. Self-abuse was giving me the blissful buzz of momentary forgiveness until the next unintentional act of self-seclusion. As violent as it often appeared, the eventual warm home-coming feeling of self-forgiveness that followed (and was always the result of) that state of self-abusive self-rage, was the equivalent of picking myself up and giving myself a hug as if some simplistic and primitive subconscious reasoning went, 'right, the self can now see and accept that that uncontrollable part has suffered for its crime against the self and by that suffering self-hate has been somehow washed away and the uncontrollable part is now worthy of self-love again'. It came as a riveting shock to me to find that as much as I had grown to love and respect myself highly, I had equally a part of me which could not forgive myself for my own unintentional self-robbery of inclusion, expression and life. Autism as enemy is one that cannot be seen. In the absence of something so clearly distinguishable as non-self, then any frustration or hurts upon the self caused by any unseen enemy may be deemed committed by some part of self or alter ego.

I also considered whether the evolution of 'characters' was a way in which some people with 'autism' managed to be more higher functioning than the degree of their autism might otherwise have allowed them to be.

Certainly most severely self-abusive people with 'autism' have not been abused by anyone external to themselves and possibly feel already abused enough by their own condition to perceive it as a form of assault inflicted upon them. Processing problems make the world overloading but even this may not be enough to cause 'war' with 'the world'. When I did realise the great source of psychological and emotional pain caused by others it was wrongly assumed this must have been the abuse by my troubled mother. My reply to this was that the greatest psychological and emotional damage happened daily, even hourly, every time I looked at a face or heard a tone that told me others found me alien and unlike them and every time I looked at or listened to others and found them incomprehensible and not 'like me'. The intense repeated reminder of this unintentional, unchallengeable exclusion and alienation suffocated hope and gave the loud and clear message that I was *not* part of their world nor they part of mine. By comparison, irregular abuse at the hands of my mother was a minor secondary factor in causing the self-protection mechanism of autistic withdrawal. When I chose not to fight my 'autism' for a right to expressive and receptive coherence, then I made all that was alien to me redundant, and was no longer closed out. In effect, I made myself a God and it was so much easier to remain a God who had made 'the world' redundant than to attempt to be a mere human being and look the daily chill of alienation in the face without hatred or resentment.

In the bad days, people blamed 'autism' on bad parenting. It is now known that this isn't true because too many people with 'autism' were born to very loving, very well adjusted people who did not abuse or neglect them.

I considered whether those people with 'autism' who had no background of abuse could have developed so-called 'multiple' or 'dual' personalities because of their own striving (or overwhelming frustration, societal or parental pressure) to function so far beyond their true integrated developmental stages that they could only achieve by fragmenting.

Within conventional (non-autism-related) theory about MP there can be the 'Host Personality', which is one's 'true' self, the 'Monitor Alter' which is part of the mind that oversees or records what is done or happens.

'Parent Alters' which are about self-parenting in some form, 'Adult Alters' and 'Child Alters'.

I think that these things are probably in all people to some extent whether they are 'autistic' or not. People who are isolated within themselves through processing-related problems might, however, be more likely to have more distinctly adult and child parts of themselves relating to different stages of development. I also think that people with very different use of memory (i.e. serial memory) may have a more highly developed part of them that could be considered a 'monitor alter'. I also think that someone whose problems of connection, tolerance and control inhibit their ability turn consistently to others for assistance may develop more highly a sort of 'Parent Alter' within themselves. Finally, people whose functional ability may be so highly reliant upon doing things *as others* rather than as themselves, may be more likely to establish secondary personalities or 'alter egos'.

Therapy for MP is highly controversial and may well have its own 'bad old days' (and may not be out of nappies yet). The other danger in applying MP therapy to someone with 'autism' is that the therapists accustomed to dealing with MP may have little experience or knowledge about the processing, accessing or monitoring problems relating to 'autism' and the intimate relationship these problems may have played in the evolution of an MP-like condition.

Certainly, non-autistic people with 'MP' might well have very different sensory perceptions, memory use and processing for personal significance from that of someone with 'autism' who has an MP-like condition, and this may make for a very different relationship between 'alters' and the self.

Generally, however, current MP therapy is about teaching the adult parts to be responsible and not reckless and about teaching the adults parts to teach and reassure the child parts within the person. It is also about using the accumulated knowledge (generally not consciously known by the other parts) of the 'Monitor Alter' (who monitors everything about everyone) in order to get it into inner dialogue with all the other parts and get generally agreement on how to live together constructively and responsibly in line with the wants and ambitions of the Host Personality (which is the 'true' self).

Within current theory on MP, 'characters', 'personas', 'faces' or 'alters' are seen as the brain's subconscious mechanisms that were 'created' or evolved as a way of coping with the demands of the world. Within 'autism', it is possible to see how 'characters' could subconsciously evolve (which does not require conscious 'imagination') to help cope with 'autism' and its associated threats to stability, consistency and security within oneself as well as confusion and fears that can result from sensory-perceptual and processing problems. Just because there is trouble with conscious processing, accessing and monitoring, doesn't mean that subconscious abilities (which is where 90 per cent of usually untapped 'intelligence' and potential 'ability' lies) is equally impaired.

It is generally accepted that MP is a mechanism that can happen in some people in order to manage very difficult circumstances. It said that the problem with 'characters' (or 'alters') is that people become addicted to them as 'the easy way out' of coping with life and building skills as one's self but doing things as 'characters' robs one of the control and consistency of one's life, belief in one's own abilities and felt emotions that might, otherwise, have come from experience.

As one becomes 'grown up', one must reassess the usefulness of 'characters' and the way they work in relation to the self. Ultimately, the intentional or unintentional, reliance upon the strategy of 'characters' can outgrow its usefulness. When this happens, one must take one's life back into one's own hands.

Ultimately, whether aware of having them or not, one has the inherent potential to take charge of one's characters because one's own subconscious mechanisms were *their* creator. Some people, however, may not have developed enough functional ability of their own and taking back their 'life' might, ironically, leave them far more disabled than they might otherwise have been, living as a 'character'. This is another aspect in which the reckless misapplication of conventional (non-autism-related) MP therapy may cause more harm than no therapy at all.

People seeking to help people with MP-related problems should be very careful about dealing with 'characters'. The other name I call characters by is 'defences' and, for me, that can be one of their most basic functions, to defend against bombardment. 'Defences' can be genius purely because they are not conscious 'minds'. Because of this, the way they work can be extremely difficult to fathom for any conscious mind, including that of the real self.

The goal of a 'defence-evolved' character may be to run the self's body and life on its own terms. These terms maybe a world of guarantees and rules that may strive to keep affect at bay. Keeping affect at bay may be the most functional way to manage information overload. Keeping affect at bay may also be the most assured way of consistently maintaining functioning on subconscious 'autopilot' (in the absence of efficient enough accessing ability to consistently consciously and voluntarily connect to the means of expression to a degree that would be self-sufficient, lead to social inclusion and ensure survival).

Stored rules and (generally involuntary) copying can replace felt morality and connection with emotion just as logic can replace personal and self-driven thought. These things are, in my experience, wholly stored and rife with copied expression and devoid of self-expression, and yet may be fiercely defended as being self-expression. Indeed, if someone has never experienced the connection between something emotionally felt or personally thought and expression (such as language or action) then 'defence-evolved' expression may be the only expression they have ever known and they well assume it to be self-expression (and be quite terrified to admit otherwise).

The ultimate goal of 'defence-evolved' characters may sometimes be to extinguish expression *as self* and connected emotion *from self*, especially if the interference of emotion is making communication disordered or functionally impractical. In place or felt emotions, a 'defence-evolved' character may use stored repertoires of 'mock-emotion' and 'mock-expression' that have been accumulated from others of from television and whilst these characters dominate, the self may not develop.

'Defence-evolved' characters may do this in response to a frustration or impatience with delayed development or as a result of the unpredictability and vulnerability of real self-development in an environment full of information overload.

'Defence-evolved' characters may subconsciously bargain with the trapped self, even creating a sense that they are needed for 'protection' yet this 'protection' may, effectively, be a sort of soul-suffocation. 'Defence-evolved' characters may take the interference of the self's emotional responses to be counter-productive to successful and consistent systems functioning. Because of this, these characters may be wholly motivated towards the breakdown of the self's belief in, or hope for, self-driven ability. By breaking down challenges at the point of motivation (belief and hope) 'defence-evolved' characters may be able to wipe out all competition for the control of functioning.

Some 'high functioning' people with 'autism' seem to live as these 'defence-evolved' characters. Some seem to function on a purely logical level without affect and without soul or true personal (non-stored) want or true personal (non-stored) like or true personal (non-stored) choice. Some may have a stored impression of pre-empted (socially expected) 'happiness' and seem 'satisfied' with their often functionally-useful and purposeful lives.

Some have used the ability to mirror others to give some semblance of 'affect', 'morality', 'opinion' and 'belief' which, though dissociated from their real selves, sometimes passes for 'normality'.

Some people with 'autism' appear still to be struggling against their 'defence-evolved' characters in asserting control over the means of self-expression and action. The result may sometimes be that they may either appear consistently 'lower functioning' or swing fiercely between living as themselves at the expense of some of their level of functioning and living as these characters.

Conventional 'MP' therapy seeks to give confirmation, even 'love' and acceptance to 'alters' in an attempt to help them 'integrate' with the self. In the case of 'MP-like' conditions in people with 'autism', these attempts may be folly, even counter-productive. In my view, 'defence-evolved' characters do not need 'love' nor know it beyond its performance even if they may find the acceptance of others reassuring of their own power to control functioning. Giving a 'defence-evolved' character a sense of importance and building upon its 'mock-identity' may merely feed its power over the real self by reinforcing the incapacity of the real self.

In my view, 'defence-evolved' characters are mechanisms and not true self-connected expression. To treat them as though they were more than this is to credit them with a right of occupation they do not have. 'Defence-evolved' characters may try to secure free reign through securing the 'love' of others but that reign may be at the expense of true self-expression and real development. Effectively, love shown to a 'defence-evolved' character is, in my view, love given to a facade, a role. What is even worse, by helping to make concrete the right to live in the shoes of the self, the love given to a 'defence-evolved' character may feel, to the real self within, like dirt thrown upon the coffin in which one is already being buried alive.

MP therapy may sometimes be able to assist 'defence-evolved' characters to behave in a better adjusted, less destructive way, but most MP therapists would have little idea of the interplay between MP and 'autism'-related problems of connection, tolerance or control.

An MP therapist may be able to encourage a 'defence-evolved' character to explore the relationship to the real self if the character were prepared to acknowledge its existence (as in the case of Willie). The problem with this is that the 'defence-evolved' character will do this from an essentially stored-copied and impersonal perspectives and generally will only explore this relationship in a way that will justify its own right to existence and expression.

Characters may not wait for the self to develop in its connections to true emotionally-connected and intentional self-expression but without connection to the inner self, the lives they appear to 'live' are lives that are disconnected from the soul. A personality without soul is a computer. A human computer will outrun an intact human being every time. Professionals attempting to take on this problem would be wise, in my view, to acknowledge their limitations. It may be that this area of 'professional help' is not yet developed enough to deal productively with this problem in people with 'autism'. Some may be better off waiting for someone to have the right tools than to go to a dentist who has only gardening tools with which to remove teeth.

'Defence-evolved' characters, alters or personalities, are essentially logic-based and, in my view, know no real compassion, even if they can be taught to seek a sort of theoretical-morality. In my view, they know no empathy, even if they can be taught to seek to be 'an understanding, caring, person'. In my view, they know no understanding, even though they can be taught to value and accumulate knowledge. In my view, they know no personal feelings, though they can portray the whole range of them from stored repertoires. I feel it is important to remember, however, that no matter how deeply expression may be in the hands of a 'defence-evolved' character, this, in my experience, is not the self and the self may still be in there somewhere, even if disconnected from the means of expression.

For better or for worse, some people will wish to explore MP theory and therapy. I heard from a woman who has some personal experience of Asperger Syndrome who happens to work as a therapist for people with MP. She has written a self-help manual which, though essentially for non-autistic people, may still have some value for those wishing to understand conventional MP theory and therapy better. I would, however, suggest that anyone reading this self-help manual, keep in mind the potential misapplications of current MP theory and therapy to people with 'autism'. The contact address via which this manual can be ordered is at the back of this book.

CHAPTER 16

Asperger Syndrome?

A young woman with Asperger Syndrome was introduced to me by her parents. 'Donna has Asperger Syndrome, just like you', they said to their daughter as she met me.

She looked relieved that I was so able. She had never met another person with Asperger Syndrome until that day. She, like her parents, had made a point of making a point that she was a very able person and not 'autistic'. For people like this, and for the young woman herself, being autistic meant not being able, being retarded and basically not having much of a right to dream of a fairly full future and equal place among non-autistic people.

This wasn't the first time I had heard this aversion, this psychological tiptoeing that fell somewhere between fear, prejudice, ignorance and snobbery. I had heard it many times in many terms: the parents who said not to mention autism to their able adult child because the child had never been told, the parents who pointed out to their child that he or she was more able than me because he or she had Asperger Syndrome rather than autism, the parents who prided themselves on how 'normal' their child appeared.

Here stood I with this young woman with wide interested eyes and a smiling face. I didn't tell her that her parents were wrong. I didn't tell her that I'd asked the person who'd diagnosed me, a man with three decades of experience with people with autism and Asperger Syndrome, whether I had Asperger Syndrome. I didn't tell her that he had told me quite clearly that in his opinion, I did not have Asperger Syndrome, I had autism.

Among some so called 'high functioning' autistic people, high functioning people with Asperger Syndrome are generally considered to be 'like themselves'. That's not hard, because although most people with Asperger Syndrome are 'high functioning', few people with classic autism are. This means that most 'high functioning' autistic people either haven't grown up around so called 'low functioning' people with autism or else they see themselves as sharing more 'interests' with high functioning people with Asperger Syndrome than with other people who share their label.

Similarly, many functionally able people with Asperger Syndrome don't find themselves to be too distinctly different from 'high functioning' people with autism. Since writing my autobiographies, I have had a huge number of letters from people with Asperger Syndrome who have written to say 'I'm just like you'. What then, from my perspective, is the difference between myself and someone with Asperger Syndrome?

Asperger Syndrome vs Autism

My husband Paul is so similar in his systems of functioning to so many functionally able other people with Asperger Syndrome, that, though undiagnosed, I consider him a person with Asperger Syndrome. I also consider him, like many other people with Asperger Syndrome, to be 'like me'. Yet, having lived with this man for almost three years, I have come to find that whilst we share many systems of functioning, there are fundamental differences between us; differences that I share with people with autism.

Though I am not qualified to discuss the difference between autism and Asperger Syndrome, I am in a position to discuss the difference between the systems of functioning of someone like me and those of someone like Paul.

The Similarities

To start with the similarities, Paul, like me, has candida albicans which is a yeast infection that he and I have probably had since childhood. Both of us have problems relating to toxicity, food and chemical allergies, vitamin-mineral deficiencies, and reactive hypoglycemia, all of which affect the supply of oxygen and other nutrients to our brains. It is these nutrients that ensure efficient information processing, accessing and monitoring.

Paul and I also both share attention problems, similar to those of someone with Attention Deficit Disorder. We also both have a visual-perceptual condition called Scotopic Sensitivity Syndrome (a bit like dyslexia) which affects how we are able to process visual information and we have the same problem on other sensory channels. The degree of these problems is, however, greater in me than in Paul.

The attention problems have been considerably improved by nutritional approaches as well as special Irlen Filters (tinted lenses) which decrease the rate of incoming visual information so it is processed more fully and is, therefore, more meaningful, significant and coherent. The capacity for these to improve functioning seems stronger for me than for Paul.

Paul and I both share information overload and sensory and emotional hypersensitivity and obsessive-compulsive tendencies related to this. We also function essentially in a mono rather than multi-tracked way and both rely on stored definitions and serial memory.

The differences

Although we both take in too much information without properly filtering it for relevance, the efficiency with which we process that information is different for each of us.

Of the two of us, my processing of incoming information is generally less efficient. I am the more literal of the two. I generally struggle to achieve complete literal interpretation of information and generally have little processing capacity left over for things like relative or personal significance. This means that everything gets processed by me with equal worth; all or nothing. It also means that I don't take things very personally and have a tendency to respond in a more objective, detached, logical way.

Paul, on the other hand, like many people with Asperger Syndrome, processes relevant and irrelevant information alike but, like many others like him, his processing is more efficient and he processes information beyond the literal level. This means that he makes a larger number of connections between what he has experienced and other things and it also means that he gets a greater sense of the relative significance or personal significance of what he experiences. Therefore, he generally responds more subjectively, in a more personally involved and less detached, or purely logical way than I do. It also means that Paul's ego (socially constructed form of 'self') is more fully developed than mine seems to be. He has more use of things like pride and impressiveness. His need for acceptance stems from a need to be valued whereas mine stems from learning that acceptance generally means that people become more predictable and less likely to provoke or hurt me.

Similarly, Paul's accessing of stored information and monitoring of expression are also more efficient and though he suffers from anxiety his is of a different nature and he does not suffer from the exposure anxiety that I do. This means that whilst he can get quite agitated, he finds the means of expressing things or getting things or doing things more easily than I do, and can also stay on his intended track with less difficulty. This also means that he doesn't have to rely so heavily upon ritual as a means of staying occupied in the absence of efficient accessing and monitoring, so his activities are generally more flexible and self-generated than mine and he appears less egocentric and more flexible.

Paul's brain triggers fewer involuntary instinctive attempts to compensate for problems of connection, tolerance and control. This means that he is not as driven to indulge compulsively in more obviously 'autistic'-like behaviours, as I find myself doing. In place of this, Paul has a greater reliance on stored information and voluntary strategies to compensate than I do. The result of these differences is that he appears to have more self-control and to behave more consistently and fully within the boundaries of socially comprehensible and socially acceptable behaviours and responses. Even if these behaviours may look formal or stored or stilted and, therefore, socially inappropriate in a particular time or place, they are generally still easily comprehensible to most people and, therefore, less disturbing or off-putting. If I were to be formal and stilted, it would be the result of the stifling effect of exposure anxiety upon expression. The same stilted formality in Paul would more likely be the result of a lack of social instinct, in spite of the want to be social like others.

Though Paul has a greater reliance upon stored information he has a lesser reliance upon rules than I do. This means that he appears to have a greater flexibility than I do. Because Paul's ability to access the knowledge he already has is more efficient and he is more able to access it voluntarily, he generally uses his vocabulary and stored phrases more flexibly and in a more consistently situation-appropriate way.

On the other hand, Paul is generally less self-aware than I am. This is probably because he is less egocentric (quite different to egotistical) than I am. This is probably because, in the absence of an ability to process incoming information efficiently, my energies were put into processing internally generated information whereas his were not. I may not have consciously known *what* I felt, but I did know that a feeling was going on. Paul, on the other hand, being able to process incoming information more efficiently, did not develop the capacity to efficiently process internally generated sensations. The result is that even though he can better name body messages and emotions, I am more aware of when I am having these sensations than he is when he is having them, even if I can't name them or tell which parts they are coming from.

It is also probably that, whilst Paul is emotionally hypersensitive, he didn't suffer from acute and crippling exposure anxiety like I did. Exposure anxiety is a suffocating and entrapping experience. If one can struggle for awareness with this condition, one is generally stuck with that awareness for a very very long time before any control over the ability to fight for its expression develops to a level where one can control the intense impulse to divert, avoid and deny expression enough to get expression through in any consistent and real way. This, more than anything else, forces intense self-awareness, if only at the preconscious, though triggerable, level.

Paul is generally more consistently aware of others, albeit often in a defensive mode. This awareness is due to him being less egocentric than I am because he has been better able to process incoming information and, therefore, less focused on internally generated information. This also means that he has a strongly developed sense of factual curiosity and enquiry, beyond purely sensory indulgences. I generally do not. Whereas I have stronger compulsions towards sensory indulgence that sometimes looks like curiosity, Paul actually thinks consciously about the things he sensorily experiences. He goes beyond the experiences themselves. Also, Paul's questions are usually about the world around him. My questions are usually in order to clarify something related to my own self-under-standing. Once I exhaust this, I usually don't have any further enquiry (this is egocentricity).

For both of us, our different problems are socially limiting. Conversation with me generally has a starting and finishing point of comparison with myself. Conversation with Paul generally starts and finishes with what is outside of him. Asked about how any of this reflects his own self-understanding or emotions, he usually flounders and can only rely on stored responses of what 'a person should think or feel about this'.

In spite of our differences, we still feel we understand the way the other makes sense of things more than we find with non-autistic people. We essentially have similar underlying problems but the level of processing, accessing and monitoring difficulty of each of us has made for very different social development, expression, use of thought, response to sensation and generally level of functioning. If we were cars, neither of us would be complete. Paul would be without steering and I would be without wheels. Paul benefits from living with me as a person who has steering and I benefit from living with Paul as a person who has wheels.

Most high functioning people with autism or Asperger Syndrome can tell who has what and we gravitate in the direction of those who most share our own system, provided the level of functioning is similar.

Professionals, on the other hand, often come across a functionally able person with autism and wrongly assume (sometimes even insist) that that person therefore has Asperger Syndrome, not autism. This type of thinking wrongly reinforces the current stereotypes and prognoses of the two conditions; that people with Asperger Syndrome are of normal or above average intelligence and people with autism are generally not and that people with Asperger Syndrome generally go on to live independant lives and people with autism do not. What I have seen, however, is something similar happening among less functionally able people.

There are non-verbal low functioning people with Asperger Syndrome who are labelled autisitic but who, often quite unlike their autistic counterparts, have excellent receptive language, can approach others in a directly confrontational way (i.e. to take a hand and remove someone from the room or have them get something) and have only minor sensory-per-ceptual problems (demonstrating far fewer 'bizarre' autistic behaviours which can stem from exposure anxiety, sensory hypersensitivity or per-ceptual problems). By contrast, children with autism with the same low level of functioning often have markedly poor receptive language both visually and auditorily, have problems with connected body sense and body perception and often cannot bear the exposure of initiating diect and personal action with another person, sometimes ending up denying the want or need they'd had and engaging instead in sensations or actions to tune out awareness.

Though both may have poor language skills, one may not speak because of a lack of social instinct in spite of the (more multitrack) capacity for the skills and lack of the want or need to use speech. The other may not use speech, in spite of intense social instinct, because the various systems aren't on line or exposure anxiety or sensory hypersensitivities make it impossible or uncomfortable either to use speech, or encourage others to. In other words, one may be a case of lack of social instinct in spite of capability, the other may be a case of inability or extreme difficulty in developing or using social skills in spite of intense social instinct. When professionals see the difference in terms of high or low functioning they may fail to see the different types of assistance these groups needs, and the fact that a low functioning Asperger can be misdiagnosed as autistic says something for the hope of many labelled 'autistic' and given hopeless prognoses.

CHAPTER 17

Seeing 'Systems'

If non-autistic people are meant to recognise the underlying problems that are hindering people with 'autism', then they need to know what to look for. I am not the definitive expert on these things but sometimes it is better to start somewhere than nowhere at all. Because of this, here is a mention of how I recognise 'systems' in other people with 'autism' who I meet.

When I meet someone else with 'autism' I do not clinically assess them according to text-book theory. Current text-book theory describes the behaviours of some people but it says little or nothing of how to recognise what systems are presently on-line or off-line or what triggers these shifts. It says little or nothing of the purpose or meaning, even 'language', of behaviours or how these are used as strategies and compensations in response to different forms of overload, sensory hypersensitivity, perceptual problems and processing, accessing and monitoring problems.

When I meet someone else with 'autism', I notice when their responses reflect my own. When their responses, connections and monitoring of sound, pitch, volume, rhythm, light, colour, form, pattern, depth, touch, intensity, variation, movement, height, interaction or expression, reflect my own pattern of responses, then I recognise whether someone is working in mono or not. When I observe their systems shifts, forfeits and shutdowns, I map out which of their systems are on-line and off-line and sometimes I find a pattern whereby certain systems continue to take precedence over others in the priorities of shutdowns.

By spending time with these people as they respond to various environmental conditions. I build up a map of what environmental factors appear to cause what sort of shutdowns in what systems and what environmental factors seem to cause more extreme overload and pervasive systems shutdowns than other things.

When I meet other people, 'autistic' or not, there is something instinctive in me that looks for where systems in them match systems in me. This is a bit like an animal sensing whether another creature is of the same or related species or not. Some animals do this by smell or sound. Some animals certainly seem able to observe the foreignness and incomprehensibility of the behaviour of creatures that are not like themselves. Many animals will observe from a position of detachment (sometimes indirectly) another animal until they sense that that animal is comprehensible and 'like me'. Perhaps, I am like this.

When I am around non-autistic people I soon know they function according to a generally alien system of functioning that makes little match with my own. I know this is because they are essentially multi-track and I am essentially mono.

When I meet a non-autistic person with autistic traits, Aperger traits, dyslexia, Scotopic Sensitivity Disorder, Attention Deficit Disorder, or obsessive–compulsive disorder I sometimes sense aspects in which these people's systems of functioning are not alien and match my own at some level. When I meet people labelled as 'autistic' who are not essentially mono and are clearly essentially multi-track then I do not sense them to be 'like me' any more than non-autistic person with no autism-related traits. Sometimes, I have met people labelled 'retarded' who are mono and their systems of functioning match my own. I do not experience these people as alien.

Sometimes, I have met people labelled 'retarded' who are not mono and I have found their systems of functioning to be as alien to me as that of non-autistic people with no autism-related traits.

Quite aside from sharing being mono or multi-track, I have things in common with people of all kinds on a personal level. I may love the smell of roses and cream cheesecake just like many non-autistic people or so-called retarded people or anyone else. I may find influence difficult to deal with, the same as many non-autistic people or anybody else. I may live in a house with someone I am close to, the same as some so-called 'retarded' people or anybody else. I may get angry, happy, sad or messed up the same as anybody else. Yet, like some animals, whatever I share in common with others, human or otherwise, what comes first for me is the recognition that I am in the company of someone who has a basic way of making sense of the world and themselves that is 'like mine'.

I think that many people with 'autism' may feel like this and it is important to acknowledge these feelings even if there are other levels on which similarities can be found. To acknowledge these feelings of alien-

ness is to verify a felt reality instead of skirting around it and unintentionally contributing to people feeling invalid or even shamed at feeling an
alienness that cannot be denied but is not verified or acknowledged. To
say, 'love me, I am not alien' means nothing when it can't change what
you feel. To say, 'I know you find me alien, but we can live together anyway
and maybe learn to trust and even love' is a starting point of equality and
acceptance and honesty which is a very good place to start if each is
equally willing to attempt to grasp the other person's ways.

Non-autistic people may not be able to measure against their own
systems of functioning the way that people with 'autism' use theirs in
terms of compensation and adaptations. Non-autistic people may not be
able to build up a detached or objective inner map of someone else as
though that person is just a collection of patterns – like a living object.
Most non-autistic people are too subjective, too personal and have egos,
all of which get in the way of these things. I try to hand them my tools
as an alien with fifty fingers handing these instruments to people alien to
me who have ten. With all the good intentions that are in me, I still cannot
give them the fifty fingers with which to use these instruments. Perhaps,
the best I can do is to make a clumsy notation of some of the compensations I know they do have that might help them to at least handle my
fifty-fingered instruments with twenty fingers instead of ten.

Keeping Notes

People often keep notes or diaries which help them to remember things
but they can sometimes use these to recognise patterns.

Some people learn how to write up experiments. People who have
done science at secondary school or university level might have done
things like this. These written experiments are part of learning to test out
different hypotheses on paper and write the results and summary and
conclusion. This approach could be used to assess different behaviours in
response to different environmental conditions, or forms of information
overload, in order to ascertain not just how to minimise overload but also
to assess how overload affects a particular person and what behaviours
are being used as possible adaptations and compensations in response to
these environmental conditions.

Some people learn how to keep diaries to help them assess things like
allergic reactions to foods. These same kinds of diaries could be used to
assess responses to different environmental stimuli and monitor progress
as different attempts to decrease overload get tried out. There are books

available on elimination diets to try to pinpoint and weed out food and chemical allergies. Not only could these be used to help many people with 'autism' whose problems are made worse by allergies but this same 'elimination' technique could probably also be used to pinpoint some of the more major sources of information overload.

If something works, keep it. If it seems to have no effect on its own, it may be that a problem is caused by the combined effect of several things rather than this one or that one.

Putting Things to Use

If you suspect that a behaviour may be an adaptation or compensation, then use your imagination to consider how you could expand upon such a strategy or compensation; how you could use it to build bridges to other skills. Do not think so much about what the person is doing but about the particular skill being used in doing what they are doing. If they are lining things up, for example, and seem indifferent to what they are lining up, then focus on the lining up rather than on what they are lining up. Consider, for example, all the useful skills in life where a skill of lining things up can be put to some use. Gradually and over time, introduce new collections of objects to be lined up that progressively resemble the things for which there is a practical need to line them up or which occur lined up in the world, in general (i.e. bowling pins, toy railway tracks, queues of dolls or cars).

If the skill is categorising, there are shelves to be tidied, clean folded laundry to be put away, cutlery to be put into sections, crockery to be put away. If the skill is disassembly or shredding, supply the sort of things that require disassembly or shredding (e.g. for recycling purposes).

If you successfully and gradually assist people who have a variety of these type of skills into using them for a whole range of practical purposes, then they may eventually be able to spend their time more constructively and develop more independence-related skills than they otherwise might have.

You could lead the horse to water and it will probably drink it. If you drag it there then it may be much less likely to.

CHAPTER 18

Education

For me, education doesn't begin at school, nor at home, nor in the community. It starts with the person. It starts with the motivation of the learner to 'HAVE'.

Education is not about mindless compliance nor about force. For me, education is something you can't force feed. It is something that has to be reached for. For me, education is something that can be offered, just like food. Yet, there is better chance that food will be taken if offered to someone who is hungry than if offered to someone who isn't. That hunger is 'motivation'.

The motivation to 'have', ideally, should be driven by 'need' or 'want' or even 'like'. 'Like' can be sensory-based and can drive 'want'.

Learning materials that are sensorily pleasurable to people with autism are more likely to be attended to and handled than those that are not. Some people with autism like the deep sound of large drums or the singular 'ping' of a triangle or the sound of tiles or beads. Some like the sound of hollow pipes or 'woody' sounds. Some like the texture of satin and shiny plastic and velvet and fur, the smell of plants or rubber or types of wood. Some like shiny metallic things or tile-like surfaces. Some like the grain of wood or lacquered surfaces. Some like mechanisms and nuts and bolts and springs and discs. Some like things that cause physical resistance when jumped upon or pressed. Some like things that swing or spin. All of these things can be considered in the purchase of sensorily pleasurable learning materials.

In the absence of 'like' or 'want', compulsion, obsession or aversion can all be motivational forces. Compulsion and obsession are attracting forces that can be used to direct someone gradually in directions that will teach them something. That may not be in the usual curriculum but life is not about the usual curriculum so unless someone needs a piece of paper more than they need practical skills, the usual curriculum may be of secondary importance to getting people involved in something practical that will help them develop.

Aversion is a repelling force. As long as the aversion is to something other than education, education can be offered up as the safe haven from what the person seeks to avoid. For example, if someone seeks to avoid being controlled and it is continually demonstrated that *chosen* attention to any learning-related activity will get them out of being controlled, then some people will take this exit.

There are many things that people with 'autism' often seek to avoid: external control, disorder, chaos, noise, bright light, touch, involvement, being affected emotionally, being looked at or made to look. Unfortunately, most educational environments are all about the very things that are the strongest sources of aversion.

If the educational environment did not insist on eye contact but focused, rather, on attention to objects, it would probably create less aversion. If it was less noisy and without bright lighting or unpredictable touch it would probably create less aversion. If it was without visual or auditory disorder and predictable and full of routine structures and patterns, it would probably create less aversion. If it allowed choice and exploration rather than controlling learners and allowing them no experiential space to have their thoughts and feelings then it would probably create less aversion.

My ideal educational environment would be one where the room had very little echo or reflective light, where the lighting was soft and glowing with upward projecting rather then downward projecting lighting. It would be one where the physical arrangements of things in the room was cognitively orderly and didn't alter and where everything in the room remained within routine-defined areas. It would be an environment where only what was necessary to learning was on display and there were no unnecessary decorations or potential distractions. It would be one where nobody unexpected would enter without everyone getting a cue and processing time to expect the change. It would be one where learning was through objects and nature and doing, not through having to rely on the interpretation of written or spoken words or having to watch someone's constantly moving, constantly changing face or body; it would be an environment where the educators wore the same clothes all the time (i.e. a uniform) so that they became visually similar and able to be relied upon. It would be an environment where the educator's volume was soft, so that you had to choose to tune in rather than being bombarded. The educator's intonation and tone of voice would remain the same so that auditorily they were perceived as consistently being the same person. It would be an environment where learners were allowed the time to have thoughts and feelings FOR THEMSELVES, without the eager tiger-like waiting of an ego-needy educator ever ready to pounce and cash-in upon, and make piercingly overt, the slightest expression of interest or attention. It would be an environment where time spent outside of the classroom was always spent in the same boundaries and at the same time for the same duration. It would be an environment where one could rely on serial memory-based routine rather than timetables to have an idea of the sort of activity one would be involved in at a particular point of the day. It would be an environment that took account of being mono and sensory hypersensitivity and information overload and didn't assume that the educator's perceptual, sensory, cognitive, emotional or social reality was the only one.

This book is a guide to some of the tools that may be used with some people with 'autism'-related conditions. It is not the job itself. The job requires that the people to do the job take a good look at the tools, how they work, who they apply to and who they do not, what to use them on and who should use them and when and for what reasons they should or shouldn't be used. The rest is up to the reader. Perhaps, with the best of intentions, the onlooker finds themselves where I once did; thrown into in the deep end where it is up to them whether to sink or swim.

Hints

Since writing my first book, *Nobody Nowhere*, I have had many letters from people asking for advice on different things they were dealing with. In this chapter, for better or for worse, I will pass on some of those things I wrote back then. I am not an expert on anything except myself and what I write should not be taken to apply to all people with 'autism'. Just because I offer the reader a taste of my views doesn't mean I force fed anybody with them. The reader is free to say, 'I don't agree with that' and that's fine. Here is a rough alphabetical list of some of the subjects the following hints cover:

- Art
- 'Bizarre' behaviour
- Body awareness
- Breath holding
- Emotions and facial expressions
- Family communication
- Fighting compulsions
- Hair washing
- Home schooling
- Indirect communication
- Lack of verbal speech
- Mirroring
- Movement, art and music
- Music
- Personality
- Proximity
- Psychiatrists
- Rage
- Self-abusive behaviour
- Self-awareness and self-expression
- Telephones
- Texture problems
- Toilet training
- Vibration
- Video communication

ART

People with visual perceptual problems may be fascinated by pattern or colour but this doesn't necessarily mean they'll 'love' art. The perceptual problems of some people with 'autism' can make art difficult if vision is too fragmented to take in any piece of work as a whole. On the other hand, this may be the very reason why some people with 'autism' have exceptional visual recall and can sometimes draw very well or can paint 'impressions' of things they've experienced by viewing or recalling things seen a fragment at a time from serial memory.

Collage can be good for some people with 'autism' who may enjoy touching surfaces because they can touch the picture and 'see' it with their hands. For some people with 'autism' who have visual-perceptual problems, collage and sculpture may be very important ways of experiencing the meaning of wholeness and connectedness of things, as their problems might otherwise get in the way of so fully experiencing something two-dimensional, such as a picture.

'BIZARRE' BEHAVIOUR

If an 'autistic' person appears to want to stand out in the rain and there is no immediate danger, instead of nagging or controlling them, it is always possible to consider going and standing in the rain with them. This way, you may help them feel less alien and they may get over 'phases' better (and there might also be less secrecy and exclusion about these phases if they are publicly 'accepted').

If a behaviour appears 'intentional', then joining someone in their so-called 'bizarre' behaviour may sometimes be a means of building trust, sharing and acceptance and this may help to avoid sending the 'autistic' person 'underground' (keeping things to themselves, in their 'own world' where it is less likely to be controlled or countered by others).

If these phrases of 'bizarre' behaviour are necessary to the grasping of a concept or some new development step, then no matter how 'bizarre' a behaviour seems to be to a non-autistic person, sometimes no amount of encouraging avoidance of the behaviour can make the need go away. Even if you successfully inhibit a passing behaviour, if it is part of a growth phase that needs to happen, then it may come up continually in various behaviour forms (some worse than those you may already be dealing with). It may sometimes be better going along with a phase to get it over with (as long as it is just a phase). In the process the non-autistic person may also learn something.

BODY AWARENESS

Mirrors may help one see where one is and how one is made up and how one moves.

Bells to wear may help one to hear where one is in space (and make a person easy to find if they don't answer or respond when called).

Self-controlled body brushing or washing with a scratchy sponge may help increase awareness of how one's body is joined together for some people. It may also help decrease tactile hyposensitivity and gradually also may be able to decrease hypersensitivity. You should, however, be very careful with these things with someone who is hypersensitive to touch as this could be a very frightening and painful process for them if it is inflicted upon them and out of their control or choice. If this is out of the person's control of (non-compliance based) choice such an infliction may result in triggering physical dissociation (disconnection from body) in people who are susceptible to this form of systems shutdown.

Two mattresses to get in between or foam rolling cushions may be used to help improve awareness of the boundaries of one's own body and may be able to help reduce both tactile hyper- and hyposensitivity in a non-threatening way for some people, provided it is within their choice and control.

A spare mattress for tramolining or a simple and safe swing may be used to help reduce stress and may sometimes assist learning by restoring an inner pattern and rhythm at times of overload (especially where there is no, or partial and unconnected, inner body sense).

A heavy coat or thick jumper may be a tool for some people with tactile or body-awareness problems in helping them increase tolerance of proximity to others and 'social touch'. Touch may not be felt so directly in this way, so the impact is less distinct and intense and may therefore be less threatening.

BREATH HOLDING

One control-based compulsion that creates other problems is to do with breathing. Compulsions to hold one's breath can interfere with the ability to experience the sensations of one's own emotions as well as with other forms of body awareness (including, for example, awareness of the need to go to the toilet or eat or the use of one's voice, lungs and mouth for expression). Involuntary compulsive breath holding can also interfere with digestion and the regular supply of oxygen to the brain, which affect both nutrition and learning (which relate to processing and information overload and systems shutdowns).

One way that may sometimes temporarily help to combat this involuntary compulsion is to make it a copying 'game', alternating between holding your breath too, blowing and breathing with rhythm (but not too deeply or the person with 'autism' may find that hyperventilation helps them 'disappear' and that will be even harder to tackle). Copying can force conscious awareness of this involuntary subconscious-driven compulsion, thereby causing it to cease for the moment (until conscious awareness wanes and the subconscious influences takes over from conscious monitoring again).

Another mechanism for interfering with unintentional, involuntary breath-holding is to use a peg on one's nose, as this forces breathing through the mouth. Doing this to someone else, however, would feel EXTREMELY invasive and controlling and could make the problem worse. Because of this, this strategy should only be chosen to be done by the person themselves (I've done it to myself when I have been fed up with this compulsion and the dizziness and lack of oxygen it causes).

Given that the main cause of this problem is, in my experience, feeling out of control, taking control away from someone is *not* going to solve this problem. Ultimately, the best long-term approach may be to look at what is making the person feel out of control. Addressing information overload on all sensory (and emotional) levels may be one of the best ways of eradicating the underlying cause of this disturbing and irritating compulsion.

EMOTIONS AND FACIAL EXPRESSIONS

The inability to understand one's own body messages, such as emotions, know how to translate these into expression and what to do about these sensations in relation to other people, is probably one of the biggest social and emotional barriers to many people with 'autism'. These problems can create an inescapable inner uncertainty-based fear that is more potent than more controllable sources of fear outside of oneself.

I think that these problems require overt explanations of emotion-related terms and the overt naming of expressions (factually and unemotionally…so as not to detract from the lesson in definition) and their related inner sensations. If someone is unable to tolerate directly-confrontational interaction, a carer could make a brief, concise, home-video that explains some of these things simply and in a logical way that takes account of the 'autistic' person's ability.

There is also a game which involves drawing one's hand over one's face to produce a different facial expression each time and naming them. Although this only explains the outward appearance of certain emotion-caricatures, and does not explain their connection to inner sensations or what one can socially do about feelings, this may be better than nothing for some people. This may help to work out the contrasts between different facial expressions, some of their theoretical labels and how to express and comprehend very basic emotion-re-lated facial expressions in others. Later, however, one could help such a person to link and name some of the INNER sensations that go with some of these facial expressions or even draw up charts or diagrams or lists, showing different things that appear to cause these sorts of feelings and expressions in the person with 'autism' (being careful not to impose an assumed non-autistic emotional reality upon this person).

FAMILY COMMUNICATION

Sometimes families have a lot of trouble coping with so-called 'able' people with 'autism'. One reason for this might be because it is very hard for them to imagine what it is like to be 'autistic'. Their brains just don't make sense of things in the same way. The differences between a non-autistic brain and an 'autistic' brain may, unfortunately, mean confusion for both sides.

The important thing for each is that they *want* to understand. If they *want* to understand, they probably *don't know how* to. This may have to be the job of the person with 'autism'. The person with 'autism' is, however, so often put in the role of learner and so rarely in the role of teacher that someone like this may never realise they can inform people and help them to understand.

If spoken words don't work for someone with 'autism', written ones sometimes might. If written words don't work, cartoons or diagrams, even poems or stories might be a start to helping non-autistic people to understand a position different from their own.

If the members of the family are not understanding someone with 'autism', some of the things that a person with 'able autism' can do are:

(1) Ask them (verbally or in writing) whether they want to know how to understand you.

(2) Ask them (verbally or in writing) to make a numbered list of three simple questions to do with things they don't understand about you.

(3) In exchange you can give them a list (verbally or in writing) of three questions to do with things you don't understand about them.

(4) Tell them (verbally or in writing) that you will take their list away with you and think about how to answer their questions (verbally or in writing). You could tell them (verbally or in writing) to take your list away and WRITE DOWN an answer to each of your questions.

(5) Take their list to a place you can be calm and think. Look at the first question and see if you could answer it (verbally or in writing) from your own way of thinking and feeling. If you can, you could write your answer or try to draw it in cartoons or diagrams – any way to answer that is easiest for you to use.

(6) Look at the second question and do the same. Then, look at the third and do the same.

(7) ONCE YOU HAVE ANSWERED ALL THREE QUESTIONS take your answers back to them (and ask when you will get the answers to your list, if you gave them one).

If this helps people to understand each other and communicate a bit better, the same thing can be done for another three questions each, perhaps on a set day each week, unless there is some immediate crisis (as opposed to a general, ongoing misunderstanding) that needs resolving, in which case this technique could be used when it is needed.

FIGHTING COMPULSIONS

Sometimes compulsions may furiously drive me to 'settle things here and now' and demand retribution and attention. In these circumstances, I have not given myself enough calm and time and space to order my thoughts correctly so it is sometimes best for everybody, myself included, to defer the issue. Though my compulsions don't like this, my policy (when not in the grip of compulsion) is, 'if it's got legs, it will wait'. What that means is that if the issue was a REAL issue rather than a compulsion-driven or anxiety-driven one, then it will wait for me once I've calmed down.

In a compulsion-driven or anxiety-driven panic I cannot be freely reasoned with, even if I insist that I can be. What I need most at these times is self-appointed TIME OUT.

To use this with someone else, the person dealing with this problem and his or her carer/s would have to agree to handle things this way. They would also have all to agree that the person dealing with this problem must trust the judgement of whoever is not in a panic (the rational person during the panic). The person in a panic would also have to be able to trust the other's reassurance that he/she would be listened to once everything has calmed down. Also, all would have to agree on a range of non-overloading, familiar, predictable, calming activities that all agree to participate in, no matter how outraged, furious or out of control. These might be activities to shift the focus to something unassociated with the panic or to establish a rhythm so that emotions be calmed enough for things to be able to be resolved. Handled properly, this may lead to getting through the panic without anyone getting hurt, feeling regret, shame, or self-hatred later.

Some ideas for activities could be sitting and listening silently to fifteen minutes of a familiar story on cassette (this might be overloading for some people), five to ten minutes of silently running on the spot or jumping, or fifteen minutes of silently listening to (non-overloading) familiar music.

At the end of these sessions, having some large cardboard and (non-injurious) crayons available to get the person to draw and headline and connect up what he or she was upset, scared or worried about may help in some cases. Seeing the person's connections and helping them to get their thoughts out in this less attacking, more controllable way may help a person to know he or she has been 'heard' because he or she can see your attention to the visible words, concepts and connections. It may also help him or her to stay calm and focused on the issue, if there was, in fact, a real one.

Though providing the opportunity to explore the possible cause for the initial panic or anxiety, it should not be assumed that there WAS any true issue to be dealt with. Sometimes, panic states may happen due to things like allergic reaction to foods or chemicals or hypoglycemia, in which case, though the panic may find an issue to focus on, there is actually NO real psychological, emotional or social issue to resolve.

If things get out of hand at any point in this process, TIME OUT can be again taken for another session – by the agreed upon rules.

HAIR WASHING

For me the anxiety about having my hair washed by someone else is about loss of control and also about an anxiety that water is free to drip on my face. If I feel in control of what is going on and feel that I am safe from getting water on my face, then, until I get to hair-drying, I'm OK.

If a person with 'autism' has anxiety about being splashed by others then this may become part of hair-washing anxiety too. Anxiety can heighten physical sensitivity too, so if you are washing someone's hair when such a person is experiencing high anxiety (due to lack of control) the person may feel his/her head is sensitive. One way to tackle this anxiety may be to give control back and reduce stress. Guiding the person's hands through actions of the hair washing may help some people feel in control and an active part of what is going on. This may also help them to map out the actions physically, establish a routine and eventually maybe even choose to take over (if you progressively 'fade out' your part in these actions so that the other person ends up pre-empting the actions and guiding your involvement rather than you guiding theirs).

Another way of decreasing some anxiety about hair washing, if the anxiety is about having one's head put back, may be to wash the person's hair whilst they are sitting up and to wash the soap off with a squeeze bottle. Making sure to do this from front to back and holding a folded cloth across the forehead to catch drips (so they don't experience a lack of control from the water or soap getting on their face), the person may feel less out of control with the whole experience.

Giving a quiet, constant, predictable, repetitive, familiar and simple rhythm and reducing all unnecessary sources of information overload whilst washing hair may also assist some people in reducing anxiety.

HOME SCHOOLING

If you can't get someone with 'autism' into a school, if you are utterly convinced the school is doing them more harm than good, if the person is being continually bullied at school or if the person is past the age where there is a place for them in the usual school systems, home schooling might have to be considered.

Teacher's aides can be privately employed to work with the person at home on a full-time basis. The local university or local Autistic Society may be able to help find someone suitable and the citizen's advice bureau may be able to help in finding someone to work as a volunteer if hiring a teacher's aide is too expensive. Advertising for a student teacher or a student who is studying in an area that interests the person with 'autism' (e.g. computer studies, art, music, mathematics) may be a way of finding someone to help.

Home teaching requires some idea of a structured programme. Some people may be willing to work one out for the person with 'autism'. In my view, a programme should be worked out by someone who knows the person with 'autism' and understands the particular individual he or she is to work with and doesn't just relate to them within the confines of 'autism'-related stereotypes or assume to know 'what (all) people with "autism" need'.

Whether the authorities are failing the person with 'autism' or not, potential shouldn't go to waste in the meantime if there is someone available to co-ordinate and implement home-learning. Even things like video learning (brief, concise, personally designed, video-documentaries can be made at home using a home video if buying video-learning packages is too expensive or too limited in the available topics) computer learning, library books and tapes can fill in some of the educational gaps.

There are also daytime or weekend social groups for people with learning difficulties or social communication problems in most populated areas and these may be appropriate even if these groups are not specifically for people with the label 'autistic'.

The local citizen's advice bureau may be able to tell you what is in your area. If there is nothing around, you could consider getting together with others in the same position and starting something, even if it is only at the weekend or once a month.

INDIRECT COMMUNICATION

'Indirectly-confrontational' communication and interaction involves not only reading a shared language of behaviour but also 'speaking' back in it. 'Directly-confrontational' communication makes people notice they are noticing and some people with 'autism' may function on a subconscious level and not be ready for 'directly-confrontational' interaction or may not have reached a stage of emotional or social tolerance to cope with the sense of 'intrusion' or 'bombardment' it can entail.

For some people, not being made to notice they are noticing may mean they will be less easily overloaded and may, therefore, come to rely less on 'disappearing' strategies. Through 'indirectly-confrontational' interaction, some may be slowly more able to dare to be consciously aware of themselves; their feelings, their wants and wider self-expression.

By very gradually over time building a bridge from 'indirectly-confrontational' interaction to progressively more 'directly-confrontational' interaction, the person with 'autism' may gradually be put through a kind of sensory/social/emotional desensitisation without feeling the loss of control and overwhelming bombardments that might have been felt if interaction had begun in a 'directly-confrontational' way. By being very gradually eased into 'directly-confrontational' interaction, the actions and expectations of others may be easier to stand as well as easier to understand.

'Indirectly-confrontational' interaction could begin by just silently being with the person with 'autism' whilst they are 'in their own company'. Being in company with oneself one has no real sense of company in the sense of simultaneous sense of 'self' and 'other'. In the company of oneself the person may not even have come to terms with the real concept of 'company' or 'social'. Once the person realises that being with you is the same as being with themselves, they may have less need to 'disappear' and their interests may gradually become more flexible to being broadened and gradually channelled into other things (though along similar lines).

Rather than moving from silence, to asserting your own presence, the bridge from 'indirectly-confrontational' interaction to 'directly-confrontational' inter-action could, for example, move through speaking minimally and quietly out loud (as though to oneself but not overtly directed as the person with 'autism') through to occasionally mentioning the person's name as you speak out loud (seemingly to yourself) within the person's presence, through to speaking in the direction of the person's foot or hand to progressively, over time, estab-lishing eye contact with the person with 'autism'.

Many non-autistic people assume that people with 'autism' will have the ability to cope with 'directly-confrontational' interaction. It is generally over-looked that communication is not just expressive but also receptive and that some people with 'autism' need to gradually build not just an expressive ability to interact in a 'directly-confrontational' way but also receptively to cope with, and process, the progressively 'directly-confrontational' interaction and com-munication of other people.

Though I have used verbal communication in this example, this progressive bridging from the 'indirectly-confrontational' to the 'directly-confrontational' can also be used to build up tolerance of affect, 'social touch', and physical proximity.

LACK OF VERBAL SPEECH

Lack of verbal language has more origins than I have any qualifications to speak about.

I have had trouble using language functionally and with intention and conscious monitoring. I have also had brief periods where I have had trouble connecting with verbal language. In my very limited personal experience, lack of speech could be due to any one or combination of the following:

- ○ lack of connection to one's own body.
- ○ difficulty sustaining two concepts or perceptions or functions at once.
- ○ difficulty sustaining simultaneous sense of 'self' and 'other' (which is necessary to having the social WANT or interest that motivates social communication).

- difficulty connecting with or grasping one's own thoughts.
- information overload and systems shutdowns.
- having no idea of a personal purpose for verbal language.
- hearing language in mono (where intonation is heard without perception of words or body language is seen but the words that were said whilst watching are heard without meaning, so that language is difficult to establish as a meaningful or reliable system).

Each of these inefficient connections has its own solution which will be different for each individual.

Some simple solutions that I have found may help make someone who is 'mono' function in a more 'multi-track' way is to cut down on the NUMBER and PACE of sound, movement, light or touch sources coming in for processing at any one time. In other words, if you are speaking, drop your intonation and movements; if you are moving, drop your sounds. Cutting down on harsh lighting (you can try coloured light bulbs or, better still, special tinted lenses), speaking slowly and clearly with as little 'fluff' and distraction as possible can all improve on processing time. These things essentially decrease information overload by directly addressing 'mono'-related systems shifts.

A few weeks of cutting out as much sound as possible may reduce overload enough so that a non-verbal person may crave sound enough to prompt it vocally. Noise is the building block of words. Without a want for making sound there may be no want for spoken audible words. You can't build a house properly without foundations.

If you think of a diet of nothing but sweets, you might be unlikely to reach out for more, but if they are all gone you might want them. I know I have burbled continuously when no-one has been talking to me but clammed up when others burble over with blah-blah. If someone seems to have no want for blah-blah, it might be worth a try to build a craving for it. A short trial could be cost-free and harmless and people can still be friendly and a family for a few weeks in non-verbal silence. Some Buddhists do it and it is meant to be good for the soul. In a verbally-silent atmosphere, the non-verbal person may feel 'normal' for a change ('normal' is to be in the company of others like oneself). That is a luxury that I think all people need but not all of them get.

MIRRORING

Mirroring can be a prerequisite to learning. It can be a step in developing awareness of 'other' and in getting observable feedback of what one's own actions or expressions look or sound like.

For someone with monitoring problems or someone whose 'mono' functioning inhibits their ability to remain properly aware of more than one track at a time, mirroring may be the only feedback of their self-expression that they may get. Whilst non-autistic people may be able to fathom their effect upon others through the reactions of others in response to themselves, some people with 'autism' may not be able to extract this information. For them, $1+1$ never equals 2. It just keeps equalling $1+1$ and they may remain effectively 'deaf to their own selfhood' even if they are expressing something.

Mirroring is about impersonally copying the actions of someone else. This can give them feedback but also, because they have already got an internal context for the behaviour they expressed, when they observe or hear it reflected back at them, they may be able to process these actions and expressions, even if they can't efficiently process actions and expressions for which they have no ready-established internal context. Finding that someone makes sense in a world which seems not to (even if they only make sense when behaving and speaking like the person perceiving them) can be a relief and a bridge to building trust.

Mirroring is about being in the company of someone AS THAT SOME-ONE. After going through a stage of being with the person AS THE PERSON and establishing yourself as a comprehensible, non-bombarding presence, you may slowly be able to break out of 'being with the "autistic" person as them' to very gradually asserting non-bombarding, unintrusive and non-overloading elements of your own personhood and individuality.

At this point, you may find that the person with 'autism' feels better with you following their lead. You may be able very tentatively and progressively, but gradually, to encourage them to 'wrestle' you socially into being with them as them again (because you being with them as them, may have felt like safe and predictable territory).

Breaking away progressively more frequently to assert the separateness between you and them may challenge them to try to reconcile and accept this in stages, but this is a very tentative balance to maintain. Activities used to establish your separateness should be things which the person with 'autism' will have demonstrated an 'interest' in and have shown to comprehend in some way. In this way the person may not be so afraid and may only have to grapple with a more minor feeling of lack of control. Hills are easier to climb than mountains.

If the person appears overloaded or too scared at losing control you can compromise by partly, but not wholly, becoming them again. Eventually any security they found in their new-found sense of company (where they know you as separate but comprehensible) may be enough to motivate them to try to cause you to take action. This would be a good move. It would be a building block to interaction. If you get to this mirroring stage you can also use it to work on language.

You could expect the possibility of aggression. Aggression can be a natural product of growing awareness and the frustration and trappedness the person may feel with this change. Some degree of frustration and trappedness MUST, in my opinion, be felt in order to use aversion (the aversion to losing predictability) as a source of motivation to a move forward (if there is an absence of general attraction-based motivation to be 'social').

During an aggressive reaction it is important first to check all sources of potential overload that could be causing problems. If overload has been minimised as much as possible, then it could be reasonable to assume that the frustration may be in response to the changes rather than overload and it may be important to channel, rather than cut off, any aggressive action. Aggression can be a step towards the birth of the mind, the emotions, want and self-initiation. It is sometimes important that it be channelled rather than stopped or cut off. Cutting the person off at this stage may sometimes leave no safe place to turn but back to oblivion, indifference and dependence (which would be familiar and therefore, feel safe but these things are not a constructive direction).

MOVEMENT, ART AND MUSIC

Including reluctant 'autistic' people in movement, art or music should take account of receptive tolerance of 'directly-confrontational' interaction as much as it should take account of sensory, emotional or cognitive processing thresholds.

A reluctant 'autistic' person may 'tune out' or 'disappear' (due to shutdowns, dissociation or withdrawal) if attempts to include them are too 'directly-confrontational'.

One 'indirectly-confrontational' way to initiate creative movement may be for the non-autistic person to move 'for him or herself' in a non-invasive, non-bombarding way, seemingly 'oblivious' to the 'autistic' person yet within their observable presence. There is, in this situation, no need to stop or change what one is doing in response to the person with 'autism' (unless he or she is in danger). In this way, it is left for the reluctant person with 'autism' to get the message that they will not be bombarded or controlled, nor unpredictably and suddenly responded to if they dare to test the boundaries of this apparent social safety. In this way, the reluctant 'autistic' person may come to know that nobody will make them notice they are noticing and the 'autistic' person may come to know that nobody will make them notice they are noticing and the 'autistic' person may gradually become progressively more 'directly' observant of what the other person is doing.

At this point, the reluctant 'autistic' person should be allowed to take the lead and the non-autistic person could gradually progressively show more 'directly-confrontational' (through unbombarding) subtle acknowledgement of the 'autistic' person's initiatives. The more predictable and familiar creative movement is (i.e. same clothes, same room, same time, same music) the safer the 'autistic' person may feel with involvement and the more likely he or she may be eventually able to be directly observant or involved in what is going on without forced compliance.

It is important to note that some people with visual-perceptual problems may have extreme difficulties processing movement if they are seeing people as collections of fragmented bits. Furthermore, people with visual-perceptual problems may have a very poor sense of depth, space and movement through space. These perceptual problems should be taken account of if it appears these are making involvement in creative movement a frightening experience for them.

Art may also be done 'for yourself' in the person's presence with no particular attention towards them or any signal of expectation that they join in (but of course casually giving them materials if they, however subtly, indicate that want or interest).

Sound/musical compositions can be repetitive but can also be about expressing emotions. To allow you to hear what the 'autistic' person has created can be an indirect sharing of emotions and true self. In this way, a musical 'dialogue' can be established back and forth in an equally indirectly-confrontational way.

It is important to take account of the particular sounds that each person with 'autism' finds non-threatening. Some people with 'autism' may particularly like the sound of drums. Others may find these irritating or disturbing but like the sound of a triangle. Some may like woody sounds. Some may like the sounds of string instruments or the piano. Some may consider the sounds of gravel, leaves, water or the tapping of tin to be as captivating/interesting/expressive, or more so, than any conventional musical instrument.

Any interest in music can be expanded upon. Getting a guitar and teaching yourself some simple chords, you can write lessons into simple compositions, even to already familiar tunes. If someone listens, for example, to the song 'Incy Wincy Spider', you can take this tune and write some of your words to the chords of this song and sing simple lessons. The lessons can be anything you want to teach, from the different steps involved in going to the toilet to getting out a snack to eat or having a bath. Things like washing hands, order of dressing, emotional expressions and how they feel, whatever involves a simple lesson or sequence, can be put to music. Verses can be added later as the songs are picked up and gradually lessons can be expanded upon.

I have a lot of difficulty establishing routines like teethbrushing in the morning if I move to a new environment. Using songs can trigger these routines. Paul and I, for example, have established a ritual of using the tune to 'The Farmer in the Dell' which follows our taking of vitamins in the morning. We put the words, 'The Brushing of the Teeth' to this tune and the song and words are cued by the vitamin taking and without fail lead me into the morning teethbrushing where it is otherwise about fifty–fifty that I forget.

If the person comes to sing known tunes, verbally, or mentally, songs can be a good way to carry along a sort of 'map' by which to trigger the sequence of steps involved in doing something. You can make home-made audio or video tapes of your made up songs and teach actions to go with the words to do with things you think need teaching or prompting. You can later do the same for stories or simple knowledge topics by expanding on verses.

PERSONALITY

Some people with 'autism' may seem devoid of personality. Other 'autistic' children and adults, especially if they seem to take on 'being' the people they are with, may seem full of personality but it may lack the flexibility of self-initiated non-triggered spontaneity, so it may seem not to be 'their own'. I have seen this happen in some 'high functioning' people who have been echopraxic or echolalic (automatically mirroring the movements and voices of others) as children and develop excellent mimicry skills in place of developing their own self-expression and (non-mimicked) social skills.

If this sounds like someone you know tactics involving teaching to copy, when employed long term, can sometimes have unfortunate effects on the person's confidence level, motivation, trust and emotional development, in spite of enabling them to achieve some level of popularity or inclusion this way.

Whilst some people are content to try to treat these patchwork repertoires as though they form their true personality, others may recognise that they are not their true self and may reach a point where they fall into a depression and get fed up with 'performing' for people (as mimicry and repertoires may feel like this). They may become prone to panic attacks, depression or rages if they realise they cannot experience the life they are 'performing' or feel others are so much more impressed with their mimicked version of 'self' than their true, probably very much less developed and less expressed, real self.

For those who wake up to the falsity and superficiality of their performances, it may feel like yet another prison. They may feel trapped upon a 'stage' and that the people around them, like wardens of their prison, keep them up there by seeming to accept them only in this form.

Many parents of high functioning people with 'autism' build their pride upon the person's ability to appear 'normal' and, intentionally or unintention-ally, display disappointment or pity if they falter in this 'achievement'. To a person with 'autism' who becomes thoroughly disillusioned and fed up with this situation, any apathy about this once pursued role may be perceived by others as a breakdown or regression, interfering with what the non-autistic people in their environment may think of as the 'autistic' person's USUAL self.

For carers who care enough to help such troubled people get real it can be hard work, but worth it to help them realise what they may already sense but not understand; that there is a distinct difference between how they 'appear' and how they 'are' inside. For some people with 'autism' this difference may be a chasm.

For some carers faced with this problem the choice may be whether they'd rather pretend that the depression, apathy, confusion or turmoil isn't happening and keep trying to stuff the person with 'autism' into a Ken or Barbie doll mould (in all its many mimicked forms) or whether they are prepared to take a look at what went on, how things got to where they did, and just who their child may really be under their success at 'acting normal'.

For those carers who have the courage and humanity and ability to swallow their pride and see the person with 'autism' for who and where they really are, there are some ways that might help some people with 'autism' to change tracks. These hints are not, however, about getting the person back onto the track of the façade they may have achieved, but to get them onto a track they may have left behind a long time ago. These hints aren't about sticking a new jumper over a tatty one. They are about unravelling the tatty jumper to the point where it might be possible to pick up the dropped stitches.

If the 'autistic' person's 'acting normal' repertoires form some kind of persona, you can encourage them to give this persona a name. If the persona with 'autism' seems to have a different face for different people, groups of people, or places and goes to great lengths to keep them separate, he or she can be encouraged to name each of the different 'faces'. After naming these 'faces', a diary or scrapbook can be made of the person's 'faces' and what areas of life each one related to, any expressions, facial characteristics, stance, tone of voice, pace of movement, and the person's own physical 'self-image' description of them. This may help some of these troubled people to piece their life together later, once they are better able to reason through all of the changes. It may give them a sense of continuity and wholeness by giving them ownership and external recognition of their patchwork of repertoires and personae.

They could be encouraged to find any photos that they perceive as being expressing of their characters and an album or scrap book could be created for each.

A drama room/corner of some sort can be set up and big boxes could be decorated and labelled for each character according to its perceived 'personality'. Anything that belonged to that character (i.e., clothes, collections, etc) could be put in its appropriate box. With a lot of structuring, this could, over time, be channelled into an interest in drama. By being able to consider their characters as 'performances', the person may come to feel more in control of when they put on characters and not feel so out of control in the hands of other people's expectations to be someone other than themselves.

If a troubled person is extremely insecure about giving up the personae totally, they might consider an interim arrangement whereby they could be one of these characters on a particular day or part of a day each week (considering this allocated time to be acknowledged as 'on stage time').

PROXIMITY

Featureless papier maché replicas of people, statues (cemeteries can be good for this), or trees, may be used to promote interaction with controllable, inanimate, human-like, forms. This could be part of a 'bridging' strategy to build very gradually the transition to toys that represent living creatures, pets and also people. People should also keep in mind that visual-perceptual problems may be a big obstacle to perceiving animals or people as whole entities. For people with severe visual-perceptual problems, perceiving animals or people in fragmented bits may make it very hard to make the move from interacting with inanimate objects to interacting with moving ones, as movement can make keeping track of things as a whole even more difficult, unpredictable and unfamiliar.

Any visual-perceptual problems should be addressed if possible and the gradual transition from inanimate to animate may be made easier if animate beings were to move in slow, concise, predictable and purposeful movements in the presence of someone with these problems. This also gives more processing time in which to make sense of who is moving towards them, why that entity is moving towards them, how they feel about that and to respond according to their own feelings or understanding.

Wearing angora, velvet, tulle, wooden beads, leather, vinyl, lace or whatever material the person with 'autism' has shown an attraction to (or at least no aversion to) may help encourage initial interest, exploration, interaction and touch. There are many ways in which materials can be incorporated in interaction – taking someone to where they are made, sold or grown is all part of learning.

The sharing of the clothing or jewellery to which a person with 'autism' has been attracted can be used as a symbolic form of interpersonal touch at a distance. I have often established a feeling of safety around people through experiencing them through their things and have also felt safe around things that were worn or carried by people I felt safe with.

If fabrics or materials are creating such a distraction that the person with 'autism' is unable to pay attention, the proportion of these things can be gradually decreased until all that is left is that the person has some sensorily pleasant association between you and those things. This is a bit like the cat that purrs around your feet, not because it likes you, but because it has come to associate you with pleasant sensory sensations caused by food. My father established a rapport with me through my associating him with the bringing of sensorily-pleasurable trinkets.

PSYCHIATRISTS

Misdiagnosis of people with able autism and Asperger Syndrome, especially in those born in the 1960s and earlier, is very common and many have been labelled as disturbed or mentally ill or as having mood or personality disorders at some point in their lives. Also, many people with 'autism' do have other non-autism-related disorders and it may be that some people have two or more conditions. The possibility of this may make some psychiatrists who have 'autistic' patients (including people with Asperger Syndrome) reluctant to assist them in getting referrals to get qualified help to do with the development of social communication skills. There is also a tendency to associate 'autism' with the so-called 'less able' or 'low functioning' stereotypes, which is not helpful.

However, people have a right to seek help for difficulties that are UNRE-LATED to mental illness, such as developmentally-related social communication skills and sensory-perceptual and body-awareness difficulties. These are things of which some psychiatrists may have little or no experience, but which experts in 'autism' or Asperger Syndrome (such as some developmental or cognitive psychologists) can often help with.

RAGES

These are a bit like the sort of feelings that drive self-abuse. For some people they may be more outward-directed and for others they may be more inner-directed.

Sometimes when I have an emotion that is too big for me it can trigger a kind of emotional 'fit'. These can be like wild rages but for me tend to be more implosive than explosive. I have found that a natural amino acid called DMG (dimethyl glycine) has decreased the frequency and intensity of these 'fits' or attacks (DMG has also worked well in controlling epilepsy in some people).

Learning to ask for help when I couldn't control myself was a really big step forward and has really made me feel more secure and able to live with these attacks when they happen. The other thing I used to do was run on the spot or jump up and down on a bed (for 15–30 minutes) when they happened. This, however, takes a great deal of mental application and, in the grip of a 'fit', my mental application is not good for much except the self-violence I am being compelled towards. I have found, though, that a stringent unbreakable rule can be formed through ritual, such as to run on the spot or jump for a fixed time during a 'fit'. Forming a triggerable ritual like this can get around the need for mental application or having a want to do this (the ritual of the rule over-rides the necessity to have to have a want to run on the spot or jump). Recently, the other most helpful thing I have found is jumping on a pogo stick (or skipping). It somehow jolts me about violently enough and uses enough energy for my brain to feels as if it has got it all out. What I have found is that these 'fits' or attacks generally have a fixed time (for me 15–30 minutes). If I can manage to keep the 'fit' at bay for that amount of time, I am usually over it quite dramatically.

This probably works for me because the rage is a the result of some intermittent bio-chemistry problem rather than a real expression of feelings. Handling 'fits' in this way can mean that they can be managed and gotten through without any of the guilt, remorse or shame that is sometimes later felt when the rage got out of hand.

If someone vomits, they shouldn't feel guilty, even if it messes up the carpet. One can take steps to mimimise the mess and not feel guilty about things one couldn't help. This approach also helps to promote understanding of the difference between oneself (as a personality and self) and these 'fits' (as one's body) and to know that as emotional as these 'fits' can be, they are not necessarily expressions of one's feelings and may only be a chemical trigger quite independent of one's real feelings.

FIGHTING SELF-ABUSE

In the grip of a compulsion to self-abuse I may be unable physically to stop the urges from being carried out. Sometimes, I have fought these psychologically as hard as possible, consciously aware that I didn't want to attack myself, yet felt the compelling urge so overwhelmingly strongly that no amount of conscious psychological reasoning or awareness could stop it.

Perhaps this is like an addiction. Certainly, giving in to the urge in the slightest way only feeds an even greater striving to go further, regardless of a psychological awareness and commitment that this is not wanted. Nevertheless, in spite of relative helplessness, one CAN decide whether one will take the responsibility to ask for physical help to stop these urges from being carried out.

When I have been in this position, I have sometimes got Paul to hold my hands if I feel the urge to use them to attack myself. I get him to hold me tightly if I feel the urge to body-slam myself. I take conscious responsibility to fight these urges because I know these compulsions are not my wants.

Involuntary compulsions to self-abuse might sometimes (in some people with 'automatic' or 'savant skills') be written or typed out of one's system (though having a pencil or pen around during this state could be a safety hazard). The same may be true of an automatic musical or artistic skill (watch out for paint brushes or pencils, though). These self-abusive drives might also sometimes be exhausted through physical exercise. In this way, one might use these 'creative' or exercise 'frenzies' to redirect the energy that would have come out in self-abuse.

Getting someone to sit upon the person in the grip of a self-abuse compulsion may be what it takes to control the situation until the 'fit' is over but I would suggest that it be within the choice and control of the person with 'autism' to choose the option, where possible.

The involuntary compulsion to self-abuse is like a 'fit' or a sort of 'compulsion-vomit'. Unlike the abuse that is related to emotional or psychological disturbance, it has no known psychological basis and the person in the grip of this compulsion may be psychologically opposed to carrying out this urge and, other than the emotional turmoil of this out of control threat for one's own body, the person may feel no emotional turmoil about anything at that time.

If constructively challenged and not indulged in, these 'fits' may only last a short time before the urge passes. For me, this can be between fifteen minutes and one hour. If I am restrained by my own choice and do not get to indulge this compulsion, emotions usually rescue me from it and once emotion gets released the energy that would otherwise be directed into self-abuse is lost.

In my view, the most important way to combat self-abuse is to prevent it in the first place. Particularly if it is resulting from information overload, then reducing this overload and improving the efficiency of information processing should reduce the intensity and frequency of these 'fits'.

The 'fits' actually seem to cause a sort of 'buzz' that makes my body feel 'purged' and 'relieved' in spite of feeling afraid and out of control at being on the receiving end of what my brain drove my body to do against my will. This 'purging' sensation may well be either an attempt to sort of 'wash out' the system of some form of information overload, or to cause a shutting down of information accumulation (by abusing the body to trigger the perception of being under attack) in order to decrease the rate of incoming information.

Not being able to fight these urges may set up an incredible feeling of being a victim of one's own self. A lot of people have been very against aversives (the use of severe preventative measures that are sometimes viewed as a form of 'torture'). I don't believe that aversives should be the first choice in managing self-abusive behaviour. I also feel they shouldn't be used in cases where the self-abuse is due to what I call 'problems of tolerance' (such as sensory or emotional hypersensitivity) where these problems could be managed by reducing sensory or emotional bombardment. There are many other things that can be done to stop anxiety from resulting in self-abuse by decreasing the sources of intolerance.

I also don't think that aversives should be used in cases of what I call 'problems of connection' (such as attention problems, perceptual problems and systems integration problems). Self-abuse, in these cases, may be due more to information overload and that can also be reduced, lessening the problem.

The only case where I feel it might be practical to use aversives is where the person themselves seems to find aversives useful in learning to fight compulsive urges to self-abuse. In my view, where the drive to self-abuse is an addictive and compulsion-driven one, and is not related to sensory or emotional hypersensitivity nor to information overload, the person experiencing self-abusive urges may actually welcome assistance outside of themselves.

I have sometimes gone to Paul and asked to have my hand slapped because I have pulled my hair, bitten a finger or punched or slapped myself because of a compulsive urge. I have got him to do this to reinforce in me a triggerable image that will come up as an association to following through with these drives. These drives are often pre-empted by a sort of 'playing out' of the sensation that will be felt when these are carried out and it is this 'taste of what it will feel like' that seems to inflate the urge to the point where it can't be psychologically fought. Being able to associate an undesirable consequence with the action, the pre-empting that addictively drives the urge to self-abuse can trigger the memory of the consequence rather than *only* triggering pre-sensations of the impending self-abuse. It is those pre-sensations (and sometimes pre-images) that actually increase the addictive drive to carry out the self-abuse. When the consequence comes up instead in response to the trigger, it gets easier to fight or even diffuse the urge to self-abuse or at least play for time to seek help.

Calcium deficiency has been found to be associated with self-abuse in some cases. I do take supplements for a calcium deficiency; my diet is anyway low in calcium due to lactose intolerance (and intolerance to soy milk as well).

It is important to point out that there are other causes for self-abuse. Some self-abuse is purely expressive. For example, when I was impacted upon by eye contact with others, this sometimes resulted in me punching myself sharply. At such times, I always glared at whoever I was making my statement to. Basically, I'd assumed they had understood that the emotional impact of this eye contact gripped my stomach with such intensity and suddenness that I felt the looker had somehow punched me by this crime of looking at me. By clearly showing them what they had caused, I had assumed they'd obviously understand (I was assuming they had a similar experience of this effect) and stop doing the offending behaviour (looking). Compliments also caused expressive self-abusive behaviour, causing me to display exactly how they had affected me. I would slap myself suddenly because compliments always made me feel slapped and I displayed this through my actions, giving the message loud and clear, 'don't do that, it feels like this'.

In cases of expressive self-abuse, providing signs to request the cessation of certain impacting behaviours such as 'no looking', 'no touching', 'no words' may be an alternative even if the looking, touching and kind words were never intended to be perceived as 'hurt' (to someone with autism, being impacted upon may be indistinguishable from physical 'hurt' which may be experienced as just another form of intense and sudden impact). Another option is to encourage the use of sound, such as drums or notes on the piano, to express impact. Movement and the use of paint can also be used to express variations in impact. The important thing to realise is that these expressions through music, movement or art need to be listened to because, by contrast, when someone uses self-abuse expressively, it almost *always* has the effect of causing a change in the other person's behaviour (for example, suddenly the impacting compliments and cooing and eye contact may stop as a struggle to control or ignore the self-abuse takes its place – for the person with autism, the expression has been effective).

Other self-abuse may not be experienced as self-abuse at all. The sensory 'buzz' effect of some self-abuse, such as biting, slapping and hair tugging may involve tingling sensations and their repetition and control over their repeated initiation in a world which seems chaotic and beyond control, may be intense reinforcements for using buzz-related self-abuse. Vibration may be a useful tool to replace reliance on self-abuse related buzzing. Push button repetitious visual or sound patterns may also help replace this reliance. It is important to realise that, as carers emphasise an end to repetitious self-stimulation involving the visual and auditory, the only buzz object that the carer can't take away may be the body. Setting aside agreed upon set times of the day for non-self-abusive 'buzzing' may be a compromise worth considering.

SELF-AWARENESS AND SELF-EXPRESSION

Mirrors, tape recorders and typewriters (or computers) could be used to help develop self-communication for some people. For someone who has no social interaction or communication, this may be the least threatening, most familiar, controllable and predictable place to start.

Costumes, foreign accents, conversation-songs, rhymes and puppets could also be used to encourage expression in a way that allows some degree of personal distance. For some people, being able to do this at their own pace may be a way to develop self-awareness in a self-controlled and self-regulated way.

TELEPHONES

Communicating via telephone (just as someone can communicate through writing or a home video) can be a safe 'bridge' to progressively more 'directly-confrontational' communication and interaction. No-one can touch you, or look at you through a phone. People on a telephone line can be 'disembodied', even 'theoretical' (as opposed to 'existing'), people. People on a telephone can be merely a voice there to speak to or only listen to or to hang up on. Communicating via telephone can maintain the tentative balance of 'self' and 'other' in people for whom the overwhelming sense of 'other' is generally at the cost of connection to 'self' and all expression that would come from self.

Phoning numbers to hear people's voices can be one way to begin enjoying listening and becoming acquainted with these tools of interaction and the initiation of interaction. One could start with the time service or the weather service which are predictable and don't need feedback. There are also story-lines, music-lines and recorded news reports for the blind.

Later, calls could be arranged with people who will speak slowly and simply, saying only one or two predictable sentences and who won't have too many language expectations of the person calling (someone who won't mind being phoned just to be listened to for a sentence or two).

Later, additional predictable sentences could be added and, eventually, simple questions requiring very simple, one word, responses. In time, a telephoning ritual could become established and the person being called could gradually increase the demands of communication to the point where telephone conversation develops some degree of flexibility and interaction.

From here, it is a short step to using play phones to speak with someone in the same room, yet maintaining 'safe' personal distance (and the right to end the interaction by the actions of 'hanging up'). This could be faded out to using any object as a 'phone' whilst speaking to someone else in the room and, later, even to miming the 'call'.

Eventually, over time, this could gradually be 'bridged' to more 'directly-confrontational' interpersonal 'fact-to-face' verbal communication. One thing to keep in mind, however, is the sensory hypersensitivity of some people to certain types of telephone bells, volumes and pitch of voice.

TEXTURE PROBLEMS

I have one particular texture problem that I call 'wool on wool'. 'Wool on wool' makes it very difficult to tolerate hair rubbing against hair or cloth against cloth so it difficult to tolerate people's hair rubbing on me or their clothes rubbing my clothes and it is difficult to tolerate putting woollen jumpers over my head. 'Wool on wool' also means that I only tolerate my hair being dried in a certain way and it can also make it hard to walk on some carpets with certain types of socks or to tolerate the dragging of fabric over carpet. These things contribute to making public transport difficult and sitting next to people (but those are hard in other ways too). It has even made eating peaches difficult (which I now cope with). The effect of these things on me, if prolonged, can be like those associated with hypersensitive hearing. In me textural adversities can cause manic behaviour and could, if inescapable and continuous, escalate to some degree of (generally self-directed in my case) aggression.

Paul has a texture intolerance he calls 'pruny'. I had the same one when I was a child (up until about ten) but I called it 'nanny'. Fortunately, I outgrew it (perhaps like some 'allergic' reactions).

'Pruny'/'Nanny' involves clammy skin-like textures touching one another, or sometimes just wet skin touching any surface that causes a squeaky sort of friction. It makes it hard for Paul at bath time or touching his wet feet or hands on his own or those of others, but it has a whole lot of other flow-on effects involving activities and 'nanny'-feeling objects. If Paul is forced to have prolonged contact or exposure to 'nanny' textures he feels compelled to get away and escape the feeling.

I heard from a naturopath once that these difficulties with textures can be caused by allergic responses to texture. If I somehow got over one texture reaction naturally and developed others, then this could well be true, as this is exactly how many of my food allergies change too. That leaves open the possibility of desensitisation to these textures and you could either discuss that possibility with a sensitive someone who deals with allergic reactions or hypersensitivities in 'autistic' people or you could, as I did with 'social-touching', create your own desensitisation program at a suitable pace.

TOILET TRAINING

First you have to work out the difficulty; going anywhere anytime, holding on forever, fear of the toilet, sound sensitivity to the flushing, going to the toilet through clothes. Once you pinpoint the toiletting problem, you have to work out what is causing it.

Going everywhere anytime can be a symbolic act of breaking free which needs to be replaced with something else before it will go away. Jumping from heights, or falling through space can also give this sensation of breaking free, and could be used to replace this 'need'. A trampoline/bed to jump on may help some people experiment with the feeling of letting go control and experiencing freedom.

On the other hand, going anywhere at anytime could just be due to lack of processing of body messages and their significance. It could also be to do with an accessing problem in doing something about the body sensations you are aware of having but haven't connected with your body and getting to the places and doing the things to deal with situation successfully. Improving the efficiency of information processing and reducing overload may help improve these underlying problems.

Holding on forever can be about lack of, or fluctuating physical awareness of, body messages. In this case, improving the efficiency of information processing and reducing information overload may help set things straight.

Holding on forever can also be about fear of losing control. To ascertain this, you can look at parallels with other behaviours to work out which of these causes it is or if it is even a mixture of both.

Fear of losing control is a difficult thing to tackle. Making the environment easier to process, giving more time and space to access connections and monitor self-expression can all be ways of reducing the feeling of being out of control. Fear of control is often related to emotional hypersensitivity. Helping people to understand their feelings, what they are called, why they are there and where they are coming from, can help some people to befriend emotions.

Fear of the toilet can be related to a hearing sensitivity to do with flushing (in which case you may find either anxiety or compulsion to do with running water). The answer to this is to establish a trust that you won't flush whilst the person is in the room (once use of the toilet is well established you can work on helping the person get accustomed to feeling in control of the sound of running water).

Fear of the toilet could be to do with sensory-perceptual problems relating to the lighting in the room, whereby being in the toilet is claustrophobic when movement is combined with a little space or the room appears particularly fragmented and disorienting. This might be solved with dim lighting or a particular colour of light bulb or special tinted glasses to correct visual-perceptual problems. Another perception-related problem may be to do with perception of relative size of the toilet bowl compared to one's body. For those with poor perception of their own body or relative size, the toilet bowl may appear to be this threatening big 'bum biter' and having seen things get flushed away in a raging torrent of water it may be easy to suspect that your own body may befall a similar fate. In this case, getting a smaller toilet seat to put over the big one and/or handles on the wall to hold onto, may help some people overcome this terrifying aversion.

Fear of the toilet could be about the tactile effect of the coldness of the bowl and the shock and imposition on a state of blissful non-awareness that this jolt to body-awareness causes. Altering the temperature or tactile effect of the seat may solve this.

Fear of the toilet could be about feeling out of control in being made to go into 'this room'. Establishing a portable but temporary toilet somewhere where the person feels safe (where they don't seem bothered or distracted or 'lost'), and establishing a new routine that doesn't create these feelings of being robbed of control, may help until they are well toilet trained.

Fear of the toilet could also be to do with the obvious and specific intent and expectations to do with the room and there being no way to drift out of awareness, thereby triggering a fear of exposure and self-expression. Allowing people to go to the toilet on 'autopilot' without praise or any other consciousness-jolting behaviour may solve this particular aversion, as might the provision of a rhythm or familiar music by which the person might be able to 'tune out' and reduce anxiety. If you need to be present you could imagine your own fear of exposure if you were being made to take a pee in front of an audience who had come to watch you and control you and wait till you went. Think of how much easier it might be for you if that audience all took out a book or some knitting or played some gentle, quiet background music you liked and knew. You could 'go into your own world' a bit more and the person with 'autism' may be more able to climb out of their own long enough to go to the toilet and get out of there.

Making the toilet a less scary place to go can improve things. Reducing echo, changing lighting, background music or altering the colour or decor are some things that could make it a place the person might feel less reluctance to go. Allowing someone to take security-objects with them may also help.

Going to the toilet in or through one's clothes can be about a lack of, or fluctuation in, the processing of body messages or accessing the connections to do something about these messages. It can also be about being in control of excretion, keeping it to oneself, enjoying the physical sensations of predictable and self-controlled warmth or damp (as one does a bath). These sensations can be replaced by other things, such as bathing in one's clothes (no problem if they were dirty) or handling clay.

It can also be about the need to break free and defy (in an obvious way) the compulsion to hold on and maintain control, in which case it is an important 'phase' but could be replaced with a more 'acceptable' way of achieving the same feeling, such as jumping from heights or letting oneself fall through space. Again, trampolining/bed jumping might be more 'acceptable' ways of getting this feeling of letting go of control.

If the person prefers to do art with excreta than to putting it in the toilet then no amount of ridicule or shouting may be able to change it. You could work out if it is the smell or texture or the scooping or the squish or the sound or the art or the familiarity of something that came from themselves, which is what makes it so attractive.

Play Doh, plasticine and bread dough, resemble the feel of poo. Mud, squashy fruit or tomatoes can feel similar and could be used to smear as a replacement for excretion. Plastic 'joke poo' looks like the real thing and may be able to help break down the war between smearer and cleaner. Any of these things might be used to break the habit even if it means letting someone carry it around in a pocket or paint the walls with it for a time.

If the person smears poo on the walls, it may not be the wall part that needs to be replaced with paper, it may be the poo part which need replacing with something similar. Presenting someone with paint as a replacement may not help. The person may not make the connection between no more poo on the walls but here is some paint and paper. Paint doesn't smell, feel or look like poo and paper has to be fetched and used intentionally – something very difficult even for some 'high functioning' people.

If you shudder at the thought of promoting smearing, consider the difference between repainting the walls and replacing clothes at the end of the year (when the child has got over this phase with something less distasteful) versus painting, cleaning and replacing things covered with poo for the next ten years – not to mention the smell.

Large mural-sized sheets of paper or plastic sheeting can be put up on the walls and clay or mud could be provided in place of poo and this could eventually be watered down and gradually replaced with brown poster paints (and then gradually with other colours).

Some people have trouble with choosing the toilet rather than the basin or bath. This can be a visual-perceptual thing where they are only processing part of the information; i.e. enamel receptacles into which fluid goes. It can also be a category thing where the person has formed the idea that all these things are interchangeable with basically similar things.

I had this with toilet paper and bathroom towels. A white towel hung on a ring between the bath and toilet, next to the toilet roll holder was an invitation to trouble. Both things were obviously for the same purpose of wiping, both were white, but the towel was softer. Naturally, and without apology I chose the towel in place of toilet paper. You can paint the toilet a different colour from the rest of the suite so it is clear that it is part of a different category and keep all choices clearly distinguished from one another.

VIBRATION

Some people love the vibration of dryers, washing machines or photocopies. I used to spend most of the wash cycle with my body lying on the top of the washing machine and did the same thing with photocopiers and dryers. In my experience, this has to do with lack of one's own inner rhythm. I think it relates to body awareness. For me, it can give a kind of reassurance, like a cat's purr.

Vibration can be used as a medium for interaction. Tapping one's throat as one's speaks can cause the voice to vibrate and stir the interest of someone with an attraction to vibration. They may take it up and, if so, it might be one aspect in which they find speaking, sharing or communication to be playful, less personal and an enjoyable sensory experience. Vibration could also be used as a non-invasive, personally detached introduction to touch for people for whom it had an attraction and caused no sensory disturbance. Massage appliances can be brought at most big electrical departments and some people with 'autism', even if intolerant to most forms of social touching, may tolerate foot or scalp massages.

VIDEO COMMUNICATION

If a person with 'autism' watches videos, one way of communicating things you think they should know or need to know, is to make a home video of these lessons using a home-video recorder. Lessons can be about naming emotions, facial expressions, toilet training, making breakfast or getting dressed. Lessons can make use of established 'interests' or collections or can be used to teach spoken or written language.

Lessons can be presented using puppets if these are not frightening. Lessons should, however, be filmed from the perspective of the person watching. If you want to teach someone about going to a certain room, you should use the camera as the subject who is going into the room (you are not seen), rather than setting up the camera to film yourself walking into the room. To the person watching, the first way can give the viewer the impression that he or she is being taken into the room. The second way creates the impression that the person doing the filming is getting closer and closer to the viewer.

Videos can be left out for the person with 'autism' to watch or put on when the person wants to watch a video. Carers could leave the room so that the person with 'autism' could watch and listen to it without fear of observation or feeling robbed of control over the experience.

A lot of my own social aversion to, and difficulty with, listening was because of it being too 'directly confrontational' to handle. When things were too 'directly confrontational', I felt I had no area of privacy in which to cope with what I thought or felt about what I was hearing or seeing. The anxiety of this contributed to problems in processing the meaning or significance of what I was seeing or hearing.

Video 'dialogue' can be established by talking (briefly, purposefully and concisely) to the 'autistic' person through the video. The 'indirectly confrontational' nature of this interaction may be unthreatening enough for them, if unobserved, to tune in. Home-video recorders can be hired quite cheaply in order to give this a trial run. If this method is useful, it might, in the long run, be cheaper to buy one. Home-made video lessons may be more situation-appropriate and cheaper than seeking out commercially-made video learning packages.

Contacts

Organisations

Alternative Approaches to Autism Consultancy (A.A.A.C.)

PO Box 1, Alfrick, Worcestershire
WR6 5YW, UK
tel/fax 0044-(0)1886 832987

AAAC is a consultancy service run by Donna Williams which seeks to provide alternative individual approaches to autism-related conditions for carers, professionals and people affected by autism-related conditions themselves. It aims to identify potential causes of autism-related problems which can then be treated, such as chemical intolerances or sensory perceptual problems. Training and instruction in 'home-based' programmes may be available to help those with autism-related conditions to achieve greater independence.

Autism Network International (ANI)

PO Box 448, Syracuse, NY 1321-0448, USA

ANI is an autistic-run international self-help and advocacy organisation for autistic people. Its philosophy and goals are:

- The best advocates for autistic people are autistic people themselves.
- Supports for 'autistic' people should be aimed at helping them to compensate, navigate and function in the world, not at changing them into non-autistic people or isolating them from the world.
- Autistic people of all ages and all levels of ability and skill are entitled to adequate and appropriate services.
- ANI works to improve the lives of autistic people who, for whatever reason, are not able to advocate for themselves.

ANI also runs an international newsletter called *Our Voice*, *by* and *for* other autistic people (diagnosed or not). They have also established an international computer-communication network for people with autism and those interested in discussing autism-related issues. They are also able to organise autistic public speakers.

Many 'autistic' people write in to the newsletter with stories, letters, drawings, poetry, tips or seeking contacts. ANI also run a confidential pen-pal list which is ONLY open to people with 'autism'-related conditions.

The Care and Action Trust for Children with Handicaps (CATCH)

Oystermouth House, Charter Court, Phoenix Way, Enterprise Park, Swansea SA7 9FS, UK
tel 0044-(0)1792 790077
fax 0044-(0)1792 772137

The Care and Action Trust for Children with Handicaps is essentially a charity for families. It does exactly what the name suggests. It *cares* for the whole family by helping them understand and come to terms with their child's problems, which in turn will help the family to care for the child in a loving, positive way. It provides *action* by teaching the family how to help the child develop to the best of his or her abilities, by campaigning for better services and, it is hoped, by changing public understanding and attitudes to allow more acceptance and integration for handicapped children.

The Centre for the Study of Complementary Medicine

51 Bedford Place, Southampton, Hampshire
SO15 2DT, UK
tel 0044-(0)1703 334752

The Centre offers non-invasive allergy testing, desensitisation and looks into the treatment of problems such as the underlying causes of food and chemical intolerances, vitamin-mineral deficiencies, hypoglycemia and candida albicans. Referrals by a GP may be covered by health benefits under an extra-contractual referal.

Communities for Autistic People Limited
Ashleigh College, 3 Elmfield Park, Gosforth
Newcastle upon Tyne NE3 4UX, UK
tel 0044-(0)191 213 0833

Communities for Autistic People Limited provides care for those with autism to enable young people to have a more independent and adult lifestyle.

CAN (Cure Autism Now)
5225 Wilshire Boulevard #503, Los
Angeles, California 90036, USA
tel 001-213 549 0500
fax 001-213 549 0547
e-mail CAN@primenet.com

CAN is a new organisation founded by parents dedicated to finding effective biological treatments and a cure for autism by funding medical research in autism with direct clinical applications. CAN's Scientific Work Group is made up of top researchers and clinicians in the field of autism, many of whom are parents of autistic children themselves. CAN believes that it is the parents who will mobilise the scientific and medical communities into action and that our hands-on involvement and funding support is crucial to finding treatment or a cure for autism in the near future.

The Interact Centre
Hanwell Community Centre, Westcott
Crescent, Hanwell, London W7 1PD, UK
tel 0044-(0)181 575 0046
e-mail jamesg@dircon.co.uk

The Centre assists people with autism to learn how to manage social and interactive information, both internal and external. It helps students to develop and use a sense of self, and brings coherence to their everyday experiences.

In Touch
10 Norman Road, Sale, Cheshire
M33 3DF, UK
tel 0044-(0)161 905 2440

In Touch was founded to bring together parents of children with special needs, for mutual support and encouragment. It also provides advice on all aspects of caring for children with special needs. There is also a newsletter available.

Irlen Centres Europe/Middle East
Ann Wright, 4 Park Farm Business Centre,
Fornham St Genevieve, Bury St Edmunds,
Suffolk IP28 6TS, UK.
tel/fax 0044-(0)1284 724301

Irlen Centres exist throughout the UK and many countries throughout the world and may be able to assist people with visual perceptual problems relating to attention problems and information overload. The addresses for other international centres can be obtained from:

Irlen Institute
Helen Irlen, 5380 Village Road, Long Beach, California 90808, USA
tel 001-310 496 2550
fax 001-310 429 8699

Irlen Centres Australasia
2 Freeman Street, Melville Heights, Western Australia.
tel/fax 010-61 9330 4922

Network 81
1-7 Woodfield Terrace, Chapel Hill,
Stanstead, Essex CM24 8AJ, UK
tel 0044-(0)1279 647 415 (10am-2pm)

Network 81 aids parents of autistic children in organising their child's education, particularly in dealing with LEAs and schools themselves.

Parents and Professionals and Autism (PAPA)
P.A.P.A. Resource Centre, Knockbracken
Healthcare Park, Saintfield Road, Belfast
BT8 8BH, UK
tel 0044-(0)1232 401 729
fax 0044-(0)1232 403 467

PAPA is an organisation based in Northern Ireland which is specifically aimed at promoting the needs of autistic people and their carers. It produces a regular Newsletter giving updates on current service developments, research and treatments, and organises annual conferences on current issues in autism.

The Scottish Society for Autistic Children
Hilton House, Alloa Business Park, Whins
Road, Alloa FK10 3SA, UK
tel 0044-(0)1259 720 044
fax 0044-(0)1259 720 051

The SSAC exists to provide the best possible care, support and education for people of all